Devon with Kids

Kate

To Sarah and Conrad, who helped with lots of research, especially on ice creams.

Discover a head for heights in Haldon Forest Park.

Introduction

Devon is a rural idyll for families; a place of thatched cottages and narrow lanes, where the grass is green, the air warm and the sea adds a touch of salt to the mix.

For children, Devon is about building sandcastles, jumping waves, rock pooling, dangling crab lines off harbour walls or splodging in fields and getting muddy. You can take to two wheels to cycle the Tarka Trail, or to the water to sail in Salcombe, canoe on the River Dart or Tamar, or windsurf on the Exe. Trains will take you puffing into heritage stations and boats will whisk you off on seafaris to spot seals or dolphins along the coastline and across estuaries.

Some families return not just year after year but generation after generation. Even for those who think they know Devon well, there is always more to discover: new walking routes, nature reserves and a growing emphasis on the environment, whether it's the geopark of the south coast, the biosphere of the north or the rolling farms and moors in between.

Pick just one square mile to make your own and you'll find plenty to keep you busy. Venture further afield and you'll find enough to keep you coming back. We certainly did.

Kate Calvert is the author of the *Harden's Baby Guide* and founder of the Family Travel website (family-travel.co.uk). She travels regularly with her two children, both overseas and in the UK.

About the book

Beach safety
The 'FLAGS' code by the RNLI (rnli.org.uk/beachlifeguards) is a handy checklist for staying safe at the beach:
F Find the red and yellow flags and swim between them.
L Look at the safety signs.
A Ask a lifeguard for advice.
G Get a friend to swim with you.
S Stick your hand in the air and shout for help if you get into difficulty.

Family rates
Unless otherwise specified, family rates quoted in *Devon with Kids* are for two adults and two children. If you have more than two children, it's always worth checking whether there are special deals for larger families.

Members' perks
Throughout *Devon with Kids*, boxes highlight properties, nature reserves and attractions that are free to members of the National Trust and the Royal Society for the Protection of Birds (RSPB). Family membership of these charities represents excellent value for money and also helps support conservation work.

National Trust T0844-800 1895, nationaltrust.org.uk. Annual family membership £82 (£61.25 for the first year if paid by direct debit) for two adults and two children under 18, under 5s free. Membership doesn't just give access to country estates but also covers the cost of parking at numerous coastal stretches managed by the Trust.

RSPB T01767-693680, rspb.org.uk. For family membership (two adults and all children under 19) you can choose how much to give, although £5/month is suggested; it's a good investment given the numerous bird reserves, particularly in East Devon.

Beach standards
Blue Flag awards are given for one season only and are awarded to beaches for the quality of facilities as well as the cleanliness of the water, so exclude wilder beaches even where the water may be clean and the scenery fantastic. The *Good Beach Guide*, goodbeachguide.co.uk, compiled by the **Marine Conservation Society**, lists recommended beaches. If you have particular concerns about water quality, you can also check the latest results at environment-agency.gov.uk.

Symbol key

Beaches
- Blue Flag award
- Café/pub/restaurant
- Beach shop
- Deckchairs for hire
- Beach huts for hire
- Water sports for hire
- Amusement arcade
- Lifeguards (summer)
- Dogs allowed year round
- Toilets nearby
- Car park nearby
- Warning!

Campsites
- Tents
- Caravans
- Shop
- Playground
- Picnic area
- Disabled facilities
- Dogs welcome
- Walk to beach
- Electric hook-up
- Family bathroom
- Baby-care area
- Bikes for hire
- Café or takeaway van
- Campfires allowed

It is up to parents to assess whether the ideas and suggestions in *Devon with Kids* are suitable or appropriate for their children. While the author and publisher have made every effort to ensure accuracy of information on activities, accommodation and food, they cannot be held responsible for any loss, injury or illness resulting from advice or information given in this book.

In particular, Devon has a high turnover of ownership of accommodation and even attractions, so standards as well as prices may change, and places which welcomed families one year may alter that policy the next.

Contents

- 5   About the book
- 8   Top 10

10 Family favourites
- 12   Yurt holidays
- 14   Festivals
- 16   Classic campers
- 18   Go historical

20 Kids' stuff

24 Dartmoor
- 30   Fun & free
- 32   Action stations
- 36   Big days out
- 36   More family favourites
- 38   Explore the moor
- 40   Sleeping
- 46   Eating

50 South Devon
- 56   Fun & free
- 58   Best beaches
- 60   Action stations
- 66   Big days out
- 70   More family favourites
- 72   Plymouth
- 74   Sleeping
- 78   Eating

82 Torbay Coast
- 86   Fun & free
- 88   Best beaches
- 92   Action stations
- 96   Big days out
- 97   More family favourites
- 100 Sleeping
- 102 Eating

104 North Devon
- 110   Fun & free
- 114   Best beaches
- 118   Exmoor National Park
- 120   Action stations
- 128   Big days out
- 130   More family favourites
- 134   Lundy Island
- 136   Sleeping
- 142   Eating

146 Exeter & East Devon
- 152   Fun & free
- 156   Exeter
- 158   Best beaches
- 162   Action stations
- 164   Big days out
- 167   More family favourites
- 169   The Blackdown Hills
- 170   Sleeping
- 174   Eating

178 Grown-ups' stuff
- 178   Inroads
- 182   Tots to teens
- 184   Festivals
- 186   Essentials
- 188   Index
- 192   Credits

Inside front cover
Map symbols

Inside back cover
Tourist information

Beach beauties
Bantham South Devon 58
Beer East Devon 158
Blackpool Sands
　South Devon 58
Branscombe East Devon 158
Combe Martin North Devon 114
East Portlemouth
　South Devon 58
Saunton Sands
　North Devon 116
Soar Mill Cove South Devon 59
Wembury South Devon 59
Woolacombe North Devon 117

Big days out
The Big Sheep North Devon 128
Dartmoor Zoo South Devon 66
Diggerland East Devon 165
Living Coasts Torbay Coast 96
Lundy Island North Devon 134
Morwellham Quay
　South Devon 66
South Devon Railway
　South Devon 67
Tarka Line North Devon 180
Tarka Trail North Devon 126
World of Country Life
　East Devon 166

Cool rides
Adventure Cottages'
　bike trailing South Devon 75
Doone Valley trekking
　North Devon 119
Granite Way Dartmoor 31
North-coast surfing
　North Devon 125
O'Connors Campers
　Dartmoor 13
Paignton & Dartmouth
　Steam Railway
　South Devon 66
　and Torbay Coast 96
Seaton Tramway East Devon 165

Tarka Line North Devon 180
Tarka Trail North Devon 126
Tree Surfers' zip wires
　Dartmoor 33

Crumbly but cool
Buckland Abbey
　South Devon 70
Castle Drogo Dartmoor 35
Coldharbour Mill
　East Devon 168
Finch Foundry Dartmoor 36
Hele Corn Mill North Devon 131
Kents Cavern Torbay Coast 99
The Oxenham Arms
　Dartmoor 44
Powderham Castle
　Torbay Coast 96
Torrington 1646
　North Devon 132
Vintage Mobile Cinema
　North Devon 133

Free attractions
Cliff kite flying East Devon 152
Dartmoor hiking Dartmoor 38
Dawlish Warren East Devon 160
Donkey Sanctuary
　East Devon 153
Following the TRAIL
　Torbay Coast 86
Jurassic Coast East Devon 152
Northam Burrows
　North Devon 112
River Otter fishing
　East Devon 154
Slapton Ley South Devon 67
Stover Country Park
　Torbay Coast 87

Local scoff
Britannia Shellfish
　South Devon 78
The Crowing Cock
　South Devon 67

Dartmouth Ice Cream
　South Devon 80
Darts Farm East Devon 174
The Holt East Devon 177
The Quay Café North Devon 144
River Cottage Canteen
　East Devon 177
Riverford Field Kitchen
　South Devon 80
Squires Fish Restaurant
　North Devon 143
Venus Café South Devon 80

Perfect pitches
Cockingford Farm Dartmoor 40
Combe View East Devon 170
Dartmoor wild camping
　Dartmoor 42
Higher Rew South Devon 74
Hole Station North Devon 136
Little Meadow North Devon 137
Old Cotmore Farm
　South Devon 74
Stoke Barton Farm
　North Devon 138
West Middlewick
　East Devon 171
Woodlands South Devon 75

Rites of childhood
Catch crabs off a harbour wall.
Hunt for fossils and rock-pool critters.
Paddle a kayak to a secret cove.
Pedal a bike along a forest trail.
Pitch a tent somewhere special.
Roast marshmallows on a campfire.
Scoff fish and chips on the seafront.
Slurp hot choc after a day's surfing.
Spot a dolphin on a boat trip.
Storm a castle's ramparts.

Top 10

Thrills & spills
Crealy East Devon 164
Kayaking North Devon 122
Kite buggying Torbay Coast 94
The Milky Way North Devon 130
Power kiting East Devon 163
River Dart Dare Devils
  Dartmoor 43
Surfing North Devon 125
The Ultimate High
  North Devon 123
Windsurfing East Devon 164
Woodlands South Devon 68

Wet & wild
Avocet Cruises East Devon 160
Chagford open-air pool
  Dartmoor 34
Greenway river crossing
  South Devon 60
  and Torbay Coast 92
Ilfracombe Princess
  North Devon 120
Powerboating South Devon 62
River Dart canoeing
  South Devon 60
Seafaris South Devon 60
  and Torbay Coast 92
Salcombe sailing
  South Devon 64
Stand-up paddle boarding
  South Devon 64
Torbay ferry Torbay Coast 92

Wild & wonderful
Barricane Beach shells
  North Devon 111
Dartmoor Hawking
  Dartmoor 32
Dartmoor ponies Dartmoor 31
Devon Badger Watch
  North Devon 124
Exe Estuary East Devon 160
Exmoor deer North Devon 118
Lundy puffins North Devon 134
Maer insects East Devon 154
National Marine Aquarium
  South Devon 72
Wembury rock pools
  South Devon 59

Woodland adventures
Bellever Dartmoor 31
Blackbury Camp
  East Devon 152
Broomhill Sculpture Gardens
  North Devon 140
Dartmeet Dartmoor 31
Escot East Devon 165
Haldon Forest Torbay Coast 99
Lydford Gorge Dartmoor 37
Stover Country Park
  Torbay Coast 87
Watersmeet Dartmoor 118
Yurtcamp Dartmoor 13

Family favourites

12 Yurt holidays
14 Festivals
16 Classics campers
18 Go historical

Yurt holidays

This is modern luxury camping – a chance to live outdoors but with a decent, dry bed for the night and the heat of a wood-burning stove. There are fire-pits, too, plus field kitchens and barbecues.

Cuckoo Down Farm Yurts, near Sidmouth, feature antique French and oriental furniture (bed linen included). There are swings, a stream to dam, wildlife to spot, chickens to feed and eggs to collect. Baby equipment and toys are bookable, along with 'Yogini' children's yoga adventures. Also near Sidmouth, **Hunger Hill Tipis and Yurt Holidays** are five-bed yurts on a smallholding with sheep, pigs, chickens and a friendly dog. There are low tables, painted Moroccan storage boxes, lanterns, Kilim cushions and sheepskins around the stove, plus hammocks outside. On the eastern edge of Dartmoor, **Yurtcamp** is set in 40 acres with 30 acres of woodland. There's a village of yurts, some in sociable proximity, others tucked between trees. The yurts are equipped with proper beds, but you can go back to basics, gathering and chopping your own wood. There are chickens (for egg collecting), a licensed café/bar serving breakfast and proper coffee, games room and woodland assault course. At **Devon Yurt**, to the west of Dartmoor, you should look out for buzzards, bats and swallows on the organic smallholding with views of Brentor. The yurts have futons, plus cot if needed, and ethnic rugs. A separate tent houses a roll-top bath heated by log burner, and there's a further tent with a loo. You can pick your own salads, dig potatoes and buy fruit and eggs at the farmhouse, which can also arrange pony rides. You can also pre-book bed linen, and organic breakfasts can be delivered to the yurt door.

Cuckoo Down Farm Yurts, Lower Broad Oak Rd, West Hill, Ottery St Mary, EX11 1UE, T01404-811714, luxurydevonyurts.co.uk. £445.
Devon Yurt, The Yurt, Borough, Kelly, nr Lifton, PL16 0HJ, T01822-870366, devonyurt.com. £525.
Hunger Hill Tipis and Yurt Holidays, nr Newton Poppleford, EX20 0BZ, T01395-568454, yurt-holidays.co.uk. £545-630.
Yurtcamp, Gorse Blossom Farm, nr Liverton, TQ12 6JD, T01626-824666, yurtcamp.co.uk. £365-625.

Festivals

Giving parents a chance to relive their youth and take the kids along too, a growing number of festivals cater for families. Some are even free. If you have little ones at single-site events with camping, take a potty, as the loos can be unpleasant for adults, let alone kids. At all kinds of festivals a sling or rucksack will be useful, if they aren't old enough to wal, and will keep them high enough so they stand some chance of seeing what is going on. So they can get into the groove too, it's a good idea to play the children some of the music before you go, but really little ones will probably need earplugs to protect their hearing. Have a contingency plan in case they get lost (find a police officer/steward/mum with kids). A useful move is to put your mobile phone number on the child somewhere (a wristband, or sticker on their T-shirt).

Kicking off the summer season in June is the **Teignmouth Folk Festival** (teignmouthfolk.co.uk), a three-day event at the Teignmouth Theatre and other free venues. Lynmouth Manor Green and various pubs and venues in Lynton are the setting for the **Lynton & Lynmouth Music Festival** (llama.org.uk), also in June. It's free and features the likes of Badly Drawn Boy, David Holmes and many more. The weekend before Glastonbury, **Gold Coast Oceanfest** (goldcoastoceanfest.co.uk) is a three-day festival held at Croyde, with a music arena and sporting events.

In July, **Chagstock** (chagstock.info), a family-friendly charity festival held near Chagford, includes a kids' play area and features music to suit a wide range of tastes, aiming to make the experience crowd-free with plenty of clean facilities. Also in July, **Beautiful Days** (beautifuldays.org), nominated for the Family Festival Award and Grassroots Festival Award, is held at Escot Park and has a retro feel, featuring regulars like The Pogues, Levellers, Hawkwind and others.

The **Dartmoor Folk Festival** (dartmoorfolkfestival.co.uk) is a weekend event held in August near South Zeal. There's a campsite, and the festival features a ceilidh, Dartmoor stepdance and broomdance championships, fair, crafts, music hall, Sunday ramble and a children's festival. See also page 184.

Classic campers

Live life in the slow lane and rent the coolest type of mobile holiday accommodation – a retro campervan. There are several companies to choose from, all charging between about £300 and £750 per week. **Classic Campervan Hire** provide classic VWs sleeping two or four with pop-up roof and including kitchen equipment, tea, coffee, sugar, washing-up materials, outdoor table and chairs, with an optional two-person awning plus airbeds, bedding and bike racks. They will pick up and drop off at Exeter train stations and airport, Plymouth train station and airport and Newquay airport. **Devon Cool Campers** offer original VWs sleeping two or four with additional drive-away awning (£20). Kitchen equipment, table and chairs, lanterns and map are all included and there are extra charges for bedding, airbeds for use in the awning and bike racks. **O'Connors Campers** run a fleet of vintage, refurbished two-, four- or six-berth VWs, equipped with everything you need from a corkscrew to washing-up liquid. You pay extra for bedding and bike hire can be arranged (loaded on the bike rack of your van with backpacks, bicycle clips, lights, combination locks, maps and a cycle-route guide). They will also do a supermarket shop before your arrival. **Southwest Camper Hire** have modern as well as vintage campers. All their vehicles are members of the Caravan Club so you can stay on Caravan Club sites for members' rates.

Classic Campervan Hire, Unit 2, Lower Westbridge Industrial Estate, Tavistock, PL19 8DE, T0800-9709147, classiccampervanhire.co.uk. £350-665.
Devon Cool Campers, The Gate House, Castle St, Bampton, EX16 9NS, T01398-331225, devoncoolcampers.co.uk. £300-750, extra £10 for collection from Tiverton Parkway train station.
O'Connors Campers, Highlands, Old Rd, High St, Okehampton, EX20 1SP, T01837-659599, oconnorscampers.co.uk. £375-725, extra £35 for collection from Exeter train and bus stations, or from Exeter and Newquay airports.
Southwest Camper Hire, The Barn, West Town, Tedburn Rd, Whitestone, EX4 2HH, T01392-811931, swcamperhire.com. £375-695.

Go historical

Give your kids a real sense of history by staying in a building that has been around even longer than their parents. You could go for something military or stately or, perhaps, one of the many workaday places where people got on with their lives.

The **Landmark Trust** offers a chance to live in historic and fascinating buildings ranging from the wonderful 1960s glass-fronted Anderton House, Goodleigh, to Crownhill Fort in Plymouth, Kingswear Castle near Dartmouth, a gatehouse, converted stables, a manor house sleeping 15, and assorted longhouses, farmhouses and cottages, all with their own past which you can explore in the reports and books kept in each building.

Not just the guardian of stately homes and wild open landscapes, the **National Trust** also owns lots of small properties that make great holiday homes. You could stay in a coastguard cottage near Clovelly, a small 15th-century manor near Challacombe, Forge Cottage at Branscombe, cottages on the estates of Killerton and Knightshayes, and more. Notably, Mill Cottage on Wembury Beach, in the same building as the café, is so close to the beach that the downstairs windows have shutters to keep the sea out during severe weather. The online search lets you request a cot, and exclude properties unsuitable for children.

Alternatively, you could opt for the **Station Officer's House**, reportedly the most southerly house in Devon, at the end of a row of coastguard houses, with plenty of sea views, five bedrooms, games, DVDs and a good nearby pub. Or try the **Wow House**, an agency specializing in traditional houses with real luxury.

Landmark Trust, T01628-825925, landmarktrust.org.uk. £145-1337 sleeping 4.
National Trust, T0844-800 2070, nationaltrustcottages.co.uk. £243-2000+.
The Station Officer's House, East Prawle, T020-7421 5567, stationofficershouse.co.uk. £700-1950.
The Wow House, T01452-715373, thewowhousecompany. com. £800+.

Crabbing

Local piers with little boat movement are the best places for crabbing.

❶ Fill a container (bucket or large food tub) with seawater from wherever you hope to find the crabs.
❷ Tie a lump of bacon, leftover fish or the like to thin string.
❸ Dangle the string into the water and wait for the crab to attach itself.
❹ Haul in and remove the crab, taking hold of the body from behind so it can't nip, and place in your container to admire.

Crabbing rules

- No more than 10 crabs in a single bucket.
- Regularly top up buckets with fresh seawater.
- Don't put tap water in the buckets.
- Don't leave buckets in the sun.
- After you've finished, put the crabs back into the water.

Rock pooling

The best time to go rock pooling is around an hour either side of low tide. A net and bucket or large food tub will give you something to put any swimmers into (only put one type of animal in the bucket at a time). Remember to check tide times (bbc.co.uk/weather/coast/tides or tidetimes.org.uk) to ensure that you do not become trapped by the rising tide. Wear shoes with good grip and watch where you are treading; it could be someone's home. Take care to disturb animals and plants as little as possible – particularly when looking under rocks – and leave creatures where you find them. See check list, below.

Species	Habitat
Barnacle	rock pool
Beadlet anemone	rocky shore/rock pool
Blenny	rock pool
Blue-rayed limpet	rock pool
Brittle star	rock pool
Brown shrimp	sandy shore/rock pool
Common blenny or shanny	rock pool
Common cockle	sandy shore
Common goby	sandy shore/rock pool
Common limpet	rock pool
Common mussel	rock pool
Common periwinkle	rock pool
Common ragworm	sandy shore
Common starfish	rocky shore
Dog whelk	rock pool
Flat periwinkle	rock pool
Green sea urchin	rock pool
Hermit crab	rock pool
Painted top shell	rock pool
Razor shell	sandy shore
Rock goby	rock pool
Sea squirt	rock pool
Shore crab	rock pool
Snakelocks anemone	rock pool
Velvet swimming crab	rock pool

Kids' stuff

Treasure Trails

An award-winning activity with treasure hunts themed as Murder Mystery, Treasure Hunt or a James Bond-style Spy Mission. In Devon there are 40 different locations to choose from, including 30 walking trails, four car trails and six cycle trails, from Ilfracombe in the north to Salcombe in the south, Plymouth in the west to Axminster in the east. You do them in your own time, using the clues provided to take you past historic and country locations. You eliminate suspects or locations until you are left with just one – either the whodunit, the location of the hidden treasure or the code to deactivate the device. Buy online or from outlets in Devon, including some tourist offices and bookshops (T07960-630900, treasuretrails.co.uk. £5/trail).

Wildlife information

Leaf Swatch Book and **Wildflower Swatch Book** (£4.99 each, The Woodland Trust), have information about each plant. **Nature Detectives' Handbook** (£6.99, The Woodland Trust and Miles Kelly Publishing) introduces children to 50 tree, bird, amphibian and butterfly species with facts and stickers. **Tree Detectives' Handbook** (£6.99, The Woodland Trust and Miles Kelly Publishing) covers British trees and shrubs with activities for every tree. **RSPB Children's Guide to Birdwatching** (RSPB) is for children aged eight to 12 years, with photos, illustrations and simple identification points. **Usborne's Spotter's Guides** (£4.99) cover 100-200 species per title. Titles include *Birds*, *Trees*, *Wildflowers*, *Shells*, *Butterflies*, and *Bugs & Insects*. **The Usborne Little Book of…** (£5.99) for younger children includes trees, birds and wildflowers. Also look out for **Collins Little Gem** guides and the publications of **Nigel Clarke**, a specialist on Jurassic Coast history and wildlife, nigelclarkepublications.co.uk.

Devon place names

It can be useful and interesting to know what place names mean.

Ber (Bere) promontory
Bury fortified place
Combe valley
Cote small dwelling
Dun fort
Lee, Ley, Leigh forest clearing
Nimed sacred grove (eg Nympton)
Stow, Stowe meeting place (holy place)
Ton originally a farm or enclosed place, eventually becoming 'town'
Tor rock tower
Tre minor farm

Ice cream

Dartmouth Ice Cream Company, dartmouthicecream.com. Outlets only in Dartmouth but great ice cream and sorbets.

Devonshire Farmhouse Ice Cream, icecreamonline.co.uk. Made in Chagford using Guernsey milk.

Dunstaple Dairy, dunstaple.co.uk. Sorbets and ice creams from near Holsworthy in North Devon.

Hockings, hockingsicecream.co.uk. Great-quality vanilla ice cream sold from vans in Bideford, Appledore, Ilfracombe, Westward Ho! and Torrington from March to October.

Langage Farm, langagefarm.com. Shops in Plympton and Yelverton. Thirty flavours made with Channel Island double cream, the farm's own clotted cream, plus frozen yoghurt.

Rocombe Farm, rocombe.com. Organic ice cream, now part of the Yeo Valley group.

Rookbeare, rookbearefarm.co.uk. Made in Crediton.

Salcombe Dairy, salcombedairy.co.uk. From the heart of smart Salcombe.

Taverners, tavernersfarm.co.uk. See page 98.

Yarde Farm, yardefarmicecream.co.uk. Based in Plympton.

Boredom busters

Buzz words
Pick a word, then turn on the radio or play a story CD and try to be the first to shout 'buzz' when the word is mentioned.

Car bingo
Give players a sheet of paper and ask them to write down 25 different numbers between one and 99. The person in the front passenger seat calls out the last one or two digits from the licence plates of passing cars. The winner is the first to cross off all their numbers and shout 'Bingo!'

Following on
Take turns to name famous people, countries or towns, each beginning with the last letter of the previous name.

Licence to thrill
Make up phrases based on the letters of licence plates. For example 234 IFS 00 could be 'Ice-cream for Sally', 'Ian fancies Susan' or 'I feel sick!'

The Minister's Cat
Players describe the cat with adjectives (able, acrobatic, etc) beginning with specified letters, losing a life if they have to move to a new letter.

Motorway snap
One player picks a colour and model of car. The next person to see a car that matches shouts snap and scores one point.

Good read
10 children's classics set in Devon

Early years
The Fossil Girl
by Catherine Brighton
(Francis Lincoln)
The true story of the 10-year-old who discovered the first complete fossil of an ichthyosaurus nearly 200 years ago.

The Lighthouse Keeper's Cat
(and others in series)
by Ronda and David Armitage (Scholastic)
Delightful adventures of the lighthouse keeper, his wife and cat, Hamish.

Ages 6-12
Friend or Foe
by Michael Morpurgo (Mammoth)
Two children evacuated to the Devon countryside enjoy farm life, but one nearly drowns on the moor and is rescued by a German soldier from a crashed bomber.

The Little White Horse
by Elizabeth Goudge (Lion)
Scary and romantic, about orphan Maria at West Country Moonacre Valley.

Mission Underground – The Making of Mr Brunel's Splendid Tunnel
by Margaret Nash (Macdonald)
Engineering by the man responsible for much of the railway building in Devon.

Tarka the Otter
by Henry Williamson (Puffin Classic)
The classic tale of an otter's life and death in Devon.

Teens
And Then There Were None
by Agatha Christie
Guests are murdered at an isolated mansion on an island like Bigbury. See page 58.

Dead Man's Folly
Evil Under the Sun
by Agatha Christie
In the first, Hercule Poirot investigates a country home like Christie's Greenway, see page 97; in the second, his coastal Devon holiday is disrupted by a murder.

Hound of the Baskervilles
by Arthur Conan Doyle
Sherlock Holmes takes to mist-enshrouded Dartmoor to solve his most challenging case.

Lorna Doone
by RD Blackmoor
(Puffin Classics)
Famous and tragic love story set around Exmoor. See page 119.

DVD
The Year of the Working Sheepdog
Shepherd David Kennard tracks his dogs and their lives on a coastal farm near Ilfracombe.

Dartmoor

Contents
- 26 Map
- 30 Fun & free
- 32 Action stations
- 36 Big days out
- 36 More family favourites
- 38 Explore the moor
- 40 Sleeping
- 46 Eating

Mystical Dartmoor river.

Restored ride at Dingles Fairground Heritage Centre.

Pooh sticks over the West Dart.

You could argue that only mad dogs and Englishmen go out in Dartmoor weather. Though very beautiful and, occasionally, sunny, it sees fog and rain even in the height of summer. However, there are things to do here year round, and the stark surroundings bring warmth – it's the kind of place where people still greet strangers as they walk or cycle past.

The national park offers plenty of pay-to-visit attractions, but it's the simple stuff like scrambling over granite tors or boulder-hopping across streams that makes the greatest impression on children.

The upland plateaux are exposed, with gorse, heather, bracken, bogs and granite tors. Dropping down, the landscape becomes lush, cocooned by tall hedges and trees arching over lanes, evoking the stories of Enid Blyton. Deeper into the woods, the mossy gnarled roots and towering trunks are more Middle Earth and Lord of the Rings territory.

Southern England's largest upland, Dartmoor covers 368 square miles, with public access to over 110,000 acres. With some roads barely the width of one vehicle, the definition of accessible depends largely on the valleys formed by the rivers that rise here. Locate these and you've understood the lie of the land.

The River Teign rises in the mid north and loops around the eastern edge of the park, joining the River Bovey to reach the sea at Teignmouth. The River Dart rises in the mid north with the East and West Dart rivers joining at **Dartmeet**, before passing on to Dartmouth. The River Plym travels southwest to Plymouth, together with the River Tavy from the park's northwest. Also shaping the park on the outer edges are the River Tamar, forming the border with Cornwall, and the rivers Exe and Kenn on the eastern side.

Another orientation aid is the main road running east to west from **Moretonhampstead** to **Tavistock**. To the north of it is the less developed and sometimes desolate part of the moor, home to more serious bogs and military firing zones. To the south, the landscape is softer, with more hedges and small villages with village greens – a flash of medieval life.

There has been human life on Dartmoor for several thousand years. Earlier inhabitants deforested the moor and left it one of the richest prehistoric areas in Western Europe with stone circles, hut circles, burial sites and old field patterns. There are also the remains of medieval occupation, 19th-century tin streaming, mining, mineral railways, tin-stamping mills and peat cutting to spot. And, if history and geology doesn't do it for your kids, there are plenty of local legends.

Out & about Dartmoor

Fun & free

Live the legend
A local man called Bowerman was out hunting when his dogs foolishly disturbed a coven of witches who in revenge turned him to stone. The **Bowerman's Nose** stone is said to be all that remains of him. Found not far from Hound Tor (see below), it makes a simple outing with easy scrambling, although you can't climb on the tor itself. You can walk from the Hound Tor car park or, for a shorter trip, park off road near Hayne Cross before walking over the top of Hayne Down. For more Dartmoor stories see legendarydartmoor.co.uk, the Fun Zone at dartmoor-nap.gov.uk, or check out the visitor centres' bookshops.

Roam a reservoir
Reservoirs offer safe walking and facilities such as water sports and public loos. In the case of **Roadford**, there's also a café and information centre. **Venford** has a 3½-mile easy walk that offers the chance to pick bilberries from July to September. The route passes man-made channels that use gravity to take water to local farms. There are also gullies (called gerts), and the remains of Ringleshutes, an opencast tin mine dating back to the 17th century or earlier. **Burrator** is one of the most attractive reservoirs and offers low-level walks. **Trenchford** is known as Little Switzerland with rhododendrons in June.

Climb a tor
You can tire everyone out over a short distance if you are going upwards. One option easily reached from the Hound Tor car park at Swallerton Gate is the top of **Hound Tor**. For a slightly longer walk head southeast on a well-used path to Greator Rocks, passing an abandoned medieval village. Here you can make out the old houses shared by humans and animals with a central fire. It involves a little climbing.

Belstone Tor from Higher Halstock.

> ❸ Children can decide whether Hound Tor really is the shape of a dog's head.

Laze the day
One of the most popular places for families is **Dartmeet**. Originally developed as a traditional beauty spot, nowadays it has a large car park and café (Badger's Holt Café, T01364-631213, badgersholtdartmoor.co.uk) that also sells fishing gear (if you want to have a go, remember to get a licence). If the weather is good you can get away from the crowd, take a picnic and find a spot on the grassy bank further upstream, where the river swirls between boulders, and eddies through natural swimming pools.

Go letterboxing
Combine orienteering and treasure hunting using clues to locate boxes hidden on the moor. Each box contains a visitors' book and rubber stamp. You can use the stamp to record the find in your own book, before adding your personal stamp to the visitors' book. For more information see dartmoorletterboxing. org, or buy a copy of *Let's Go Letterboxing: A Beginner's Guide* by Janet Palmer. A catalogue of letterbox clues is available from Tony Moore (25 Sanderspool Cross, South Brent, TQ10 9LR).

Spot the animals
Look for signs reading 'Sheep Lying On Road' and spot the different types of sheep and cattle. For more details see the section on farming history at dartmoor-npa.gov.uk, or the packs for sale which list the different types. There are also the ponies (dartmoor-npa.gov.uk/laf-ponies.htm), supported by the **Dartmoor Pony Trust** (wdpht.co.uk). The Trust offers free guided walks with a pony at **Bellever** for groups of six or more (T01626-355314). For £75 per family or group of six there are Pony Power sessions, including hands-on tuition in how to approach, catch and groom a pony and learn about its role on the moor, before taking it for a walk along the **Brimpts Tin Mine Trail**.

Applaud a clapper bridge
Earlier inhabitants have left traces of unexpected skills. **Postbridge** is the place to see the biggest and most impressive of their charming bridges, built of huge granite slabs around the 13th century. Nearby is **Bellever Forest** with a picnic site, two Forestry Commission nature trails plus hut circles and other prehistoric monuments.

Cycle the Granite Way
This 11-mile section of the Devon Coast-to-Coast cycle route runs between **Okehampton** and **Lydford** (devon.gov.uk/granite_way-2.pdf). There's a castle at each end, a steam-train ride in summer between Okehampton and **Meldon** (bikes carried free), and a visitor centre at Meldon (teas served in a former buffet car). You run along an old railway for the first six miles then across the Meldon Viaduct before continuing along the former Southern Railway to Lake Viaduct, then down a gravelly footpath to Bearslake Inn. The route continues on a road to Bridestowe station before a final mile on rail-track bed.

A new cycling map with safe, traffic-free cycling options is available from the National Park Visitor Centres and also check out the **Drakes Trail** at drakestrail.co.uk. For bike rental see page 32.

Feel the frisson
Conan Doyle based the detective thriller *The Hound of the Baskervilles* on the moor, probably around **Grimspound**, a prehistoric settlement on one of the bleaker parts, an easy walk from the road. The remains of the huts are located east of the B3212 between Two Bridges and North Bovey. There's also Foxtor Mire, reputedly the model for Grimpen Mire. Conan Doyle wrote the story while staying at the Duchy Hotel in Princetown, now the **High Moor Visitor Centre**, see page 38.

Out & about Dartmoor

Action stations

Climbing
Dart Rock Climbing Centre
Dart Mills, Old Totnes Rd, Buckfastleigh, TQ11 ONF, T01364-644499, dartrock.co.uk. £7 adult, £5 child (under 16), £20/taster, £50/family taster.
Climbing centre suitable for novices up. Over-fives can climb under the supervision of a registered adult climber, or there are dedicated supervised kids' sessions for two hours on Saturday mornings (5-10s) or Sunday mornings (10-17s). There are also taster sessions for all ages. Children aged 12-17 may climb unsupervised with parental consent after passing an assessment.

Cycling
Devon Cycle Hire
Sourton Down, nr Okehampton, EX20 4HR, T01837-861141, devoncyclehire.co.uk. £14 adult/day, £10 child, £8/buggy, £8/tag-a-long, £5/child seat.
Near the Granite Way and will also deliver bikes to you. Helmets and tandems also available.

Falconry
Dartmoor Hawking School of Falconry
Puddaven Farm, nr North Bovey, TQ13 8RJ, T01647-433640, dartmoorhawking.co.uk. £120 family or up to 6 people, minimum age 6.
Private falconry school offering hands-on experience and hunting days. A two-hour falconry introduction is available as an exclusive family session, flying anything up to the size of an eagle owl.

Yarak Birds of Prey
T01884-277297, yarakbirdsofprey.co.uk. Experience days £110/£180 person/2 people, £80/afternoons only, minimum age 6.
Barn owls, kestrels, Bengal eagle owls, eagles and Harris hawks, and classes to learn how to handle the birds and have them flying to you.

Horse riding
The sheer extent of public land makes Dartmoor great riding country, see dartmoor-npa.gov.uk/vi-horse-riding.htm. There is also the opportunity to learn carriage driving.

The Dartmoor ponies are wild but you can take one for a walk with the Dartmoor Pony Trust.

Babeny Farm Stables
Poundsgate, Newton Abbot, TQ13 7PS, T01364-631296, babenystables.co.uk. £20/1 hr, £30/2 hrs, minimum age 7.
Riding on the moor, with novice, intermediate and advanced hacks, plus full-day rides.

Cheston Farm Equestrian Centre
Wrangaton, TQ10 9HL, T01364-73266, chestonfarm.co.uk. £35/assessment lesson, £30/45 mins, £40/hr, minimum age 8.
Riding school with indoor and outdoor arena offering private lessons.

Dartmoor Driving
Holne, nr Ashburton, TQ13 7SP, T01364-631438, dartmoordriving.wordpress.com. £95/holiday carriage drive for up to 4, £55 person for 2 on half-day course, minimum age 8.
Half-day carriage drives for four or more (can swap passengers half way if it's too cold for the little ones). Plus more serious introduction to carriage driving, starting with a single pony and trap and covering how to harness, put to the vehicle and drive.

Dartmoor Riding Centre
Widecombe-in-the-Moor, TQ13 7TF, T01364-621281, dartmoorstables.com. £35/hr, £50/2 hrs.
Complete beginners and families are welcome. Rides on the moor are tailored to the small group (four or less), and are faster for the more experienced. All

Multi activities

The Dartmoor Centres
Dartmeet, Yelverton, PL20 6SG, T01364-631500, devon.gov.uk/devondiscovery. £130 for up to 8 people.
Two residential centres run by Devon County Council with accommodation and moor-based activities. Families can book for a morning or afternoon of caving, mountain biking, archery, orienteering or climbing, with qualified instructors and all equipment provided. A day-long navigation course for ages 16 and over leads to a bronze or silver navigation qualification.

Isca Outdoor
T01392-494053, iscaoutdoor.co.uk. £75/half day, £135/full day for up to 3 people.
A family programme of activities on the edge of Dartmoor, from half day to full weekend. Activities include caving (at Buckfastleigh), climbing (at Chudleigh), navigation and bushcraft, aiming to provide a variety of physical, adventurous and fun activities. Bunkhouse accommodation is also available.

Moorgate the Dartmoor Experience
T07740-514421, moorgatedartmoor.co.uk. £30 person for family of 4.
Two brothers, one a Scout leader, offer day walks, letterboxing, guiding and weekends for less experienced walkers. Location depends on the weather.

The Rock Centre and Tree Top Adventures
Chudleigh, TQ13 0EE, T01626-852717, rockcentre.co.uk. £7.50 person/hr for groups of 4+.
Mix and match activities at this indoor and outdoor rock-climbing centre that include climbing, abseiling, caving and tree-top adventure treks with seven circuits starting with an easy one for kids. Also campsite £2.50 person and tipi hire £10 head in grassy glades surrounded by trees, with one shower, toilets and gas barbecue.

Tree Surfers
Woodlands, Tavistock, PL19 8JE, T01822-833409, treesurfers.co.uk. Ropes Course or Canopy Zip Tour £22 adult, £19 child; Tree Jump £10.
Ropes courses include swings, bridges, wooden walkways and zip wires; children under 12 must be accompanied by an adult. Canopy Zip Tours see instructors guiding your almost bird-like moves from tree to tree (minimum height 1.4 m). On the higher course guides use harnesses and rope pulleys to control landings (minimum height 1.5 m). Or try a Tree Jump (minimum height 1.4 m).

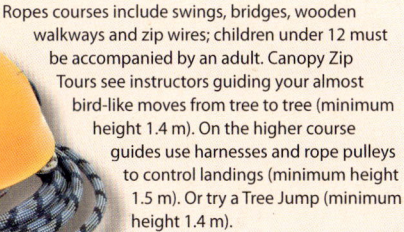

Out & about Dartmoor

instruction plus hats and boots provided. Lessons in the arena by arrangement.

Eastlake Riding Stables
Nr Belstone, EX20 1QT, T01837-52513, eastlakeridingstables.co.uk. £10/30 mins, £17/hr, £30/2 hrs, inc hard hats, minimum age 3. Offering shorter rides.

Finlake Riding Centre
Chudleigh, TQ13 0EH, T01626-852096, finlakeridingcentre.co.uk. Ride £3/10 mins (2-4), £10/30 mins, £17/hr, £22/1½ hrs; lesson £16/30 mins, £30/hr; Sat kids' club 1000-1600, £20.
Based at the Finlake Holiday park (devon-connect.co.uk), with riding on the 130-acre parkland, bridle paths and lanes. Offers leader rides for children (four or over) and quiet treks for those with little or no experience, to faster more exhilarating outings venturing further.

Skaigh Stables
Belstone, EX20 1RD, T01837-840917, skaighstables.co.uk. £36/2 hrs.
Daily Dartmoor riding mornings and afternoons, adventurous for experienced riders, gentle for novices. Offers some help but not lessons.

Llama walks
Dartmoor Llama Walks,
Ponsworthy House, Ponsworthy, nr Newton Abbot, T01364-631481, dartmoorllamawalks.co.uk. £35 for a cream tea and walk.

Will tailor-make walks according to the ages of the children and your needs, with the option of a llama-transported picnic.

Navigation
Compassworks
Wingreen, Petrockstowe, nr Okehampton, EX20 3HQ, T01837-516386, compassworks.co.uk.
From £99/2 days inc some meals. Courses on how to navigate using map and compass, leading to bronze, silver and gold in the National Navigation Awards System. Suitable for families. Also hand-held GPS training.

Vertical Frontiers
Lower Pudsham, Buckland-in-the-Moor, TQ13 7HW, T07709-432014, verticalfrontiers.com.
Rock climbing and navigation courses plus guided walks, tailored to the participants but best for children over eight accompanied by parents. Costs depend on size of group and activities but from £50 per person.

Outdoor swimming
Ashburton
Love Lane, TQ12 6JT, T01364-652828.
Heated pool dating back to the 1930s.

Bovey Tracey
New Recreation Ground, Newton Rd, TQ13 9BD, T01626-832828, boveyswimmingpool.co.uk.
Heated pool.

Buckfastleigh
Victoria Park Lodge, Plymouth Rd, TQ11 0DB, T01364-642222.
Heated pool built in the 1900s.

Chagford
Rushford, T01647-432929, chagfordpool.co.uk.
The UK's largest outdoor river-fed pool beside the River Teign, plus paddling pool built in 1934.

Kingsteignton
Meadowcroft Drive, TQ12 3PB, T01626-366480.
Heated pool.

Don't miss Castle Drogo

Drewsteignton, EX6 6PB, T01647-433306, nationaltrust.org.uk. Mar-Nov Mon, Wed-Sun 1100-1700, more restricted opening at other times. Castle and grounds £7.45 adult, £3.72 child, £18.63 family Grounds only £4.50 adult, £2.50 child.

The last castle built in England, this fine Lutyens' 1910 reconstruction of a baronial hall was commissioned by a self-made millionaire grocer with pretensions, who wanted a comfortable version of an ancestral home complete with portcullis, 2-m-thick walls and arrow slits. The lion was adopted as the family emblem – something to spot as you go round. Sitting above the dramatic Teign Gorge, there's plenty to discover such as a very early telephone and lift, giant pestle and mortar, great old-fashioned bathtub, family photos, old gramophones, and dolls' houses. Also check out the Bunty House in the garden where the grandchildren used to play. As well as a children's quiz and family trail, there are family events from March to December with trails, re-enactments, themed weekends and daily school-holiday activities. Outdoors you can hire a croquet set and play a game on the lawn, and there's a children's play area plus picnic area and tea room.

The estate offers dramatic walks with fine views over the River Teign, tumbling through boulders in the wooded valley. This is steep in places and can be slippery in the wet. A circular route of just over three miles goes from **Fingle Bridge** upstream beyond Drewe's Weir (watch out for leaping salmon in autumn), along the high wall of the deer park and across a footbridge. Look out for deer and birds, including woodpeckers. A walk downstream along the north bank will bring you back to Fingle Bridge. Slightly off the route in Whiddon Deer Park on the estate are intriguing sculptures by Peter Randall-Page (peterrandall-page.com).

Moretonhampstead
Community Swimming Pool Trust, Court St, T01647-440134. Volunteer run, solar-heated pool with refreshments and grassed areas.

Traditional skills
The Husbandry School
Mapleton, 30 West St, Ashburton, TQ13 7DU, T07980-253677, husbandry.co.uk. £15/drop-in sessions, £45/day, £250/week per family for Wellie Stompers.
An off-grid centre running courses in traditional arts and crafts from felting, basket and willow working, through to food growing and rural skills like hedge laying and clay-oven building. Week-long Dirt to Dinner courses are about growing and cooking food and are suitable for older children. Wellie Stompers is a version for parents and younger ones.

Wild Woods 'n Willow/ Wood & Rush
1a The Square, Chagford, TQ13 8AA, T01647-231330, wildwoodswillow.org.uk. £60 family, £25 unaccompanied child (8-14).
An organization aiming to reconnect children with nature, running bushcraft days at various venues around Chagford, for families or unaccompanied children. Skills include fire lighting, food foraging and basket making. Suitable for children from two, if accompanied.

Also woodandrush.net. From £40 adult, £20 child. Wood- and rush-basketry courses on a smallholding where the willow grows. Suggested minimum age 10 for full days or younger for half days.

Water sports
Roadford Lake
South West Lakes Trust, Broadwoodwidger, nr Okehampton, PL16 0JL, T01409-211507, swlakestrust.org.uk. Open 0900-1700. £32/taster session, £45/multi activity, £145/RYA sailing, minimum age 8. Campsite £6 adult, £3 child (5-14), £14 family, £2.50/electric hook-up.
The largest inland water in the southwest, where an angling and water-sports centre offers brown-trout angling, sailing, windsurfing, rowing, kayaking and camping. Tuition, self-launch and hire available. On the other side of the lake is a restaurant, picnic spot and walking paths.

Out & about Dartmoor

Big days out

Becky Falls Woodland Park
Manaton, nr Bovey Tracey, TQ13 9UG, T01647-221259, beckyfalls.com. Feb-Nov 1000-1700. £6.50 adult, £5.50 child (5+), £22 family.
A 50-acre park with attractive falls, marked walks and nature trails (including a competition with prize for every child), an animal centre with goats, rabbits and rescued birds of prey, animal encounters daily between July and September, plus weekends and school holidays, summer pony rides, cute and cuddling animal shows, children's crafts, a picnic area and bouldering space.

Dartmoor Railway
Okehampton Station, EX20 1EJ, T01837-55637, dartmoor-railway.co.uk. Apr-Nov 1000-1800. Whole line day return £6 adult, £4 child (5-15), dogs, bikes and under 5s free.
Passenger-train services started again in 2009 on this 15-mile line, once part of the main line from Waterloo to Plymouth. It's now operating between Sampford Courtenay and Meldon, via Okehampton with its 1950s-style station with buffet (Fri-Sun) and model shop (daily). From Meldon you have access to the Dartmoor National Park (there's a free *Railway Walks* leaflet when you pick up your ticket), or stroll up to the viaduct for views of Yes Tor and High Willhays.

More family favourites

Canonteign Falls
Christow, nr Chudleigh, EX6 7NT, canonteignfalls.co.uk. Mar-Nov 1000-1800. £5.75 adult, £4.50 child (4+), £19.50 family, closed for safety in heavy rain.
Set in stunning woodland scenery (baby carriers recommended), England's largest man-made waterfall is a Victorian folly, created to give work to unemployed miners. The 80-acre site offers a children's assault course, playground and trampolines, a giant caterpillar swing, and forest garden with information on wildlife and conservation. There's also a snack bar and lakeside café.

Dingles Fairground Heritage Centre
Milford, Lifton, PL16 0AT, T01566-783425, fairground-heritage.org.uk. Apr-Oct Thu-Mon plus school holidays 1000-1730. £7 adult, £5 child (3+), £21 family.
This quirky National Fairground Collection features moving and static fairground exhibits, industrial and road steam engines, plus vintage vehicles and machinery. There are working rides (check website for times) much longer than a regular one, so great for those who want to spend hours on the dodgems (£1).

Finch Foundry
Sticklepath, Okehampton, EX20 2NW, T01837-840046, nationaltrust.org.uk. Mar-Nov Mon, Wed-Sun 1100-1700. £4.20 adult, £2.10 child.
For the mechanically or historically minded, here is a water-powered foundry, set up during the Napoleonic Wars to make mining and agricultural tools. It also repaired them, sharpening up to 400 tools a day using the three waterwheels to drive a huge tilt hammer and grindstone. There are hourly demos by volunteers, a professional blacksmith, quiz and trail for children, exhibition, foundry garden, kick-about space, picnic area, tea room, and the start of the 'four village trail' walk.

Traditional West Country fairground sign.

Ingenious marble run at the House of Marbles.

House of Marbles
Bovey Tracey, TQ13 9DS, T01626-835285, houseofmarbles.com. Mon-Sat 0900-1700, Sun 1000-1700. Free entry.

Effectively a shop, this one-time pottery has built a success story on three small museums of glass, games and marbles. Most fun are the mechanical marble runs, glass blowers in action and games to play in the garden. Nearby Bovey Heath is a Devon Wildlife Trust nature reserve.

Lydford Gorge
Lydford, EX20 4BH, T01822-820320. Gorge Apr-Nov daily 1000-1700; waterfall only Nov-Mar daily 1030-1500. £5.27 adult, £2.90 child, £14.50 family.

The whirlpools, waterfalls and rocky scenery along the River Lyd include the spectacular 30-m White Lady waterfall. With lagoons and deep rock pools it's a place for real wild swimming. In the 17th century it was the hideout of a large family of outlaws who stole sheep from Dartmoor farms but by the 19th century had become a 'Little Switzerland' attraction. Today it is complete with café using local food. There are some short circular walks (leaflets available from the shop) and you can 'walk the plank' over the Devil's Cauldron whirlpools, or take the Railway Trail (good for pushchairs) with hides for watching wildlife such as lizards, badgers, butterflies and deer, as well as bugs, beetles and other mini-beasts in the woods. A leaf display at the entrance helps identify the different kinds of trees. Also look out for regular family events. Lydford village has a 12th-century castle on a motte.

Miniature Pony Centre
North Bovey, TQ13 8RG, T01647-432400, miniatureponycentre.com. Apr-Nov 1030-1630. £6.95 adult, £5.95 child (3-16), £24 family.

Real life My Little Pony, with Shetland ponies, donkeys (foals in spring and summer), pygmy goats, guinea pigs, rabbits, gerbils and more. There's a good adventure playground, indoor play areas for littler ones, assault course, nature trails by the lakes, daily bird-of-prey display, and, at Sandy Farm, sessions on farm skills like driving tractors, loaders and trailers, sorting hay and feeding the animals. You can also ride a pony (£1.50) with rosettes for all riders.

One of Devon's best value days out

ROSETTE WITH EACH PONY RIDE

Find us on the B3212, two miles west of Moretonhampstead towards Princetown.
Tel: 01647 432400 www.miniatureponycentre.com

THE ORIGINAL
MINIATURE PONY CENTRE
DARTMOOR

Visit us on beautiful Dartmoor for a fun day out. There's lots to see and do for all the family.

- Miniature ponies, donkeys and other horse breeds • Children's pony rides (aged between 2-9 years) • Pygmy goats, pigs, lambs and many other animals • Mini tractors • Daily birds of prey display
- Paddock View cafeteria • Indoor and outdoor play areas • Lots of other activities throughout the day

Open every day from Easter to Autumn half term inclusive from 10.30am - 4.30pm. (July and August 10am - 5pm).

Explore the moor

Once the children have stopped yearning for the props of civilization, they'll find that the moor is a great place to listen to skylarks, watch sheep being silly, mess about over stones and go slightly feral.

The Dartmoor National Park Authority organizes an annual programme of more than 400 guided walks, including family strolls, as well as children's activities lasting two to three hours (£3), such as pond dipping, story walks, discovery trails, and Dartmoor play days, suitable (but not exclusively) for children aged seven to 14. Of the authority's three information centres the most comprehensive is the **High Moorland Visitor Centre** at Princetown (T01822-890414, daily from 1000, free admission). There are displays on the history, culture and wildlife of Dartmoor, and information on walks and other activities. There is also information and screens for children to play with at Haytor (T01364-661520) and Postbridge (T01822-880272). The Ranger Ralph Club is for children aged five to 12. Members receive a goody pack, quarterly newsletter and a membership card allowing them to attend special events for free. It's the cost of just four second-class stamps, more details at dartmoor-npa.gov.uk/funzone, which also offers online games on subjects such as farming and climate change.

Ditch the car

The Authority sells detailed directions for numerous walks, some specifically for families, along with identification cards for spotting granite artefacts (stone corbels or apple crushers, quarried and prepared for use but not shipped), prehistoric remains, birds, wildflowers and more, to keep children interested. Audio walks can be downloaded from dartmoor-npa.gov.uk/vi-audiowalk.

Easy walks start at the three National Park Visitor Centres. Three options around **Haytor** are the Haytor Granite Tramway Walk (2½ miles), Haytor Rocks Walk (just over one mile) and Hound Tor Walk (seven miles). Around **Postbridge** you could try the Bellever Forest Walk (four miles), Archerton Walk (just over one mile) or Waterfall Walk (five miles). Near **Princetown** there's the Nun's Cross Walk (six miles), North Hessary Tor Walk (two miles), or King's Tor Walk (five miles on hard surface, so good for buggies). Alternatively, Abbeyford Woods near **Okehampton** (T01409-221692, forestry.gov.uk) have specially adapted paths suitable for buggies and a picnic area.

There are a variety of long-distance routes you could opt for. The **Dartmoor Way** is a circular route of more than 90 miles of generally easy walking around the moorland edge, via Okehampton, Chagford, Moretonhampstead, Buckfastleigh, Princetown and Tavistock. It can be accessed by bus and/or train routes, so you can pick a section to suit. There are also bus routes to take you on to the moor, so you simply walk back to your starting point. The summer Haytor Hoppa from Bovey Tracey is specifically designed for this, stopping at **Haytor Information Centre**, Widecombe-in-the-Moor, Hound Tor Rocks, Manaton and Becky Falls. There's also the Transmoor Link route between Exeter and Plymouth and the Cross Moor Link between Bovey Tracey and Okehampton via Moretonhampstead, with five trips a day at weekends. For more details check dartmoor-npa.gov.uk.

Walkers and climbers at Haytor.

Beware the moor

Whenever you walk on Dartmoor, take more care than seems necessary. The weather can change before you get to safety, mists are common, and every year people have to be rescued. Wear suitable clothing and footwear, take waterproofs, a map and compass, and know how to use them. Tell someone your route and expected return time before you set out and check the weather forecast.

To the north of the moor, between Two Bridges and Merrivale in the south and Okehampton in the north, are the military ranges, which are patrolled and marked by flags. They are generally not operational during the holiday season, but check firing times at dartmoor-ranges.co.uk.

Finally, if children know that animals can die after eating litter, they are less likely to leave it, so it's worth telling them. Feeding the ponies is a particularly bad idea as they are wild and even if they don't get sick from your snacks, they can bite and kick.

Sleeping Dartmoor

Pick of the pitches

Barley Meadow
Crockernwell, EX6 6NR, T01647-281629, barleymeadow.com. Mar-Sep. From £7.10 adult, £2.45 child, plus £6.46 non-member fee.

This small, immaculate, family-run Camping and Caravanning Club site in the northeast of Dartmoor National Park is just five minutes' drive from Fingle Bridge, a mile's walk from the popular Drewe Arms and a short stroll to the Two Moors Way. Campsite comforts include fire-pits, a games room, children's wooden play trail and a shop selling fresh-baked croissants.

Beara Farm Camping Site
Colston Rd, Buckfastleigh, TQ11 0LW, T01364-642234. Year round. £5 adult, £1 child (1-5), £1.50 child (6-10), £2.50 child (11-15).

Voted a top-10 Venture site by the AA, this Camping and Caravanning Club member offers just 25 pitches in a 3½-acre level meadow, 20 m from the River Dart with a steam train on the opposite side. Includes barbecue and spring water.

Churchill Farm Campsite
Buckfastleigh, TQ11 0EZ, T01364-642844, Easter-Sep. From £10-12/pitch, £1 dog.

Between Buckfastleigh and Buckfast, a relaxed, simple site on a working farm with views towards Buckfast Abbey (within walking distance). Eggs and lamb from the farm are sold. There are 20 pitches in 2½ acres with a central area where children play together (no ball games).

Cockingford Farm
Nr Widecombe-in-the-Moor, TQ13 7TG, T01364-621258. Mar-Nov. £3.50 adult, 50p child (4-10), £1 child (10-15), under 4s free.

A lovely, simple site in a deep cut in the moor between Widecombe- and Buckland-in-the-Moor, protected by hills and narrow roads (think hard before taking a caravan). It's popular with families, who return, sometimes generation after generation, and is something of a hidden gem.

Harford Bridge Holiday Park
Peter Tavy, Tavistock, T01822-810349, harfordbridge.co.uk. Year round. From £11/pitch.

Award-winning park with views of Cox Tor and the River Tavy as a boundary. Facilities include a hard tennis court, children's enclosed play area, table tennis and games room, television room and library, recreation green (no football and hard ball games), and two permanent barbecues. Holder of a David Bellamy Gold conservation award.

West Banbury Farm Cottages

10 charming self-catering cottages
Sleeping 2-8
Heated indoor swimming pool
Children's play area
Ideal location for Dartmoor,
North Devon Coast and Cornwall
Children and dogs welcome

t: 01566 780423
e: westbanburyfarm@btinternet.com
w: www.westbanbury.co.uk

Langstone Manor Park
Moortown, nr Tavistock, T01822-613371, langstone-manor.co.uk. Mar-Oct. £12-15/pitch (2 people), £3-4 child (3+).

Set in the grounds of a manor house in Dartmoor National Park, Langstone offers picture-perfect pitches in the shelter of grand trees, or terraced sites with views across the moor. A cosy on-site bar serves evening meals. There are nearby sales of organic vegetables and eggs.

Hayford Bridge Holiday Park.

Lydford Caravan & Camping Park
Lydford, nr Okehampton, EX20 4BE, T01822-820497, lydfordsite.co.uk. Mar-Nov. £4.70-7.10/pitch, £4.20-5.60 adult, £1.30-2.15 child.

With 90 pitches, a David Bellamy Gold-award site near the Granite Way cycle route. There is a dedicated dog walk (they are not allowed on the nearby village recreation ground) and barbecue area.

Parkers Farm Holidays
Ashburton, TQ13 7LJ, T01364-654869, parkersfarm.co.uk. Easter-Nov. £7-24/pitch (2 people), £2 child (3+).

Well placed for exploring the moor or making a break for the beaches in the South Hams, this terraced site is a guaranteed hit with the kids. In addition to trampolines, a playroom, restaurant serving home-cooked family food, farm walks are available where children can meet cows, pigs, goats, ponies, rabbits and other furry friends.

Runnage Camping Barns
Postbridge, Yelverton, PL20 6TN, T01822-880222, runnagecampingbarns.co.uk. Easter-Oct, at other times call first. Campsite £4.50 adult, £2.50 child (3-10), £3.50 child (11-15), £2 dog. Camping barns sleeping up to 15 £7.50 person, bunkhouse sleeping 12 £70/night, £10/central heating.

On a working beef and pedigree-sheep farm, surrounded by forest, moor and farmland, the campsite is divided between two meadows, the Walla Brook beside

Rain check

Arts & crafts
- **Duchy Square Arts Centre**, Tavistock Rd, Princetown, PL20 6QF, T01822-890828, duchysquare.org.

Cinemas
- **The New Carlton Cinema**, Market St, Okehampton, EX20 1HN, T01837-658586, cromer-movieplex.com.
- **The Wharf**, Canal Rd, Tavistock, T01822-611166, tavistockwharf.com.

Indoor swimming pools
- **Endsleigh Swimming Pools**, Cadleigh Park, Ivybridge, PL21 9JL, T01752-898903.

- **Meadowlands Leisure Pool**, The Wharf, Tavistock, PL19 8SP, T01822-617774.
- **Parklands Leisure Centre**, Simmons Park, Okehampton, EX20 1EP, T01837-659154, leisureconnection.co.uk/Centre/2/65/okehampton.html.

Museums & visitor centres
- **Bovey Tracey Heritage Centre**, The Old Railway Station, St John's Lane, TQ13 9GP, T01626-835078, devonmuseums.net/bovey.
- **Dartmoor Prison Museum**, Princetown, PL20 6RR, T01822-322130, dartmoor-prison.co.uk.

- **High Moorland Visitor Centre**, Tavistock Rd, Princetown, PL20 6QF, T01822-890414, Dartmoor-npa.gov.uk/vi-highmoorlandcentre.htm.
- **Museum of Dartmoor Life**, 3 West St, Okehampton, T01837-52295, museumofdartmoorlife.eclipse.co.uk.
- **The Robey Trust**, Parade Business Park, Pixon Lane, Tavistock, PL19 9AX, T01822-615960, therobeytrust.co.uk.
- **Tavistock Museum**, Court Gate, Guildhall Sq, PL19 0AE, T01822-612546, tavistockhistory.ik.com.
- **The Valiant Soldier Heritage Project**, 79 Fore St, Buckfastleigh, TQ11 0BS, T01364-644522, valiantsoldier.org.uk.

Sleeping Dartmoor

Go wild camping

Dartmoor is one of the few places in the UK where you can camp wild, except for a few restricted areas (not in enclosed areas or archaeological sites) and as long as you are out of sight and at least 100 m from the road. Campervans are not permitted and National Park Rangers do enforce the rule. You are even allowed to use suitably placed camping stoves – although no fires to protect insect and plant life – so you can lie and look up at the stars and think what life was like for the people who lived there in the past. A guide is available from National Park Visitor Centres or at dartmoor-npa.gov.uk/vi-wildcamping.htm.

Melted marshmallows at camp.

one, with use of toilets and showers in the camping barns. There are 30 Dartmoor ponies that roam free on the moor but occasionally turn up at night. Barbecue chops, burgers and sausages available from the shop. Camping barns sleep up to 15 and a bunkhouse offers six beds per room.

Woodovis Park
Gulworthy, nr Tavistock, PL19 8NY, T01822-832968, woodovis.com. Apr-Nov. £5-16/pitch, £7 person (5+), all-weather super pitches £4 extra.

Fourteen acres of park on the edge of the Tamar Valley, with five-star grass, all-weather pitches, indoor heated pool, shop selling local produce (bread and croissants baked on the premises), children's play area, including a real tractor, and games room with pool, air hockey, etc. The local Chipshop Inn includes a restaurant and bar menu plus skittle alley. Bike hire delivery can be arranged and there's an open field as play space with picnic table. Mobile homes are also available.

Best of the rest

Beechwood
Postbridge, PL20 6SY, T01822-880332, beechwood-dartmoor.co.uk. From £28 adult, £12-15 child (3-14), £4 child (under 3).

Off the main cross-moor road, a B&B with five acres of meadow where children can run wild, a garden, plus cosy old-style sitting room for guests. Accommodation includes a family room and two twin bedrooms making a family suite. Meals available.

Bellever YHA
Postbridge, PL20 6TU, T0845-371 9622, yha.org.uk. Year round. From £50/4-bed family room, £1 discount if arriving by bus, bike or on foot. Available as Rentahostel in winter.

The YHA's first purpose-built hostel, part of a Duchy of Cornwall farm, offers easy access to Bellever Forest and Tor, good for family rambles. Home-cooked evening meals with local ingredients available, plus wildlife garden, birdwatching, and pony trekking groups.

Burnville Farm
Brentor, Tavistock, PL19 0NE, T01822-820443, burnville.co.uk. B&B £70-80/night.

On the edge of the moor in lush landscape, a delightful period house, beautifully decorated, with views across farmland to the moor. Children are welcome in two rooms, one en suite. There are four attractive self-catering options too (booked through Helpful Holidays, see inside the back cover), two with swimming pools, and all with access to a tennis court.

Action bases

Okehampton YHA
Klondyke Rd, EX20 1EW, T01837-53916, adventureokehampton.com. Feb-Nov. Accommodation only Okehampton from £14.95 adult, £11.50 child; Bracken Tor from £16.95 adult, £12.95 under 18. Activity break £62-228 adult, £53-192 child (under 14), water-sport day £25 person.

In a converted Victorian railway shed on the edge of Dartmoor, this is not just a youth hostel but a licensed adventure centre with campsite, adventure playground, bike hire and climbing wall. You can try rock climbing, abseiling, canoeing, gorge scrambling, pony trekking, archery, treasure hunts, raft building, archery, survival skills and more. The hostel also manages the newly converted Bracken Tor Hostel at Saxon Gate, nearby, a 100-year-old Arts and Crafts house, plus annexe, with four acres of grounds leading straight onto the moors and access to the same activity programme.

River Dart Country Park
Holne Park, nr Ashburton, T01364-652511, riverdart.co.uk. Apr-Sep daily, Oct-Mar weekends only. £15-25/pitch (2 people), £6-7 extra person.

The spacious campsite in this woodland country park has a shop, outdoor heated swimming pool, tennis courts, games room and café. It is just a stroll away from numerous on-site and free activities, including an assault course, pirate ship, toddlers' beach and wooden play fort. For those nine or over, from mid-July to end August there are also CRS Adventures (T01364-653444) offering a day rock climbing and abseiling, canoeing on the Dart Estuary or caving (£30 per day, pre-booking essential). Through spring and summer school holidays CRS also runs Dare Devils – instructor-supervised adventure activities including indoor climbing and bouldering, canoeing on the lake in Native American-style canoes, mega zip wire, water zorbs and a high ropes course. Self-catering cottages (sleeping six to nine people) and luxury B&B in Holne Park House (holnepark.co.uk) are also available.

Spirit of Adventure
Powder Mills, nr Postbridge, PL20 6SP, T01822-880277, spirit-of-adventure.com. 2 days £120 adult, £90 child; accommodation only £14 adult, £11 child (under 18).

A granite barn on the site of an old gunpowder factory, pretty much in the middle of the moor, has been converted into a bunkhouse. There's a pottery and craft centre next door, which serves cream teas (Jun-Sep) in the courtyard using local cream. On offer are family-adventure weekends of two or three days, featuring rock scrambling, climbing, abseiling, kayaking and raft building.

Sleeping Dartmoor

Farm favourites

Dartmoor and West Devon Farm Holiday Group
dartmoor-farm-accommodation.co.uk.
B&B and self catering on Dartmoor and West Devon farms.

Kilworthy Farm
Nr Tavistock, PL19 0JN, T01822-614477, kilworthyfarm.co.uk. £27.50-35 person, around half price per child (to 14), evening meals £15.
Grade II Victorian factory farm buildings offer a family area with two rooms, or a single room made up to take children as well. There are also farm animals, garden space, board games, pool table, plus night-time outings by Land Rover to see the wildlife. Meal options (on request) include packed lunches and cream teas.

Dartmoor Holiday Cottages
Nr Bridestowe, EX20 4NS, T01837-861233, dartmoor-holiday-cottages.co.uk. £370-635/week sleeping 4.
Six cottages in a converted stone barn on an ancient working farm, dogs and horses welcome. There is a farm trail for visitors to follow, cots, high chairs and freezer meals.

Hammerslake
Ellimore Rd, Lustleigh, TQ13 9SQ, T01647-277547, lustleighbedandbreakfast.co.uk. B&B £60-85/room, £20 child in no-frills bunkroom for kids.
Off the beaten track, a hillside property with a big garden and attractive rooms. Popular with children. Evening meals available at The Cleave pub in Lustleigh.

Splashing out

Bovey Castle
North Bovey, TQ13 8RE, T01647-445000, boveycastle.com. From £180/room to £1500/suite, also 14 granite lodges sleep up to 8.
1906 luxury is offset by grounds where children are encouraged to set up camp and build dams. Along with a daily falconry display, prices include mountain bikes, croquet, a walks booklet, tennis, boules, cricket nets, jungle camp, trampoline, table tennis and tennis. As well as a billiard room, golf course and spa, there's a playroom for childen aged two to eight (£20 per session) and, in the holidays, rangers offer children aged seven to 14 activities like woodland camps, riding, volleyball, abseiling, raft building, tree-top adventure, survival skills, fly fishing and even ferret racing. For rainy days there are arcade games, pinball, X-box, dressing-up chest, karaoke machine, train set, Scalextric, Lego, board games and more, including a swimming pool.

Higher Westcott Farm
Westcott, nr Moretonhampstead, TQ13 8SU, T01647-441205, higherwestcottfarm.com. £80-115/room, afternoon tea £5 person, 3-course dinner £30/inc sparkling wine and canapés.
A boutique B&B run by owners with a small son who welcome families. Elegant and small enough that you can curl up in front of the fireplace and enjoy the honesty bar while the children sleep upstairs, or watch one of the selection of DVDs.

The Oxenham Arms
South Zeal, EX20 2JT, T01837-840244, theoxenhamarms.co.uk. B&B from £52.50 person.
A chance to step back in time in a 12th-century building where the stone floors have been worn away over the centuries. Just seven rooms, all too small for added beds, but children are welcome in the restaurant and attractive grassy space with tables at the back.

An autumn walk around Dartmoor.

Eating Dartmoor

Local goodies

Dartmoor is a great place to find local food, and most towns have a good butcher who also sells other local produce, as do shops like the Co-op in Moretonhampstead.

Delis

Ashburton Deli
16 North St, Ashburton, TQ13 7QD, T01364-652277.
A traditional deli with imported as well as local produce.

Black's Delicatessen
28 The Square, Chagford, TQ13 8AB, T01647-433545, blacks-deli.co.uk.
Offers both local bread and cheese, look out for the goat varieties.

Country Cheeses
Market Rd, Tavistock, PL19 0BW, T01822-615035, countrycheeses.co.uk.
Specialists in local cheeses, with shops in Tavistock, Topsham and Totnes, now also commissioning their own bespoke cheeses.

The Fish Deli
7 East St, Ashburton, TQ13 7AD, T01364-654833, thefishdeli.co.uk.
Fish from local boats, cooked fish dishes, plus deli items like olives.

Mann & Son
43 Fore St, Bovey Tracey, TQ13 9AD, T01626-832258.
Started as a farm shop, a family-run deli selling a wide range of local foods, especially cheese.

NH Creber
48 Brook St, Tavistock, PL19 0BH, T01822-612266, crebers.co.uk.
Established in 1881, the current Mr Creber stocks a huge range of cheeses plus home-cooked meats, pâtés, and other deli staples.

Farm shops

Dartmoor Farmers
dartmoorfarmers.co.uk.
Lists where to buy produce (largely meat) from the moor.

Lifton Strawberry Field Farm Shop
Lifton, PL16 0DE, T01566-784605, liftonstrawberryfields.co.uk.
Soft fruits, other fruit and vegetables (some pick-your-own), on-site bakery with steak pasties, meat pies, bread, scones, cakes, biscuits, jams, chutneys, apple juice, crisps, cereals, West Country confectionary, ice cream and more. There's also a restaurant for lunches.

Ullacombe Farm Shop and Barn Café
Haytor Rd, nr Bovey Tracey, T01364-661341.
Also has a great café, plus animal barn. You drive past some of the produce growing in the field.

Quick & simple

This is farming country and local food is both sustainable and high quality. As well as meat, look out for local honey, cider, milk and other dairy produce.

The traditional eating place for visitors has been the tea shop, although some can be too old-fashioned and formal for today's children. There are also pubs where portions cater for outdoor people and are generous.

Café Green Ginger
26 East St, Ashburton, TQ13 7AZ, T01364-653939, cafegreenginger.com.
In a period town house, on offer are salads, home-made soups, cakes, and generous cream teas. Friendly service and the kitchen is happy to cater for kids.

The Castle Inn
Lydford, EX20 4BH, T01822-820241, castleinnlydford.co.uk.
Built in 1550 with slate floors, stone walls, high-back settles, bronze and silver coins from the time of Ethelred the Unready and Norman scrolls above the

---

Farmers' markets

Ashburton Tucker's Market, Tuesday-Saturday.

Bovey Tracey, Saturday fortnightly.

Moretonhampstead, Tuesday.

Okehampton, third Saturday.

Tavistock pannier market, second and fourth Saturday. Friday produce and WI goods.

Widecombe-on-the-Moor, fourth Saturday.

Fresh produce makes for great meals in Devon.

EATING Dartmoor

The Elephant's Nest Inn.

fireplace. There is good homemade food and bar snacks. Families are welcome in the snug bar at the back or in the lounge if eating.

Dartmoor Tearooms and Café
3 Cross St, Moretonhampstead, TQ13 8NL, T01647-441116, dartmoortearooms.co.uk.
A changing blackboard menu, plus teas, from scones and cream to carrot cake.

The Drewe Arms
The Square, Drewsteignton, EX6 6QN, T01647-21224, thedrewearms.co.uk.
A thatched pub built to house the workers who built the Norman church. Run by the same family for more than 100 years, there are plain walls and benches, no bar but drinks carried from the servery. It's a place to show children how simple life used to be. Also has B&B accommodation and bunkrooms.

The Elephant's Nest Inn
Horndon, Mary Tavy, Tavistock, PL19 9LQ, T01822-810273, elephantsnest.co.uk. Daily 1200-1500 and 1830-2300 (Sun 2230).
A 16th-century country inn with traditional bar but decorated with elephant-theme items. Log fires, thick stone walls, slate floors, plus large garden. Children are allowed in two rooms off the bar. A monthly-changing menu features local produce. Accommodation is available in three en-suite double/twin rooms.

Peter Tavy Inn
Peter Tavy, nr Tavistock, PL19 9NN, T01822-810348, petertavyinn.com.
A charming 15th-century pub in a pretty village on the western flank of Dartmoor.

The Ring of Bells
North Bovey, TQ13 8RB, T01647-440375, ringofbellsinn.net. Easter-Nov daily 1100-2300, lunch and eves rest of year.
A 13th-century coaching inn in a pretty village with a good choice of beers, plus restaurant and bar meals, and a small courtyard outside.

Riverside Mill
Bovey Tracey, TQ13 9AF, T01626-832223, crafts.org.uk.
Run by the Devon Guild of Craftsmen, it serves main meals, cakes, Fairtrade coffee and snacks, using seasonal and locally sourced produce in a building with an exhibition space and impressive craft shop.

Royal Oak
Meavy, Yelverton, PL20 6PJ, T01822-852944, royaloakinn.org.uk.
Excellent pub on the western side of the moor beside an attractive village green with small rooms and decent food.

Rugglestone Inn
Widecombe-in-the-Moor, TQ13 7TF, T01364-621327.
A simple, small pub with open fires plus home-made food. Children are welcome and, in

good weather, can enjoy a large, grassed seating area across a shallow stream.

Warren Inn
Postbridge, PL20 6TA, T01822-880208, warrenhouseinn.co.uk. High on the moor, the fire always burns next to the lino floors, designed to cope with walkers' boots. Uses local suppliers for food. Children welcome and also dogs on leads.

Posh nosh

Agaric
30 North St, Ashburton, TQ13 7QD, T01364-654478, agaricrestaurant.co.uk. In a town becoming something of a foodie haunt, this is an elegant Michelin-listed restaurant which also rents four classy rooms in a refurbished Georgian house, including one king size suitable for families with sofa bed and cot (£130 plus £10 for children). Just let them know in advance if taking children and to make any special requests. Main courses from £14.95.

Prince Hall Hotel
Two Bridges, PL20 6SA, T01822-890403, princehall.co.uk. A restored Victorian home in a dip in the centre of the moor. Excellent food served in the bar, on the patio or in the restaurant. Light lunch fishcakes £8.95, home-made chips £2.95. Also eight rooms from £70 per adult, £30 per child (aged 10 to 13), and £25 per child (under 10). The large bell outside the front door was originally used to warn residents of prisoner escapes.

The White Horse
7 George St, Moretonhampstead, TQ13 8PG, T01647-440242, whitehorse-moretonhampstead.co.uk. A once spit-and-sawdust pub but now listed by Michelin for its food, it also offers good beer and live music. The enormous super-thin pizzas go down well with children. Wash down with a juice from Luscombe's. A large courtyard at the back.

Riding across Dartmoor.

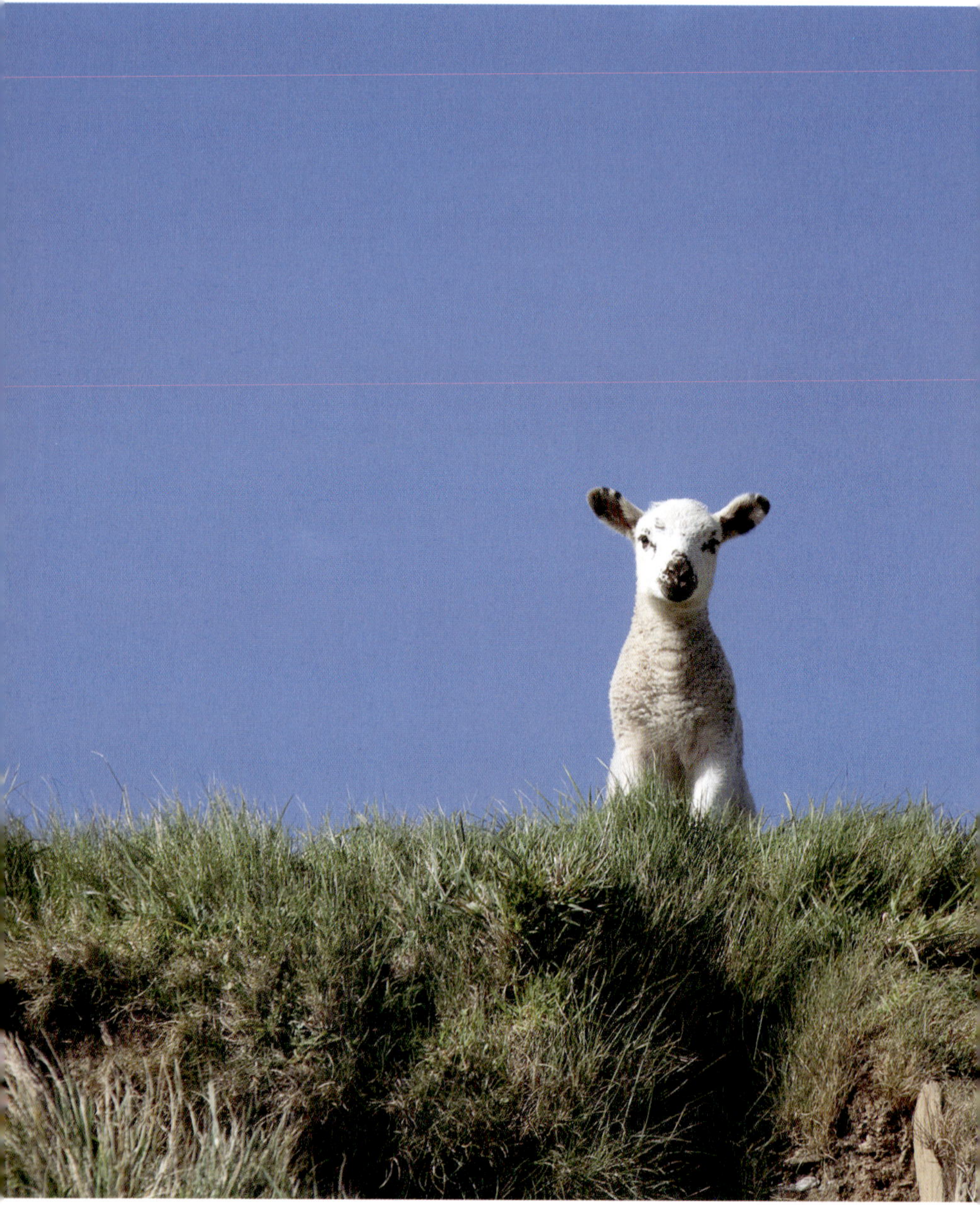

Contents

- 52 Map
- 56 Fun & free
- 58 Best beaches
- 60 Action stations
- 66 Big days out
- 70 More family favourites
- 72 Plymouth
- 74 Sleeping
- 78 Eating

South Devon

South Devon lamb.

You must

❶ **Catch** a crab (or several) at Dittisham.

❷ **Run** across the sands of Bantham.

❸ **Find** a blenny in the Wembury rock pools.

❹ **Paddle** a canoe in the Dart Estuary.

❺ **Follow** Francis Drake to Plymouth Hoe and Buckland Abbey.

❻ **Learn** to sail in Salcombe.

❼ **Ride** the rails up the Tamar Valley.

❽ **Go** wild at Woodlands Leisure Park.

❾ **Meet** the denizens of the deep at Plymouth Aquarium.

❿ **Eat** a Dartmouth ice cream.

Ashburton
Woodland
Denbury
Abbotkerswell
Coffinswell
Kingskerswell
Buckfast
A38
Buckfast Butterflies
& Dartmoor Otters
Ipplepen
Barton
Buckfastleigh
South Devon
Railway
Broadhempston
North
Whilborough
Shiphay
A381
Dean
Pennywell
Farm
Compton
A380
Torquay
Torre
Staverton
A384
Cockington
Dean Prior
Dartington
Marldon
Didworthy
Hollicombe
Rattery
Shinner's
Bridge
Berry
Pomeroy
Blagdon
Paignton
Tigley
A385
Totnes
Paignton &
Dartmouth
Railway
Tor Bay
South Brent
A385
Collaton
St Mary
A38
Belsford
Dart
Goodrington
heston
Avonwick
Lincombe
Harberton
Sharpham
Vineyard
ittaford
Stoke
Gabriel
Ashprington
4
A3022
North Huish
Diptford
Galmpton
Churston
Ferrers
Ugborough
Harbertonford
Tuckenhay
Greenway
Cornworthy
A381
121
Crabadon
Washbourne
Dittisham
1
Curtisknowle
Allaleigh
Hillhead
B3196
Capton
Halwell
A379
Brownston
Moreleigh
B3205
Avon
Woodlands
Leisure Park
8
A3122
Dartmouth
10
Kingswear
Woodford
Blackawton
Warfleet
3392
Millcombe
Bowden
A379
Loddiswell
Woodleigh
Mew Stone
A381
East Allington
Aveton
Gifford
Stoke Fleming
t Ann's
Chapel
Blackpool
Strete
Bigbury
Goveton
Churchstow
Harleston
Slapton
A379
A381
West
Alvington
Sherford
Slapton Sands
Bantham
Kingsbridge
Frittiscombe
Start Bay
Buckland
A379
Stokenham
Thurlestone
South
Milton
Frogmore
Charleton
Chillington
Woolston
Torecross
Kernborough
Beeson
A381
Galmpton
Beesands
South Pool
Hope
Malborough
It Tail
Kellaton
Salcombe
6
East
Portlemouth
Bolberry
Hallsands
South
Allington
N
Soar
Overbeck's
East Prawle
Start Point
Lannacombe
Bay
2 km
2 miles

Children will play on the beach till the sun goes down.

There are plenty of places to go boogie-boarding all over South Devon.

As a contrast to the semi-wilderness of Dartmoor, South Devon has been tamed a little but, unlike neighbouring Torbay, has not seen great tourism development. Here there are still long stretches of coast for exploring, running, splashing, generally having fun and taking advantage of the mild microclimate, both in and out of the water.

Covering 130 square miles of coastline and countryside and no fewer than five estuaries (the Avon, Erme, Dart, Salcombe-Kingsbridge and Yealm), the South Devon Area of Outstanding Natural Beauty is a magnet for holidaymakers. As well as the beaches of the South Hams, highlights include numerous family-friendly walks and towns and villages that are small and charming. There's **Kingsbridge**, traditionally the South Hams' market town, and **Totnes**, a more obvious centre of alternative living, full of intriguing shops, while Dartmouth, with its half-timbered buildings and narrow streets, dates back to its 14th-century heyday as a trading port and is a place to go crabbing, watch the yachts from the Embankment and perhaps listen to the band on the bandstand in the summer. **Salcombe**, home to Salcombe Dairy ice cream, is the place for smart yachties, who gambol across the protected estuary waters but leave the place largely closed out of season. To the west is the busy conurbation of **Plymouth**. South Devon is somewhere to try a bit of this and that, ramble, explore and potter, out and about.

Out & about South Devon

Fun & free

Dawdle around the Dart
The **Dart Valley Trail** runs for approximately 16 miles, taking in both sides of the River Dart. A shorter section is Kingswear to **Greenway**, around 4½ miles on the eastern side through thick ancient woodland along the river and a good place to spot wildlife. **Dittisham**, on the opposite bank from Greenway, offers an attractive field by the river with a play area that's good for just kicking a ball around. Mix and match with river rides, see page 60. Try the small passenger ferry between Dittisham and Greenway – summon by ringing the bell – or even hire your own boat.

See the strength of the sea
Put a shiver up your spine with a visit to **Hallsands**, once upon a time a coastal fishing village, home to 160 people, strung out along the cliffs and protected by a large shingle bar. Almost 100 years ago it was destroyed by storms and you can see the stark remains from a viewing platform at South Hallsands. At **Beesands**, just further north, a sea wall protects a similar village, built in the late 18th century when the threat of pirates had diminished. There's a small play area, a pebble beach to crunch over, maybe boats to watch. You can stop off at The Cricket Inn (T01548-580215, thecricketinn. com), founded by a man whose daughter was the last inhabitant of Hallsands, or pick up a snack from the Britannia Shellfish Café, see page 78.

Revel in a ria
Because there is no river flowing into it, the **Salcombe Estuary** is known as a ria. Protected from the open sea, this is both a local nature reserve, full of marine wildlife and a place to find good and sheltered beaches like East Portlemouth, Sunny Bay, South Sands and Mill Bay on the opposite side from Salcombe, all boasting golden sands. It's easy to nip between the beaches and Salcombe by ferry, see page 63.

You can also dally around the water's edge at South Pool, at the far end of the inlet opposite Salcombe, where there's a tidal ford and stepping-stones for splashing about. Here too is the Millbrook Inn (T01548-531581, millbrookinnsouthpool.co.uk), winner of Community Pub of the Year 2009, and runner up in the UK Gastro-pub Challenge, with simple as well as fancy food and live jazz on Sundays.

For something more demanding try the walk from East Portlemouth to Mill Bay beach, partly following the coast path and passing along open coast through grass, heath and scrub with fine views to Bolt Head. There are occasional sightings of whales and basking sharks here. You can continue as far as the former Gara Rock Hotel, returning inland along the tree-lined bridleway which follows the valley down to the sand and rock pools of Mill Bay, and then to East Portlemouth where you could refuel at the Venus Café, see page 80.

Sometimes the Devon sea looks like a mill pond.

Be impressed
The nine-mile **Revelstoke Carriage Drive** (southdevon aonb.org.uk) was built in the 1880s for the local Lord of the Manor who showed it off to visitors. Today the drive features a surfaced track on part of the South West Coast Path near Noss Mayo, along the cliff tops with great sea views. You may not be able to proceed along in a carriage, but park at the Warren National Trust car park (Warren Cottage was where the carriage visitors were given lunch) and take a stroll to enjoy the vistas. Mew Rock, named after the old term for a seagull, is now used by nesting cormorants which, if not flying low over the water, necks outstretched, may be standing, holding their wings half open to dry them after diving.

Take an arty amble
For an unusual twist on the South West Coast Path, dip into the 10-mile **Plymouth Waterfront Walkway**, which meanders around **Plymouth Sound** (by foot or water taxi if you prefer), and uses art, sculpture and poetry to showcase its heritage and history. A free MP3 pod-cast with commentary by Edward Woodward can be downloaded from southwestcoastpath.com. The walk can also be combined with a visit to the excellent **National Marine Aquarium** and other attractions in Plymouth, see page 72.

See the light
From the **Start Point** Lighthouse car park, the old lighthouse road (suitable for pushchairs) descends to Start Point with views across the bay to Slapton. Watch out for seals which sometimes sun themselves on the rocks below, plus basking sharks near the base of the cliffs, while further offshore, the submerged sandbank of the Skerries often attracts plunge-diving gannets. From the car park there is also a sign to Mattiscombe, a quiet and secluded beach. The path, almost directly south, has views to Prawle Point, the most southerly headland in Devon. Getting down to the beach is a bit of a scramble, but fun from the cliff-top path and there's sand, rocks and pools to enjoy once you are down.

Not free, but the 45-minute Lighthouse Tours offer a chance to explore the cylindrical kitchen and to listen to tales of storms and wrecks in Start Bay (T01803-770606, trinityhouse.co.uk, Jul-Aug daily 1100-1700, times vary rest of year. £2.80 adult, £1.50 child (5-16), £7.50 family, 1 m minimum height, no carrying of babies or children).

Pedal the Plym
The **Plym Valley Cycle Track** (NCN route 27) is seven miles long and passes Plym Bridge at Plym Woods (also good for walking). It's is a family-friendly route, easily reached from the A38, with a sealed surface and section over Roborough Down. There's also easy family cycling from **Coypool** (look out for the steam railway workings) to **Clearbrook** near Yelverton, along a former railway line over many spectacular viaducts where you may see peregrine falcons.

The **Erme Plym Trail** links with the **Erme Valley Trail** (Ivybridge south to Ermington) at Sequers Bridge, forming part of a coast-to-coast walk across Devon, with a branch reaching the coast at Wembury.

Go great guns
For those who want to relive war times recent and more historic, there are all kinds of pillboxes and fortifications created to defend against invasion. On the coast by **Kingswear** there are Second World War gun emplacements to admire at **Froward Point**. Then cross the river and either walk or catch the ferry from Dartmouth quayside to explore **Dartmouth Castle**. The first fortification to be built for firepower, this castle features a large canon on view outside (T01803-833588, english-heritage.org.uk, Apr-Oct daily from 1000, Mar-Nov weekends only; £4.50 adult, £2.30 child if you want to go inside).

Out & about South Devon

Best beaches

Bantham

It's impossible to hold your children back at Bantham. The moment you walk through the dunes to reach this beach beauty west of Kingsbridge, they'll be off, sprinting across acres of soft, rippled sand, splashing in shallow tidal lagoons or skipping through waves clutching a surfboard. Apart from toilets in the car park, facilities are few, but part of Bantham's free-spirited appeal lies in its wild, unspoilt nature.

Beesands

A mile-long, fine-shingle beach, backed by the freshwater lake of Widdcombe Ley. There's also Britannia Shellfish, see page 78.

Bigbury-on-Sea

This large sandy beach is effectively a sand spit pointing from the mainland to Burgh Island. A low-tide causeway or sea tractor offers access to The Pilchard Inn (T01548-810514, burghisland.com/pilchard), a reputedly haunted, 14th-century smugglers' pub serving soup, baguettes and bar snacks at lunchtime, plus Friday-night curries. During summer there is a limited passenger-ferry service, linking Bigbury-on-Sea with Bantham on the other side of the estuary.

Blackpool Sands

Driving south from Dartmouth, the A379 dips towards Start Bay where you'll find this immaculate turquoise cove (blackpoolsands.co.uk) nuzzled between headlands. Privately owned, the sand may be gritty at high tide (pretty useless for sandcastles) and the car-park attendants don't always excel in the charm stakes, but you can't deny the almost-Mediterranean beauty of the place, backed by trees. The swimming is sheltered, there are lifeguards in summer, a lost-child collection point, a freshwater paddling pool, deckchairs for hire, a large beach shop to buy bucket, spade, sun block, etc, and a lovely grassy area behind the beach for picnics, that is if you can resist the excellent Venus Café, see page 80.

Bovisand

Bovisand, near Plymouth, has a wide expanse of sand at low tide – perfect for ball games.

Challaborough

Just west of Bigbury, this sheltered, sandy cove has rock pools at low tide. Sailing, surfing and canoeing are popular and there is a good coastal walk to Ayrmer Cove.

East Portlemouth

A string of sandy beaches facing Salcombe, including Fisherman's Cove, Smalls Cove and Mill Bay (see below), East Portlemouth offers a Venus Café with terrace overlooking the water. A foot ferry operates between here and Salcombe; Sunny Bay is further along.

Hope Cove

This is the kind of place that lodges in childhood memories. A sleepy fishing village, fabulous rock pools, ample sand for beach cricket, gentle waters in which to swim and paddle a canoe, a harbour wall to fish from… all within the wide sweep of Bigbury Bay.

Lannacombe

Hidden down a long lane, just to the west of Start Point, Lannacombe is a peaceful beach with sand and rock pools. There's not much left of it at high tide and parking is limited.

Mill Bay

You won't find a beach in Devon with softer sand or more sheltered swimming than privately owned Mill Bay opposite Salcombe. A shallow stream on the left side of the bay is ideal for damming, while walkers can set off on a superb cliff-top jaunt as far as Gara Rock, before looping back to the beach car park. You'll only find toilets here but there's a café just up the lane above the jetty for the Salcombe to East Portlemouth ferry. Less than a mile from East Portlemouth, it's a steep climb to get there.

Salcombe North Sands

Lying just beyond the ruins of Salcombe Castle, North Sands is snug between wooded headlands and has limited parking, a shop and café.

Salcombe South Sands

Towards the mouth of Kingsbridge Estuary and Bolt Head, South Sands, with Lifeboat House selling ice creams, cream teas, sailing and wind surfing lessons, has fine sand, good, safe bathing, and can be reached by road, footpath or ferry from Salcombe.

Slapton Sands

A three-mile ridge of shingle and gritty sand stretching across the southern edge of Start Bay, Slapton Sands is popular for water sports and there's a good fish and chip shop at Torcross. Allied forces used the beach in 1943 to rehearse for the D-Day invasions. Behind is Slapton Ley Nature Reserve, see page 67.

Soar Mill Cove

If you're after a secluded smugglers' cove with caves, cliffs and rock pools, look no further than this stunning cove. It's easily reached from Soar, but the longer walk across Bolberry Down (T01752-346585, nationaltrust.org.uk) is all part of the adventure of a day here; alternatively there is a short tarmac path from the large car park. The sandy beach promises superb strandline treasure hunting and has streams ripe for damming.

Thurlestone & South Milton Sands

These are two big, open sand/shingle beaches; on the largest stands Thurlestone Rock sea stack. Rock pooling is excellent at low tide, while surfing, windsurfing and canoeing gear can be hired in summer. **Yarmer Beach** is also great for rock pooling.

Wembury

Near Plymouth, this is a real rock-pooling hotspot. In fact, it's such a good place for inter-tidal critters that it forms part of the Wembury Voluntary Marine Conservation Area. Best of all is that it's also home to the Wembury Marine Centre (T01752-862538, wemburymarinecentre.org, Easter-Oct, free admission), an ideal place to learn about the ecology and importance of rock pools. The centre organizes guided rock-pool rambles (£1 per person) where you'll search for rarities like the bloody-eyed velvet swimming crab and tompot blenny, as well as old favourites such as shore crabs and beadlet anemones. For more on rock pooling, see page 20.

Wonwell

This is a sandy beach on the east side of the Erme Estuary. Mothecombe, also sandy, lies opposite.

Out & about South Devon

Action stations

Boat trips

African Queen
Dartmouth, TQ6 9AL, T0800-211 8500, theafricanqueen.co.uk. Family rates negotiable.
Family cruises and fishing trips upriver or out to sea with a husband-and-wife team, aboard a 15-m-long ex-Royal Navy boat. From two hours to full day to catch a mackerel, see a dolphin, or spot a shark.

Dartmouth Boat Hire
Kiosk, North Embankment, T01803-834600, dartmouth-boat-hire.co.uk. 4-person boat £25/hr, including fuel, life jackets and charts.
Wooden motorized self-drive cabin cruisers ideal for exploring the River Dart from Dartmouth to Totnes. Skippered rigged inflatable (RIB) rides also available.

Falcon Charters
Dartmouth, T01803-839245, dartboat.com. Departures 1100 and 1500 for 2- to 3-hr trips. From £10 per person, family rates available.
Seafaris on the Dart Estuary and along the South Devon coastline aboard the 9-m *Falcon*, with the emphasis on wildlife watching.

Greenway Ferry
TQ1 2BG, T0845-489 0418, greenwayferry.co.uk. Dittisham to Greenway return £3 adult, £2.50 child, £5 inc bike. Rambler Dartmouth, Dittisham and Greenway £8.50 adult, £6.50 child. Also water-taxi services.
For the Dittisham to Greenway ferry just ring the riverside bell and you get to travel in a lovely, traditional wood-built boat. For other routes to Dartmouth and beyond, see page 63.

Salcombe Boat Hire
Salcombe, TQ8 8BX, T01548-844475, salcombeboathire.co.uk. Easter-Oct daily, hourly from 1100. Boat hire from £35/hr for 6 people.
Explore the sheltered estuary waters of Salcombe and Kingsbridge either on an organized cruise or on your own. Each fibreglass self-drive hire boat comes with lifejackets and a detailed chart to help you find the best spots for seals, beaches and pubs.

Whitestrand Boat Hire
Whitestrand Quay, Salcombe, TQ8 8ET, T01548-843818, whitestrandboathire.co.uk. Daily 0900-1800. 2-hr mackerel fishing trips £15 adult, £10 child; motor boat and Laser Pico dinghy hire from £25/hr, £85/day; rowing boat hire £20/hr, £75/day; double canoe hire £13/hr, £55/day.
Great range of options for getting you afloat from three independent businesses, from stable two-person kayaks to a 5-m Fastliner with cabin and outboard engine. Mackerel fishing trips take place four times daily (May-Sep) on the skippered *Calypso*.

Bushcraft

Wildwise
Foxhole, Dartington, nr Totnes, TQ9 6EB, T01803-868269, wildwise.co.uk. Family camp £335 for 2, £450 for 3, £565 for 4; Wild Ones (8-12) and Teen Spirit (13-16) Weekends £195; Prehistoric Weekend £185.
Aiming to communicate that the natural world is essential, accessible and enjoyable for all, courses include a dangerous weekend for boys, family bushcraft days, family wildlife tracking and more.

Canoeing

Backwater Adventures & Essential Adventure
Bovey Tracey, T01395-200522, backwateradventures.co.uk. £30 person, minimum age 8.
Canoe trips of five hours on rivers Dart, Teign and Exe, plus Exeter Canal, including bushcraft and survival skills, whitewater kayaking, open-canoe training plus guided trips and some scheduled archery and air rifle sessions (even for kids). Courses are tailored to requirements.

Canoe Adventures
Beside the Maltsters Arms, Tuckenhay, TQ9 7EH, T01803-865301, canoeadventures.co.uk. From £19 adult, £16 child (3-16).
Guided paddling trips of four or five hours exploring the secret creeks of the Dart Estuary in 12-seat Voyager canoes. Each canoe comes with steersman, equipment, flint and steel lit

brazier, barbecue and shelter, tea, coffee and hot chocolate. Family paddles are available, catering for all ages, from babies upwards.

Canoe Tamar
Tavistock, T01822-833409, canoetamar.co.uk. £22 person, under 5s free.
Paddling the River Tamar between the quays of Morwellham and Cotehele (on the Cornish side of the river) using stable, Canadian canoes and run by the same people as Tree Surfers, see page 33. Time and direction depends on the tide.

leaving only ripples

CanoeAdventures
For all ages why not try guided 12-seat Voyager canoeing offering you excellent fun on the wonderful River Dart in South Devon
01803 865301
www.canoeadventures.co.uk

Green Tourism GOLD

Keeping warm at Wildwise.

Out & about South Devon

Singing Paddles
Kingsbridge, T0775-442 6633, singingpaddles.co.uk.
From £20 adult 2 hrs, £10 child for canoe trips and bushcraft.
Tailor-made canoeing trips on the Kingsbridge and Avon estuaries, suitable for all ages and covering technique, safety, navigation, plus games. Also bushcraft, learning to build shelters, light fires and cook over them.

Horse riding
Dittiscombe Equestrian Centre
Slapton, nr Kingsbridge, TQ7 2QF, T01548-581049. £10/half hr, £20/hr, £25/day. Minimum age 5.
BHS-approved centre offering individual or group lessons and hacking, from complete beginners to experienced riders. Indoor and outdoor schools, tuition, plus full days with stable management, lessons and a ride.

SRS Training
Nr Totnes, TQ9 6AU, T07974-813389, srs-training.co.uk. Starter hack £30/1¼ hrs, £28/Nature Play half day, £40/pony day.
A riding school and training centre for land-based skills, offering lessons, pony days (or half days), starter hacks and steady hacks for experienced riders. Also nature play for children aged seven and over, having fun petting and looking after the guinea pigs, ferret (which plays like a cat), ducks, geese, furry degus, sheep and goats.

Outdoor swimming
Tinside Lido
The Hoe, Plymouth, PL1 2PA, T01752-261915, plymouth.gov.uk. May-Sep daily weather permitting. £3.40-6.50 adult, £2.40-4.25 child (5-15), £9.70-17.05 family.
Below the Hoe at sea level, a large saltwater pool with three fountains and views across Plymouth Sound from a Grade II-listed Art Deco building. Entry to the Mount Wise 25-m fun activity and paddling pool is free of charge.

Powerboating
RIBS 4 Kids
Salcombe Powerboat School, Bolberry House, Bolberry, TQ7 3DY, T01548-842727, salcombepowerboats.co.uk. £160/day, minimum age 8, level 2 from 12 years.
Full-day RYA course in handling a RIB.

Sailing
Dittisham Sailing School
Anchorstone Café, Dittisham, TQ6 0EX, T01803-722365. Easter-Nov. Lessons £38/2 hrs, boat hire £20/hr.
From the café next to the pontoon, tuition from six years in a range of dinghies from Toppers up, plus boats for hire, including motorboats from half day to a week.

ICC Salcombe
Island St, Salcombe, TQ8 8DT, T01548-531176, icc-salcombe.co.uk. 2-day courses Fri-Sun from £160 non-resident adult, £144 non-resident child, £135 resident adult, £122 resident child, minimum age 8.
The Island Cruising Club operates from the retired Mersey ferry *Egremont*. You can join live-aboard sailing courses or take a launch from Whitestrand Pontoon. ICC offers the full range of RYA sailing courses, lasting from two days to a week and suitable for water-

CANOE TAMAR
Family canoe trips on the River Tamar
01822 833409
www.canoetamar.co.uk

Don't miss the waterfronts

The harbour at Dartmouth.

The deep estuaries from Dartmouth to Totnes and Salcombe to Kingsbridge, along with the Avon at Bantham and Yealm between Newton Ferrers and Wembury, define the South Hams almost more than the coast. They all prevent easy road transport so it's a good move to ditch the car and take to the water. You can then explore inaccessible corners, fine beaches and enjoy the waterside views – perhaps taking binoculars and snacks with you.

Around Salcombe, particularly in summer, it's a good idea to take the foot ferry to **East Portlemouth**, for example (T01548-842061, year round daily), giving access to the secluded but popular beaches of Mill Bay, Sunny Cove and Smalls Cove (see pages 58-59). Operating from Salcombe to South Sands is the **South Sands Ferry** (T01548-561035, southsandsferry.co.uk, Easter-Nov every 30 mins). **Rivermaid** (T01548-853607, May-Oct) covers the waters from Kingsbridge to the coast and all the creeks in between, reached at high tide in a purpose-built passenger vessel.

The **Avon Estuary Walk** provides a waymarked nine-mile trail around the estuary if you and, more importantly, the kids are feeling energetic, with a summer-only foot crossing between Bantham and Bigbury-on-Sea (Cockleridge, T01548-561196). Bantham Copse is National Trust land but a more likely attraction is the large sandy beach 300 m from the parking.

Riverboats run between Totnes and Dartmouth, Dartmouth town and Dartmouth Castle, and also Dartmouth and Greenway. It's a lovely way of getting around and a chance to admire wildlife and greenery so lush in summer that it has stood in for the Amazon on film. Passenger and vehicle ferries operate year-round services between Dartmouth and Kingswear (dartharbour.org/harbour-river-guide/ferries). **Dartmouth Lower Ferry** (T01803-861234. £3.20 per car, foot passengers £1 adult, £0.50 child) crosses between Lower Kingswear and Dartmouth carrying up to eight cars and towed by a small tug. River taxis like **Ferry Rat** (T07818-934869) link smaller points like the Buckfastleigh–Totnes rail route to the Steamer Quay at Totnes.

Out & about South Devon

confident children. Boat hire and private tuition (for half or full days) is also available.

Salcombe Dinghy Sailing

Salcombe Tourist Information Centre, TQ8 8DE, T01548-843927, salcombedinghysailing.co.uk. £45/1½-hr tuition, £85/day tuition, from £130/day sailing with tuition, £65/half day Wayfarer hire. AALA licensed. Learn to sail with RYA-qualified instructors over a series of sessions, plus some taster sails. Family sailing sessions operate from Whitestrand Pontoon or East Portlemouth beaches. Alternatively, hire a boat from half a day to a week for a more leisurely exploration of the Salcombe Estuary.

Southsands Sailing

Southsands, Salcombe, TQ8 8LN, T01548-843451, southsandssailing.co.uk. Taster sessions from £35/2 hrs, courses from £190/RYA children's course, minimum age 8.
Here is a catamaran school with sailing, plus stand-up paddle boarding and kayaking at an AALA-licensed centre (also RYA and BCU), offering two-hour taster sessions to two-day courses. Also hires out sailing dinghies, single or tandem kayaks, and catamaran dinghies.

Surfing

The main surfing area is at Bigbury-on-Sea/Bantham, with some also at Wembury.

Discovery Surf

Bigbury, T07813-639622, discoverysurf.com. Year round. £38/2-hr lesson, discounts for more, minimum age 6.
Surf lessons at Bigbury-on-Sea for all ages and levels, with an emphasis on small groups, plus a summer Fun Hour where kids can learn about sea safety and use surfboards to build a raft.

Lushwind Watersports

Blackpool Sands and Bigbury, T07849-758987, lushwind.co.uk. £38/2-hr taster session, from £11/hr kayak hire, tuition from age 8.
Kayaking, windsurfing (an RYA-recognized centre), plus stand-up paddleboard hire and trips, week courses are available. The Venus Riders package for £80 includes food from the café at Blackpool Sands or Bigbury, and four hours' tuition in paddle boarding, surfing (Bigbury only), windsurfing or kayaking over one or two days at either or both beaches.

Multi activities

Mountain Water Experience
Courtlands, Kingsbridge, TQ7 4BN, T01548-550675, mountainwaterexperience.co.uk. £25/half day. Minimum age 8.

Includes rock climbing, abseiling, coasteering, kayaking and caving, in, around and even under the Devonshire countryside. Offering residential or non-residential, half- and full-day activities for families. Locations vary depending on the tide.

Learn to surf with Discovery Surf School.

Out & about South Devon

Big days out

Dartmoor Zoo
Sparkwell, Plymouth, PL7 5DG, T01752-837645, dartmoorzoo.com. Daily from 1000. £8.95 adult, £6.95 child (4+), £29 family. Perhaps better known as 'Ben's Zoo' from the BBC TV series which followed efforts to re-open this small zoo (read *The Story* on the site), the 33 acres are now home to an observation tower and more than 200 animals, from tiny stick insects to Solomon the Lion, just one member of the UK's largest collection of big cats. There are bears, wolves, seals, llama, deer, ostriches and prairie dogs. Close Encounters of the Animal Kind takes place daily at 1400 in the education barn, with pythons and spiders as well as tame foxes and occasionally big cat cubs, plus birds of prey flying demonstrations at 1200 and 1600. There are also picnic areas, a shop and restaurant.

Morwellham Quay
Nr Tavistock, PL19 8JL, T01822-832766, morwellham-quay.co.uk. Easter-Nov 1000-1700. £9.50 adult, £7 child, £24.50 family, £3.50/parking. Now part of the Tamar Valley Area of Outstanding Natural Beauty, Morwellham Quay was for 1000 years a centre for shipping silver, tin and copper. Deserted by 1900, today the award-winning industrial museum is part of the Cornwall and West Devon Mining Landscape UNESCO World Heritage Site. Costumed-staff show how things used to be done by the Victorians and visitors can dress up themselves to join in. There's a railway ride into an old mine, woodland trail, kitchen gardens, Victorian cottages and workshops, smithy, boat building, including a 100-year-old gaff-rigged ketch, horse and cart rides, working hydro-electric station, and the ship's chandler's shop selling lots of old-fashioned sweets. A rolling restoration programme includes on-going excavations. The Ship Inn is now serving good local food from the farm.

Paignton & Dartmouth Steam Railway
Queens Park Station, Torbay Rd, Paignton, TQ4 6AF, T01803-555872, River Link T01803-834488, pdsr.co.uk. Trains Apr-Oct, boat Dartmouth–Totnes year round. Paignton–Dartmouth return £12 adult, £8.50 child (3-15), £30 family; Round Robin £19.50 adult, £12.50 child (3-15), £58 family. Spend a day riding waves and rails with this seven-mile holiday line along the coast from Paignton to Kingswear, passing over three Brunel viaducts, crossing to Dartmouth on the passenger ferry, then taking a River Dart Cruise to Totnes, stopping off as and when you like. A Round Robin ticket covers all sectors and links back to Paignton by bus service 100 from Steamer Quay in Totnes (open-topped when weather permits). Check the website for specials like Pirate, Ice Cream, Murder-Mystery and Thomas days.

Pennywell Farm
Buckfastleigh, TQ11 0LT, T01364-642023, pennywellfarm.co.uk. Feb-Nov daily 1000-1700. £10.50 adult, £8.50 child (3-16). This all-springing, all-prancing farm park should keep you busy for a whole day with different activities every half hour. Lambs, chicks, rabbits and miniature pigs are just some of the cute-and-cuddlies, with pony rides, falconry displays and deer feeding also available. It's not all wild and woolly, though, as rides for all ages are included in the admission price, such as quad bikes for children over six, go-carts for those over eight, and Rainbow Railway for all ages along with a Tractor Village. During school holidays there are on-site entertainers such as jugglers, storytellers and more. There is pond dipping, a wonderful willow maze, plus a chance to learn about growing food. If it rains, you can take cover in the animal barn or farmyard theatre.

South Devon Railway
Buckfastleigh, TQ11 0DZ, T0845-345 1420, southdevonrailway.org. Mar-Oct, limited timetable in other months, departure times vary. Buckfastleigh–Totnes return £10 adult, £6 child (5-14), £29.80 family.

Buckfastleigh Station oozes nostalgia as the Great Western Railway steam locos hiss and puff next to the cosy waiting room and old trolleys piled with trunks. However, there's more to this beautiful seven-mile section of track alongside the River Dart than just another ride on a choo-choo. At Buckfastleigh you will find a museum, gift shop, café, picnic garden, play area, a maize maze and riverside walks – not quite enough to fill a whole day until you discover the South Devon Railway links two additional attractions. At Buckfastleigh (the route also stops at Staverton), **Dartmoor Otters & Buckfast Butterflies** (T01364-642916, ottersandbutterflies.co.uk. Apr-Oct 1000-1700) features an underwater viewing area for European, Asian and North American otters, as well as a tropical house for butterflies, leaf-cutter ants and terrapins. Feeding times are daily at 1130, 1400 and 1600 and there's a hospital for sick otters. At the other end of the line the **Rare Breeds Farm** at Totnes (T01803-840387, totnesrarebreeds.co.uk. £4.50 adult, £3.25 child, £14 family) is a place to cuddle, fuss over and

Visit Slapton Ley

Why? A shingle bar in this National Nature Reserve is all that separates the largest freshwater lake in the southwest from the sea, the bar showing the links between seabed features and shoreline landforms. You can look out for the wildfowl, check out the old Sherman tank (this is where Allied forces practised for D-Day Landings during the Second World War) and, if the weather is good, pop over the pebbles for a paddle.

Where? Next to the A379, with the village of Slapton just inland and Torcross at the southern end.

How? The **Field Studies Council** (field-studies-council.org/family) manages the site and there are hides, a nature trail and interpretation panels, along with toilets and picnic sites so you can explore at will. Alternatively, the **Slapton Ley Field Centre** (TQ7 2QP, T01548-580685, slnnr.org.uk) runs guided walks from May to September on topics such as local birds, shelter building, badgers, bats and eels (£10 adult, £7 child, £30 family). Round off with food at Torcross. There's fish and chips at the **Start Bay Inn** (T01548-580553, startbayinn.co.uk) run by a Rick Stein food hero and also offering a family room, although others swear by **The Crowing Cock** (formerly The Sea Shanty, T01548-580747) who offer eat-in or takeaway. Or you can try the Sea Bay Café or Rocket Café.

Alternatively, the Field Studies Council runs residential courses year round on natural history and art, plus family activities. Sand Sea and Surf, (£345 adult, £245 child over 8) combines adventure activities like kayaking, coasteering and body boarding with relaxing beach and wildlife activities. Start Bay Stores at Torcross sells beach gear.

The shingle bar protects Slapton Ley from the sea.

Out & about South Devon

feed an array of beasts. There are owls, red squirrels, goats, sheep, rare-breed chickens, a hedgehog rescue centre and more. Discounted joint tickets are available for the railway and either attraction. As an add-on, on some days you can catch an onward bus from Buckfastleigh station to the town and Buckfast Abbey, free to train ticket holders.

Tamar Valley Line
National Rail Enquiries, T08457-484950, firstgreatwestern.co.uk. This is one of the prettiest national rail routes, running from Plymouth to Bere Ferrers (quayside 10 mins from the station), Bere Alston and Gunnislake, all of them on the **Tamar Valley Discovery Trail**, passing orchards and market gardens. En route, across the magnificent Calstock viaduct, the train crosses into Cornwall and Calstock village with riverside picnic and play areas, where the National Trust medieval estate of Cotehele is accessible by a 1½-mile river walk.

Woodlands Leisure Park
Blackawton, nr Totnes, TQ9 7DQ, T01803-712598, woodlandspark.com. Mar-Nov daily from 0930. £11.45 person, £43.80 family, children under 92 cm free.
Deer grazing in leafy paddocks offer a deceptively tranquil entrance to Woodlands' 90 acres, but step through the gates of this 10-zone theme park and whether

Fun on the bumper boats at Woodlands.

Out & about South Devon

it's the indoor play zones or outdoor rides, life becomes a blur. Without resorting to electronic thrills, rides include the 500-m Tornado Toboggan, White Knuckle Swing Ship and three water coasters. There are also pedal boats, zip wires, a commando assault course plus plenty of less intense attractions for younger children, such as a Wild West play town. Calming moments can be sought at the fun farm (home to Terence the Champion Turkey) and falconry centre with free flying displays, while wet weather will see everyone bolting for the biggest indoor play area in the UK. You can combine the fun with accommodation at an award-winning campsite, see page 75.

More family favourites

Buckland Abbey
Yelverton, PL20 6EY, T01822-853607, nationaltrust.org.uk. Mar-Nov Fri-Wed 1030-1730, limited opening rest of year. £7.40 adult, £3.70 child, £18.40 family.

This converted monastery was the home of adventurer Sir Francis Drake after he was knighted, and there are rumours that Drake (first to sail around the world and responsible for the defeat of the Spanish Armada) still haunts the building with his 'hell hounds'. Perhaps his drum really does sound when England is in danger, in which case Drake is supposed to come back from the dead. There are workshops in the ox sheds, with demonstrations of Tudor crafts like woodturning, a kitchen with clues to 400 years of history, and a herb garden with 40 different authentic medicinal and cooking herbs. Children can try on traditional Tudor costumes while meeting Drake's servants, and discover how to find their way at sea with replica Tudor navigation equipment. There are four woodland walks, a picnic area, quarry orchard, as well as a restaurant (restricted menu Nov to Mar).

❸ Modbury, between Plymouth and Salcombe, boasts of being the UK's first plastic-bag-free town.

National Marine Aquarium
Plymouth. See page 72.

Overbeck's
Sharpitor, Salcombe, TQ8 8LW, T01548-842983, nationaltrust.org.uk. House/museum Mar-mid Jul and Sep Mon-Fri and Sun 1100-1730, mid Jul-Sep daily 1100-1730, Oct Mon-Thur and Sun 1100-1630; garden daily 1000-1800. £6.40 adult, £3.20 child, £16 family.

The seven acres of grounds here feature exotic gardens and views over the estuary, but this is an indoor option too, home to an Edwardian scientist and inventor called Otto Overbeck, and possibly a ghost called Fred (children can

Buckland Abbey.

win a ghost-hunter's certificate by finding him). Overbeck's inventions included the popular 'rejuvenator' meant to make people young by giving them an electric shock… There are also shark's teeth, a crocodile skull, birds' eggs and hyena droppings in one of those idiosyncratic natural history collections. A polyphon is a giant, old-fashioned music jukebox and there are clues to a secret children's room with old games and toys. At the back is a youth hostel, see page 77.

Sharpham Vineyard
Sharpham Estate, Ashprington, Totnes, TQ9 7UT, T01803-732203, sharpham.com. Café, T01803-732178, thevineyardcafe.co.uk. Mar-May and Sep-24 Dec Mon-Sat, Jun-Aug daily 1000-1700.
Not just a vineyard but a centre for cheese, with walks on a gorgeous estate which points into a sharp bend on the River Dart. From Easter to September there's an outdoor café offering a cheese or fish platter, starters and puddings, plus great views. When bored the children can play in the nearby field, admire the Jersey and Guernsey cows, and peer into the creamery to look at cheese in the making. Booking is recommended. Estate wine and cheese are sold to take home.

Rain check

Cinemas
• **Alexandra Cinema**, Market St, Newton Abbot, TQ12 2RB, T0871-230 3200, scottcinemas.co.uk.
• **Apollo Cinema**, Esplanade Rd, Paignton, TQ4 6AG, T0871-223 3475, apollocinemas.com.
• **The Barn Cinema**, Dartington Hall, Totnes, TQ9 6DE, T01803-847070, dartington.org/arts.
• **Central Cinema**, Abbey Rd, Torquay, TQ2 5NQ, T01803-380001, merlincinemas.co.uk.
• **The Flavel**, Flavel Place, Dartmouth, TQ6 9ND, T01803-839530, theflavel.org.uk.
• **Plymouth ABC Cinema**, Derry's Cross, Plymouth, PL1 2SW, T01752-663300, ents24.com/web/cinema.
• **Plymouth Arts Centre**, Looe St, Plymouth, PL4 0EB, T01752-240240, plymouthartscentre.org.
• **Reel Cinema**, Fore St, Kingsbridge, TQ7 1PP, T01548-856636, thereelcinema.co.uk.
• **Vue Barbican Leisure Centre**, Barbican Approach, Plymouth, PL4 0LG, T0108-224 0240, myvue.com.

Indoor activities
• **Bang Wallop**, 2 Island Sq, Island St, Salcombe, TQ8 8DP, T01548-843100, bangwallop.co.uk. A photography studio and school, offering photography lessons in the school holidays (£45 for two hours, maximum 10 children).
• **China Blue**, Station Rd, Totnes, TQ9 5JR, T01803-860908, china-blue.co.uk. A chance to paint your own piece of pottery.
• **Chocaholics Café**, see page 79. Chocolate courses for kids.
• **Riverford Field Kitchen**, West Barn, Buckfastleigh, TQ11 0JU, T01803-762074, riverford.co.uk, £24 child. Pick-and-cook afternoons are run for children every school holiday, including half terms.

Indoor swimming pools
• **Central Park Leisure Pools**, Outland Rd, Milehouse, Plymouth, PL2 3PU, T01752-566410.
• **Dartmouth Leisure Centre**, Townstal Rd, TQ6 0JL, T01803-837010, toneleisure.com.
• **Ivybridge Leisure Centre**, Marjorie Kelly Way, PL21 0SL, T01752-896999, toneleisure.com.
• **Plympton Pool**, Harewood Park, PL7 2AS, T01752-283275.
• **Quayside Leisure Centre**, Kingsbridge, TQ7 1HH, T01548-857100, toneleisure.com.
• **Totnes Pavilion and District Swimming Pool**, Station Rd, TQ9 5JG, T01803-862992, toneleisure.com.

Museums
• **Ashburton Museum**, 1 West St, TQ13 7DT, T01364-653595, ashburthon.org.
• **Dartmouth Museum**, 6A The Butterwalk, TQ6 9PZ, T01803-832923, devonmuseums.net/dartmouth.
• **Kingsbridge Cookworthy Museum**, 108 Fore St, TQ7 1AW, T01548-853235, kingsbridgemuseum.org.uk.
• **Plymouth City Museum & Art Gallery**, Drake Circus, PL4 8AJ, T01752- 304774, plymouthmuseum.gov.uk.
• **Salcombe Maritime & Local History Museum**, The Old Council Hall, Market St, TQ8 8DE, devonmuseums.net/salcome.

Let's go to...

Plymouth

Heavily bombed in the war, you could argue that subsequent planning did Plymouth even fewer favours, but the fabulous location overlooking the deep bay called the Sound, makes up for it, and recent investment is looking good.

National Marine Aquarium
T01752-600301, national-aquarium.co.uk, daily from 1000, £11 adult, £6.50 child 5-16, £30 family. There's easy parking just behind in the Barbican car park.
Once you've visited this water wonderland, boasting over 4000 creatures from 400 species, other aquaria might strike you as damp squibs. Not only will you find Britain's deepest tank (holding 2.5 million litres of water), but there are also around 70 sharks and a loggerhead turtle that was rescued after being washed up on a Cornish beach in 1990, alongside stunningly beautiful little jellyfish and rather ugly frogfish, among others. The aquarium is divided into distinct zones: Atlantic Reef, Mediterranean Sea, Weird Creatures, Coral Seas and The Shallows, with plenty of talks though the day as this is not just entertainment but a conservation and research centre. As captivating as these, often huge, displays are, it's the Explorocean zone that steals the show. Delving into oceanography with more than a splash of fun, its interactive exhibits include Mini SubMission, an underwater assault course using remotely operated vehicles. Equally high-tech is the 4D cinema where you get sprayed as a whale breaches and rocked in your seat when a shark nudges past. It's an all-day ticket so you can visit, then wander Plymouth and come back later.

Boat trips
To see sea life in the wild the Aquarium has teamed up with **SeaTrek** (T01752-266420, seatrek-plymouth.co.uk, from £24 adult, £12 child) which offers guided outings of 1-2½ hours from the Barbican (waterproofs and lifejackets supplied) in a rigid inflatable boat. Get up close to the shipwrecks and reefs with a hydrophone for listening to marine life (and ships and submarines), an underwater camera, binoculars and underwater viewing boxes to spot anything from oystercatchers and gannets, to dolphins, grey seals and sharks.
  Alternatively, **Sound Cruising** (T01752-408590, soundcruising.com) explores the Tamar upriver; under Brunel's bridge, to places like Calstock and Morwellham Quay (see pages 68 and 66), along the coast and River Yealm, or just cruises the harbour to take in sights of the naval dockyard and any warships moored up.

Around the town
You might find entertainment in the space outside the Aquarium, or in the irresistible attraction of watching smelly fishing boats go about their business, or even a wild cormorant learning to defend dinner from marauding gulls. The pedestrian harbour bridge may swing into movement while you wait, but once the gates open again it offers a quick route to the ancient **Barbican** area. Here buildings include the **Elizabethan House** (32 New St, T01752-304774, plymouth.gov.uk/museums; Mar-Oct Tue-Sat), a chance to go back to the times of Sir Francis Drake

and explore the restored kitchen and gardens of a sea captain's house. There's also the **Merchant's House** (33 St Andrew St, T01752-304774;. Mar-Oct Tue-Sat), the home of a famous Elizabethan 'privateer' and now venue for an Edwardian chemist's shop, Victorian schoolroom and a display on Plymouth in the Blitz.

Around the corner from the Barbican, facing the Sound, is the Art Deco **Tinside Lido** (see page 62) or climbing up to the Hoe behind, past the impressive and still-occupied **Royal Citadel** (guided tours Mar-Sep), you reach not just fabulous views over the water with its navy vessels and cruise liners but the red-and-white-striped **Smeaton's Tower** (T01752-304774), the re-erected base of the old Eddystone Lighthouse with 93 steps to the top.

There are more forts in Plymouth, including one rented as a holiday home with the Landmark Trust (see page 19), or for a taste of more gracious living, on the outskirts above the River Plym is **Saltram House** (Plympton, PL7 1UH, T01752-333 500, nationaltrust.org.uk; house Apr-Sep Sun-Thu 1200-1630, Oct Sat-Thu 1130-1530; garden and gallery Apr-Oct Sat-Thu 1100-1700, shorter hours rest of year; park daily dawn to dusk; house and garden £8 adult, £4 child, £20 family; garden only £4 adult, £2 child). It's a magnificent Georgian mansion, often used as a film set, in a rolling and wooded park dotted with follies. There's a regular programme of events, and activity rooms and trails for children. Admire the Chinese wallpapers, ornate ceilings and paintings, including those by local boy Sir Joshua Reynolds, as well as the variety of little buildings in the garden. The parkland offers cycle paths as well as walks and a play area. There's also a gallery selling local arts and crafts, and a children's menu in the licensed tea room.

Grab a bite

You can eat in the Aquarium or there are alternatives around the Barbican. **Monty's Bistro and Café** (13 The Barbican, T01752-252877) is just across the swing bridge, close to the Mayflower Steps where the Pilgrims set sail. It's open for breakfast, coffee, lunch and dinner. More of an institution is **Cap'n Jaspers** (T01752-262444) on Whitehouse Pier, visited by local fishermen as well as visitors and offering breakfast rolls, hot dogs, burgers, teas and coffees. Rather different again is **Duttons Café Bar** (T01752-255245) on Madeira Road, at the foot of the citadel on the Hoe, with views out over the Sound, offering crab sandwiches or fish soup, enjoyed outdoors in summer, plus cream teas inside or out seven days a week. Alternatively, if you want to go smart there's **Urban Brew** (T01752-227598) at Royal William Yard, serving coffee, paninis, wraps and sandwiches, next to one of the area's best art galleries.

Shark and diver.

Lionfish.

Sleeping South Devon

Pick of the pitches

Alston Farm
Nr Salcombe, TQ7 3BJ, T01548-561260, alstoncampsite.co.uk. Mar-Nov. £10-20/pitch, £0.50-2 child (under 12).

On the flat base of the valley, with sloping fields for tents. It's a little eccentric and there's not much in the way of facilities but the 12 acres adjoining the Salcombe Estuary are sheltered and pretty, with hedges, woodland, and plenty of wildlife. Fresh vegetables are available from the farm.

Bolberry House Farm Caravan & Camping Park
Bolberry, nr Hope Cove, TQ7 3DY, T01548-561251, bolberryparks.co.uk. Easter-Oct. £11-22/pitch (2 adults, 2 children).

This small, friendly park occupies a choice spot in the South Hams and has the sea views to prove it. There are fine cliff walks across Bolberry Down which can be used to access beautiful beaches like Soar Mill Cove. The campsite has lots of space for children to play and an added bonus of a fish and chip van calling by once a week.

Higher Rew
Marlborough, TQ7 3BW, T01548-842681, higherrew.co.uk. Apr-Sep. £10-17/pitch, £2-3 adult, £0-1.50 child.

A lovely four-star but simple and relaxed family-run site on five gently sloping acres above the Salcombe Estuary, booked well ahead by returning families. About one mile from South Sands and a ferry to Salcombe town, it is also within walking distance of Soar Mill. A play barn includes table tennis, skittle ally, pool table and covered play area for children under 11. There's a tennis court for hire, plenty of space for children to play, including a field for kite flying and dog walking, plus weekly visits from hog roast and fish and chip takeaways.

Karrageen Holiday Park
Bolberry, nr Marlborough, TQ7 3EN, T01548-561230, karrageen.co.uk. Mar-Oct. £12-20/pitch, £3-5 adult, £1 child.

For fabulous views of the valley or down to the sea, this is the place. On two fields above Hope Cove, the main five-acre field has been terraced and tree-lined and there are two large open areas for children to play safely. As well as camping pitches, static caravans are offered. The shop includes basic camping equipment.

Leonards Cove
Stoke Fleming, Dartmouth, TQ6 0NR, T01803-770206, leonardscove.co.uk. Easter-Oct. £7.50-15/pitch (+ 2 people), £2 child.

With a choice of static caravans, self-catering lodges and pitches for 40 tents and 14 touring caravans, Leonards Cove has a cliff-top position just half a mile from much-loved Blackpool Sands. Stoke Fleming (within easy walking distance) has shops, a pub and restaurant.

Old Cotmore Farm
Stokenham, nr Kingsbridge, TQ7 2LR, T01548-580240, holiday-in-devon.com. Mar-Oct. £11-16/pitch, £2-3.50 child (15-18), £1.50-2 child (under 15).

On a 16th-century farm in 22 acres with just 30 pitches and just a mile walk to Beesands, this site sees many repeat customers. There's a children's play area plus table tennis, table football, an open field for ball games plus dog walking. Also available are cottages with attractive traditional decor (oldcotmorefarm.co.uk).

Slapton Sands
Slapton, TQ7 2QW, T01548-580538, campingandcaravanningclub.co.uk. Mar-Oct. From £5.53 adult, £2.45 child, £6.46 non-member fee.

A well-run Camping and Caravanning Club site. overlooking Start Bay and close to the shingle beach of Slapton Sands and the nature reserve at Slapton Ley.

Woodlands Caravan Park

Blackawton, Totnes, TQ9 7DQ, T01803-712598, woodlands-caravanpark.com. Apr-Nov. £13.50-21/pitch, £7.50 person, under 2s free.

Right next to the amusement park (see page 68, free entry when staying two nights or more) and regularly winning awards, this site is geared to provide everything parents and children need, such as spacious pitches, immaculate facilities, ample laundries, luxurious showers, games/TV room, plus services like a freezer for ice packs, gas exchange and battery charging. There are three sections, Falcons View and Hillcrest Parks, with landscaped and terraced lawn or all-weather pitches, and Well Park with good views and non-allocated, sometimes sloping, lawn pitches.

Best of the rest

Adventure Cottages

Wheeldon Farm, nr Halwell, TQ9 7JY, T01548-821784, adventurecottages.co.uk. £340-1195/week.

This restored barn complex with self-catering cottages sleeps four to eight. There's an indoor pool, friendly animals and a games room. What will really get your kids begging to return though is the junior motorcycle

Farm favourites

Carswell Farm Cottages
Holbeton, nr Plymouth, P18 1HH, T01752-830020, carswellcottages.com. £275-795/week sleeping 4.

Lovely cottages with private gardens on this family-owned organic dairy farm near the coast path and just 15 minutes from the beach. You get a complimentary jug of milk when you arrive and there's a selection of local organic meat in the freezer – just pay in the honesty box. You can also order Organic Devon breakfast hampers. All the cottages come with TVs, a selection of CDs and DVDs, books, toys, games, stair gates, cots, high chairs, along with the names of recommended local babysitters. You can watch the milking and enjoy the wildflower meadow, with apple trees, a hazel copse, grassy areas, some children's play equipment; and there's the start of a new wildlife trail.

Fowlescombe Farm
Nr Ugborough, PL21 OHW, T01548-821000, fowlescombe.co.uk. £400-995/week sleeping 4.

This organic working farm, along with two architect-designed cottages, offers indoor games and toys, a cot, high chair, bed and stair guards, plus a raft of outdoor activities (and off-road pram to take little ones around them). There's a farm adventure pack including sheets with I Spy, pond-dipping kits, identification charts and nets, plus outdoor toys, enclosed garden and access to lots of farm walks. In the mornings children can learn how to feed chickens, peacocks, goats and pigs and can collect the eggs, before watching the sheepdogs at work. The farm's award-winning meat and ready-made meals are available from the freezer.

Knowle Farm
Rattery, nr Totnes, TQ10 9JY, T01364-73914, knowle-farm.co.uk. Year round. £285-1735/week.

Six cottages in 44 acres for children to explore with a walking trail, kingfisher at the pond, roe deer in the fields, a nuthatch in the woodland and, sometimes, an otter on the River Harbourne. There are the farm's resident kune kune pigs, donkey, rabbits, alpacas, sheep, chickens and ducks available for regular feeding and petting. Inside, there's a 10-m heated swimming pool, patio, play barn with soft play, table tennis, pool and other kids' games.

Feeding the ducks.

Sleeping South Devon

academy in a soundproof arena (minimum age seven). Just watch them get to grips with accelerating up the hills and braking into corners, clad in gear to look like Power Rangers. Tutoring is by the extraordinarily patient brothers who used to compete themselves.

Dittiscombe Cottages
Slapton, TQ7 2QF, T01548-521272, dittiscombe.co.uk. £300-820/week sleeping 4.

Stone cottages with private gardens in 20 acres that include a play area under trees with a picnic table, swings, slide, climbing wall, sandpit and a living-willow wigwam, plus a separate flat area for ball games. A 'Dittiscombe Wildlife Detectives' pack in each cottage encourages children to look for the local plants and animals on mini safaris around the nature trail, past ponds and through woods, with a list of the wildlife you might spot including little owls, barn owls, jackdaws, bats, pied wagtails and bees.

Flete Estates
Haye Farm, Holbeton, PL8 1JZ, T01752-830234, flete.co.uk. £646-1474/week.

Here are eight self-catering properties across a 5000-acre estate in an area of Special Scientific Interest on the Erme Estuary. Properties range from coastguard cottages through to a fine house sleeping 17, each with cot and high chair, and babysitting can also be booked. There's a no-dogs policy on private Mothecombe beach from May to October although they are allowed on any other estate beaches.

Lower Coombe Royal
Nr Kingsbridge, TQ7 4AD, T01548-852880, lowercoomberoyal.co.uk. £375-2695/week.

High quality, eco self-catering in eight acres of gardens, slowly being restored, and home to woodpeckers, owls, foxes and, sometimes, even a buzzard. For children, there's a tailor-made climbing frame with lookout tower, Wendy house, sandpits, croquet or net-games area, rope swing, tyre swing, hammocks, rope ladder, trees to climb and dens to make. There's also a nature trail developed by Wildlife Wonders.

Sharpham Barton Family Camp
Coachyard Cottage, Sharpham, nr Ashprington, TQ9 7UT, T01803-732324, sharphamfamilycamp.co.uk. £140 adult, £75 child (3+), special offers for teen helpers.

This family camp for a week in August on a bio-dynamic farm takes no more than 250 people and features Steiner kindergarten teachers, a 'making things' marquee, bushcraft, woodwork, story blankets, indigo-dyeing, and more. Teens have their own yurt and campfire and, for adults there are activities like willow sculpture, art class, bread-making, talks and therapies. There's evening entertainment for all, including an end-of-week cabaret. Visitor tents are arranged in villages with a central camp fire for cooking if you wish, or a café offers breakfast, lunch and dinner. All on-site activities are included

Dartington Hall.

in the price; off-site activities such as rock climbing, caving and canoeing are additional.

YHA Salcombe
Sharpitor, TQ8 8LW, T0845-371 9341, yha.org.uk. £15.95 adult, £11.95 child (under 18), £44.95 family.
Part of the National Trust Overbeck's site (see page 70), rooms have two to eight beds with fabulous views, plus cot available and children under three welcome. Links to neighbouring activities like sailing from South Sands, below.

Cool & quirky

Dartington Hall
Nr Totnes, TQ9 6EL, T01803-847 1000, dartingtonhall.com. B&B £120/night inc 1 zed bed, £15/extra zed beds.
This restored 14th-century complex, complete with Great Hall used for arts performances, welcomes all ages with plenty of space for younger ones in the gorgeous grounds and estate. Dartington Youth is a summer-holiday programme offering arts, crafts and music. Accommodation includes suites, and zed beds can be added for children up to 12 years. Meals are available in the White Hart, see page 81.

Fingals
Coombe, Dittisham, TQ6 0JA, T01803-722398, fingals.co.uk. £90-160 person, £15 child sharing.
An English and mildly eccentric option ("a bit bonkers", according to Vic Reeves), with a Fairtrade folly in the garden, plus meals eaten together in the wood-panelled dining room where children are welcomed or offered an earlier high tea. There's a family suite or self-catering barn, a pool in summer, and ducks roam the grounds.

Hazelwood House
Loddiswell, nr Kingsbridge, TQ7 4EB, T01548-821232, hazelwoodhouse.com. £85-245/room, £15 child (3-12) sharing, under 3s free.
Only some of the 14 rooms (some sleeping four) come with a bathroom, and no bedroom door locks at this hotel with its house-party atmosphere. There's a hall with piano, drawing room, study/TV room and dining room, plus 67-acre grounds including river, boathouse and chapel.

The Tamar Belle
Bere Ferrers Station, Yelverton, T07813-360066, tamarbelle.co.uk. B&B from £25 person, self-catering £20 person.
The four vintage train carriages offer a dining coach, saloon/lounge, plus two sleeping cars, re-built to modern standards with heating and insulation in the ex-LNER teak Corridor Carriages which once served the East Coast line along with locos like the Flying Scotsman. Compartments offer double or twin beds and en suite, plus interconnecting rooms for families. There's a galley kitchen for self-catering (only one person at a time), or lunch, afternoon tea and dinner is served Pullman-style, and in the morning there is a filling Platelayer's Breakfast. A converted Guards Brake Van alongside is good for older children as a den and sleeping van, with two first-class-style seat units on which to make the beds. There's also a free visitor centre covering local interests with displays on the railway plus a children's playroom including a model railway and signal box where an interactive computer simulates the workings of a real one.

Splashing out

Thurlestone Hotel
Thurlestone, TQ7 3NN, T01548-560382, thurlestone.co.uk. B&B from £92-186 adult, £28 child (3-7), £38 child (8-12) sharing.
This is not merely a luxury family hotel, it's a luxury family hotel with an Egon Ronay Henry the Duck award for excellence in catering and facilities for children, such as children's crafts, bug hunting, magic, nail art, movie nights and more. Not impressed? Then consider that it occupies a priceless location just five minutes' walk from a prime stretch of rock-pooling and sand-digging heaven. The hotel also boasts a children's Dolphin Club, tropical gardens, playground, two swimming pools, tennis courts, croquet and a nine-hole golf course.

Eating South Devon

Local goodies

Delis

Britannia Shellfish
Beesands, TQ7 2EH, T01548-581186, britanniashellfish.co.uk.
Fresh fish and seafood right by the beach, selling snacks such as pasties, half pint of prawns or fresh cooked scallops, beurre citronne, clotted cream, plus an outdoor café open daily in the summer.

Country Cheeses
1 Ticklemore St, Totnes, TQ9 5EJ, countrycheeses.co.uk.
One of the group of excellent shops specializing in local cheese.

Dartington Cider Press
dartingtonciderpress.co.uk.
A centre including local food shops.

Effings
50 Fore St, Totnes, TQ9 5RP, T01803-863435, effings.co.uk.
A highly regarded deli, with five tables for delicious lunches.

Holliss Filling Station
Townstal Rd Garage, Dartmouth, TQ6 9LW, T01803-832091, holliss.co.uk.
Privately owned petrol stations and convenience stores at Dartmouth and Halwell, or wherever you see the BP and Spar fascias combined in the South Hams.

Portlemouth Pastries
15 Church St, Kingsbridge, TQ7 1BT, T01548-8544073.
Fresh pasties, pies, puddings and cakes.

Red Earth Deli
1 Duke St, Kingsbridge, TQ7 1HU, T01548-856100.
Also with an outlet at Stokely Barton Farm Shop, see page 79, a specialist selling foods such as pâtés, dips, soups and frozen meals.

Riverford Goes to Town
38 High St, Totnes, TQ9 5JA, T01803-863959, riverfordfarmshop.co.uk.
A high-street convenience store, also serving food to take away.

Seeds Bakery
22 Duke St, Dartmouth, TQ6 9PZ, T01803-833200.
Organic bread, cakes and savouries, plus local ham, cheese, bacon, organic vegetables and groceries.

Deliveries

Green Table
T01548-560850, thegreentable.co.uk.
A cookery school run by TV chef Lesley Waters, also delivering ready-made dishes.

Kate's Cuisine
T01548-521753.
Ready-made dishes delivered to holiday accommodation, including frozen meals, summer barbecues, sponges or fruit cakes (decorated for special occasions).

The Local Food Company
T01392-248485, thelocalfoodcompany.co.uk.
Delivers fresh, local and organic food direct to your door, including prepared ready meals.

Riverford Home Delivery Torbay & South Hams
T01803-732786, riverford.co.uk.
Organic vegetable boxes, meat boxes and many other products delivered free of charge to holiday lettings on Friday and Saturday.

Farm shops

Aune Valley Meats
Loddiswell Rd, nr Kingsbridge, T01548-550413, aunevalleymeat.co.uk.
Not just meat but eggs, cheese, smoked goods, fruit and vegetables.

Churston Traditional Farm Shop
Brokenbury Quarry, Dartmouth Rd, Churston (nr Brixham), TQ5 0LL, T01803-845837, churchston traditionalfarmshop.org.uk.
Beef butchered on site, fresh local fish, cooked crab, local vegetables, home-baked pasties and cakes, preserves, chutneys, cheeses, wines and staples like fresh-baked bread and milk.

Countryman's Choice
Farm Shop, Cadleigh Park, nr Ivybridge, PL21 9JZ, T01752-895533, countrymanschoice.co.uk.
A big shop with a butcher, local cheeses, bread and on-site

baked cakes, pies and pasties, fruit and vegetables, plus local preserves.

Dean Court Farm Shop
Dean Court, Lower Dean, Buckfastleigh, TQ11 0LT, T01364-642199, deancourtfarmshop.co.uk. Along with a café, a large shop sells groceries, dairy products, fruit, bread, organic vegetables and hand-prepared local meats.

Kitley Pick Your Own & Riverford at Kitley
Church Cottage, Yealmpton, PL8 2HB, T01752-880189, T01752-880925, riverfordfarmshop.co.uk. Selling a wide range of local ingredients and prepared foods.

Oak Tree Gardens
Ashprington, nr Totnes, TQ9 7UU, T01803-732451. Jun-Oct. Pick-your-own raspberries, tayberries, gooseberries, blackcurrants and redcurrants, plus vegetables like peas and broad beans.

Farmers' markets
Buckfastleigh, Thursday.
Dartmouth, second Saturday.
Ivybridge Glanvilles, third Saturday.
Kingsbridge, first and third Saturday.
Plymouth, Saturday fortnightly.
Totnes, last Saturday.

Riverford at Staverton
Riverford Farm, Staverton, nr Totnes, TQ9 6AF, T01803-762523, riverford.co.uk. The original shop, established in 1984, selling a full range of fresh, local food seven days a week.

Stokeley Barton Farm Shop & PYO
Stokeley Barton, Stokenham, TQ7 2SE, T01548-581010, stokeley.co.uk. Food from Ken Durrant butchers, Red Earth Deli, Britannia of Beesands fish, and more than 30 other local suppliers, along with produce from the farm's own market garden and pick-your-own operation. A café, general store and garden centre as well.

Quick & simple

Castle Tearooms
Dartmouth Castle, Castle Rd, TQ6 0JN, T01803-833897. Summer 0900-1730, winter 0930-1700.
A nice spot for a snack, offering sandwiches, jacket potatoes, pasties, cakes and desserts.
Use the car park or you can visit as a stop on a circular Little Dartmouth walk of around three miles, starting at the National Trust Redlap car park.

Chocaholics Café
Salcombe Chocolate Academy, Island St, Salcombe, TQ8 8FE, T01548-844811, salcombechocolateacademy.co.uk. Michelin-starred chocolatier Miguel Blanchet serves hot chocolate, tea, coffee and fresh, locally made pastries, baguettes and handmade chocolates using Fairtrade 70% cocoa and local ingredients where possible. Also available are 90-minute chocolate truffle-making courses for all age groups.

Crabshell Inn
Embankment Rd, Kingsbridge, TQ7 1JZ, T01548-852345.
Pub nosh where seafood platters are a speciality (crab £48 for two, book two days ahead), but the real lure is the quayside setting where kids can dangle crab lines and might catch sight of a local seal. Also sandwiches, jacket potatoes and kids' meals.

Dartington Cider Press Centre
Shinners Bridge, TQ9 6TQ, T01803-847500, dartingtonciderpress.co.uk. Mon-Sat 0930-1730, Sun 1030-1630.
Local organic food café, a branch of Cranks vegetarian restaurant and a takeaway, with picnic area, along with a great toy shop, play area, 'access-for-all' riverside walk and cycle path to Totnes. Ham and cheese baked potato or baguette £5.95, penne with tomato sauce for kids £3.50, cream tea £4.50.

Eating South Devon

Dartmouth Ice Cream
The Good Intent, Lower St, Dartmouth, T01803-832157, dartmouthicecream.com. Possibly the best ice cream in Devon (or so our kids thought), with forest fruits, ginger and other fancy flavours, plus home-made clotted-cream fudge.

The Old Mill Café
Church Rd, Wembury, T01752-862314, oldmillwembury.co.uk. Closed during winter, but the Beach Shop remains open for hot drinks, local pasties and ice cream. In a stunning position on Wembury Beach and offering home-made cakes and cream teas.

The Picnic Boat
Dartmouth, T01404-42449, thepicnicboat.co.uk. Mar-Dec. It's hardly the high seas and it's definitely not the *Jolly Roger*, but there's no denying that a pirate party aboard the delightful *Picnic Boat*, pottering up the River Dart, is a perfect treat for mini mermaids and wannabe Blackbeards. Cruises last three hours and cost £250 for up to 12 passengers, including skippered boat hire, a hearty pirate feast, plus crabbing lines and bait. If that all sounds like a mutiny-in-the-making, opt for a more sophisticated alternative, such as a Devon cream-tea cruise or luxury picnic.

Riverford Field Kitchen
West Barn, Buckfastleigh, TQ11 0JU, T01803-762074, riverford.co.uk. Apr-Oct lunch daily, dinner Fri and Sat, Nov-Mar lunch only half terms and weekends. Booking required. Lunch £15.95 adult, £7.95 child, free under 3s; farm tours £5 adult; £4 child; early supper 1730 £16 adults, £10.50 child; Pick and Cook session 1600-1800 £24. Close to the A38, an award-winning licensed restaurant on the farm, where you share a table with fellow diners. Produce is straight from the fields outside (book a tour first, see page 71) with a set menu of five vegetable dishes and one meat dish (or vegetarian if you ask when booking). The dishes are generous and there's pudding and BYO £4 corkage. With the informal and communal style, children fit right in and, although there are no special child dishes; everything is passed around to share, so you can serve them as much or as little as they like.

River Shack Café
Stoke Gabriel, T07775-890959, therivershack.co.uk. Mar-Oct daily 1030-1730, plus Fri evening for summer barbecues.
Local suppliers are used as much as possible at the River Shack. Apple juice and cakes are from the village, seafood is from Brixham (crab sandwiches £5.90) and meat and dairy products are from Devon farms (minute steak ciabatta £5.90). The views across the River Dart and Mill Pool are gorgeous, not that the kids will notice as they'll be too busy catching crabs from the quay. It's such a hotspot for hauling in the crustaceans that the River Shack sells crab lines, nets, buckets and bait.

The Venus Café
Bigbury-on-Sea, T01548-810141; Blackpool Sands, T01803-770209; East Portlemouth, T01548-843558, venuscompany.co.uk. Mar-Jun and Sep-Oct Mon-Fri 1000-1700, Sat-Sun 0900-1700; Jul-Aug daily 0900-1800; Nov-Mar daily 1000-1600.
Something of a bright star in the South Hams, the Venus Company operates award-winning cafés at Bigbury-on-Sea, Blackpool Sands and East Portlemouth, as well as Tolcarne in Cornwall. You can eat al fresco at the outside tables, or take food with you to the beach. Children's box meals (from £3.95) offer a sausage roll or chicken drumstick, French fries, orange squash plus activity book. There is also a good range of paninis (£4.50), salads, burgers, sandwiches, ice creams and a tasty crab bisque soup. But Venus is more than just good, wholesome nosh, as the company carries out regular beach cleans and has teamed up with local wildlife trusts to support environmental education. You can also buy beach clothes, water-sports gear, and buckets and spades at their beach shops.

The Waterman's Arms Country Inn

Bow Bridge, nr Ashprington, TQ9 7EG, T01803-732214.
On the River Dart in a lovely, out-of-the-way setting, there's smart accommodation and a good quality kids' menu offering dishes such as a Sharpham organic cheese burger with organic beef (sourced from half a mile away), served with chunky chips and mature cheddar cheese, plus home-made coleslaw, ice cream and toy (£6). There's also pasta, chicken, sausage and mash, etc. Locally sourced food includes sandwiches, baked potatoes and fish and meat dishes.

Willow Vegetarian Restaurant

87 High St, Totnes, TQ9 5LW, T01803-862605. Mon, Tue, Thu 1000-1700, Wed, Fri, Sat also 1830-2130.
Offering a relaxed mid-morning break as you wander the High Street, or a more extensive meal. Children are welcome, there's a walled garden for eating outside, and Friday is music night.

Also recommended
Avon Mill Café

Loddiswell, T01548-550338, avonmill.com. Daily 1000-1700.
Devon cream teas and deli.

Church House Inn

Harberton, TQ9 7SF, T01803-863707, churchhouseharberton.co.uk.
Good family room in an ancient village pub.

George Inn

Main St, Blackawton, TQ9 7BG, T01803-712342.
In a South Hams village, warmed by a wood-burning fire and said to be haunted. There's a separate room for family dining.

Posh nosh

The Oyster Shack Salcombe

Island St, Salcombe, T01548-843596, oystershack.co.uk. Wed-Sun 1200-1500 and 1800-2100.
One for grown-ups, the Shack has oysters in numerous guises (from £1.95 each), cooked, if squeamish about raw, plus a superb range of other seafood dishes. A Small Fry menu is available for lunch and there's a sister restaurant in Bigbury.

Resnova Floating Inn

Dartmouth, T07770-628967, resnova.co.uk. Tue-Sun.
Catch a water taxi to this Dutch barge moored in Dartmouth harbour and tuck in to everything from bangers and mash to fresh lobster.

The White Hart

Dartington Hall, nr Totnes, TQ9 6EL, T01803-847 1000, dartingtonhall.com. Mon-Sat 1100-2300, Sun 1200-2230; lunch 1200-1400, light meals 1200-1700, dinner 1800-2100.
The bar in these ancient buildings has always been a bit more gastro than pub, although there's a decent selection of beer and cider. The attractive flagstone floor, limed oak settles and log fire make a good venue for ingredients like locally cured ham, speciality cheeses and fresh Devon fish. Children are welcome and you should find something suitable for them like Dartington beef burger with fries, £11.95.

The Winking Prawn

North Sands, Salcombe, T01548-842326, winkingprawn.co.uk. Easter-Oct daily 0845-late, winter 1030-1700.
Located across the road from North Sands, this popular brasserie has a great selection of mainly seafood dishes. Daytime snacks range from tuna salad (£4.25) to whole cracked crab (£13.60), while the dinner menu pushes the boat out with a seafood platter costing around £20. Probably best for kids is the barbecue menu (from 1630), including a choice of king prawns, rib-eye steak, salmon and chicken, served with salad and new potatoes.

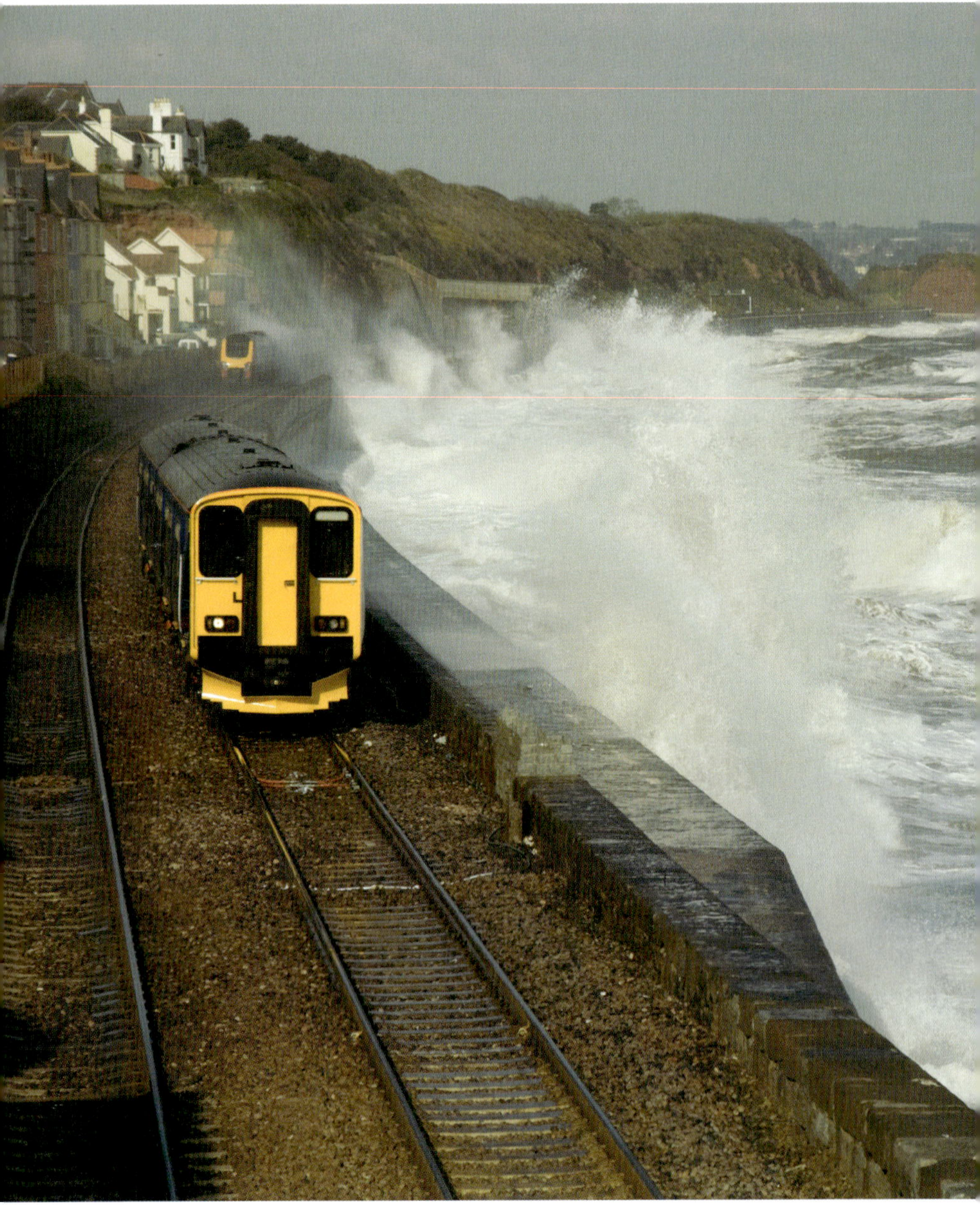

Torbay Coast

Contents

- 83 Map
- 86 Fun & free
- 88 Best beaches
- 92 Action stations
- 96 Big days out
- 97 More family favourites
- 100 Sleeping
- 102 Eating

Race through the waves by rail.

You must

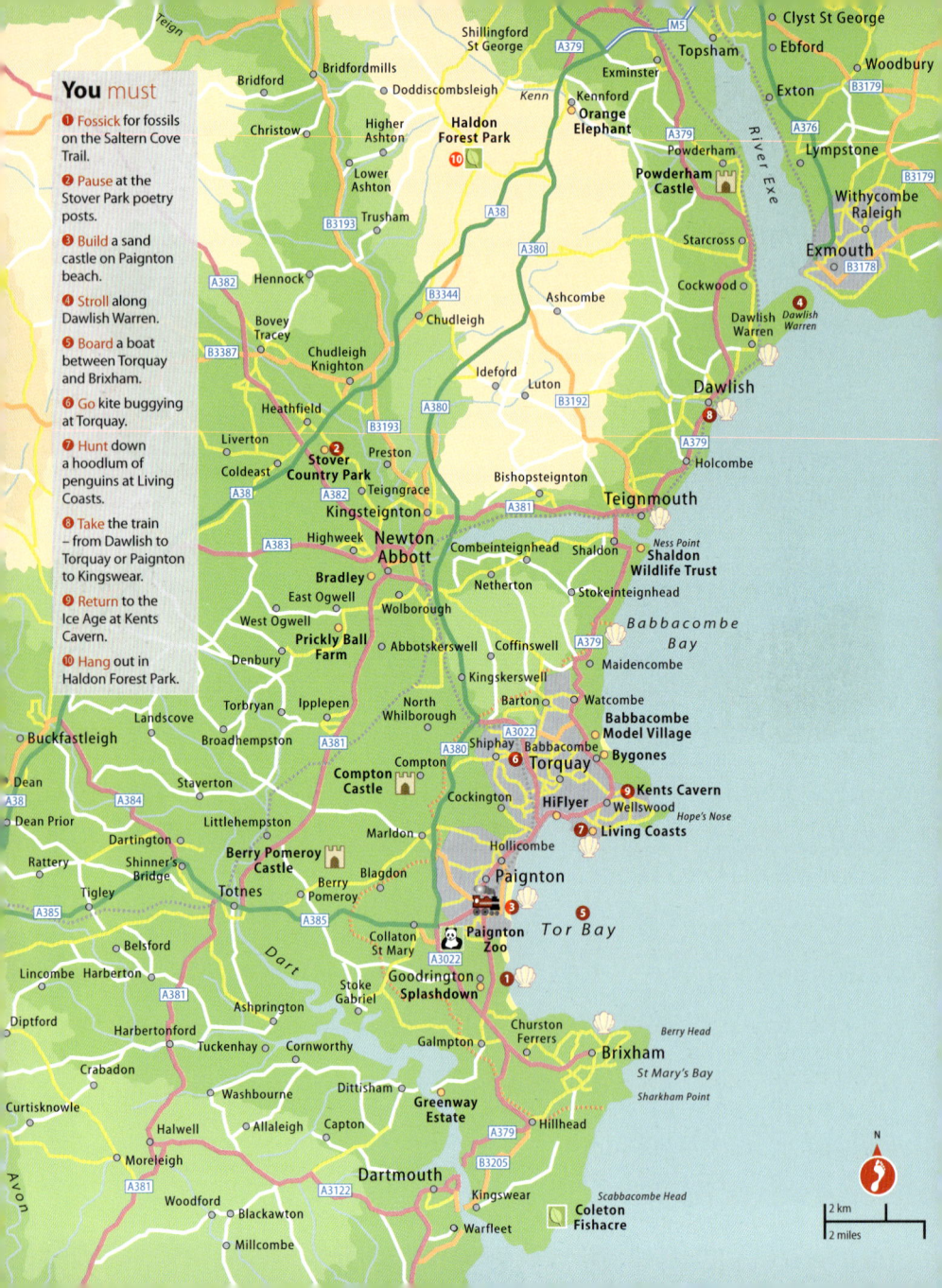

1. **Fossick** for fossils on the Saltern Cove Trail.
2. **Pause** at the Stover Park poetry posts.
3. **Build** a sand castle on Paignton beach.
4. **Stroll** along Dawlish Warren.
5. **Board** a boat between Torquay and Brixham.
6. **Go** kite buggying at Torquay.
7. **Hunt** down a hoodlum of penguins at Living Coasts.
8. **Take** the train – from Dawlish to Torquay or Paignton to Kingswear.
9. **Return** to the Ice Age at Kents Cavern.
10. **Hang** out in Haldon Forest Park.

The coast between Dawlish and Brixham is the place for an urban coastal holiday, complete with Walls ice cream, fish and chips, and crazy golf. Sheltered from the prevailing southwesterlies, there are water parks, go-karts and buckets and spades, along with the pink sand the locals claim is the best ever for sandcastles.

I spy at the seaside.

However, alongside this, a new spirit is abroad, seen in the refurbished harbour in Torquay and renovated Cary Arms at Babbacombe. As retro becomes chic, it looks like the in-crowd are coming, enjoying the calm waters, scudding yacht sails and regular visits of tall ships.

The **English Riviera**, the bay between Torquay and Brixham, is also the world's only urban geopark, a status conferred by UNESCO because of its prehistory of corals, desert, dinosaurs and the earliest humans. The red rocks date from 270 million years ago and at the bottom of **Hope's Nose**, next to Torquay, you can see fossilized coral remains. The limestone grasslands at **Berry Head** on the southern peninsula beyond Brixham and Walls Hill are, like Hope's Nose, home to vast quantities of wild fowers, and places to spot butterfies and lizards basking on open rocks.

Inland, there are a growing number of attractions, from the poetry trail of **Stover Park** to the rather wilder interests of **Haldon Forest**. Then, of course, there are the beaches and, when it comes to splashing about, the coast from Torquay to Brixham offers 20 in just 22 miles, with the highest concentration of Blue Flags in England. The main resorts offer easy access but the coves between steep, red cliffs are spectacular. There is also an underwater reserve with corals and seahorses and, if you look across the water, you may even spot a dolphin.

Out & about Torbay Coast

Fun & free

Trace the TRAIL
Linking Shaldon, Teignmouth and Dawlish for seven weeks from mid-July to early September, **TRAIL** (trail.org.uk) is a **Trail Recycled Art in Landscape** project, featuring dozens of structures created by local and national artists as well as Devon community project groups. Predominantly from waste materials and designed to highlight concerns about the environment and climate change, the fun, beautiful and quirky works pop up in unexpected places like pub gardens and along the seafront, where kids revel in working out what they're made from, or what they are supposed to be. Also look out for associated one-off events like the wearable art show.

Yo ho ho and a bottle of rum
The sunny **Ness** bathing beach behind Ness Point is reached through an old smugglers' tunnel, giving the opportunity for extensive echo testing as you walk through. Book the beach for an evening barbecue (form under 'beaches' at teignbridge.gov.uk) and relive the old days of piratical misbehaviour, maybe with a copy of Kipling's *Smugglers Song* ("If you wake at midnight and hear a horse's feet…"). A short walk away in genteel **Shaldon**, a fishing village turned Georgian resort, you can see where rum, tobacco and lace were bought. Or you can forget the smugglers and just admire the critters at the small but entertaining **Shaldon Wildlife Trust** near the tunnel entrance, see page 91.

Industrial heritage
The **Templer Way** (devon.gov.uk/templerwayleaflet.pdf) is a walk tracing the business activities of the Templer family over 18 miles from the open moor of Dartmoor, through woodland, meadow, tram tracks and urban land, to the estuary foreshore by Shaldon. Walking towards the coast, it's an easy downhill route, although you could pick just part of it. One section passes through **Stover Country Park** (see page 87; Stover House, which was the Templer family home, is now a school). The Heritage Trail then goes either to Ventiford where the tramway and canal met, or to Locks Bridge where there are remains of the old lock gates. It continues alongside the now disused **Stover Canal** and past **Jetty Marsh Nature Reserve**. If on reaching the River Teign you realize you've missed the tide, you can catch the train from Newton Abbot.

Park life
Just a mile from the beach, **Cockington Country Park** near Paignton (TQ2 6XA, T01803-606035, countryside-trust.org.uk) is part of an estate including a listed thatched village, and is a world away from the busyness of the neighbouring resorts. The 450 acres of charming parkland are a place to sit and watch cricket, stroll woodland walks, admire the ornamental lakes, or drop by the play area. There's an organic garden demonstration, tea rooms and craft studios. In summer the site is also the venue for open-air theatre performances like *Alice in Wonderland*, *The Three Musketeers* and *The Mowgli Stories*.

Explore the seashore geopark
Find evidence of ancient sand dunes in the red sandstone around **Roundham Head**, and flash floods in the rocks and stones at the eastern end of **Goodrington Sands** (see page 90). Also check out the fossils at the foot of **Hope's Nose**, evidence of tropical seas, scorching deserts, raised beaches and drowned forests. It's all part of the UNESCO-designated **Global Geopark** (englishrivierageopark.org.uk). The area also includes 16 marine sites of national importance such as **Saltern Cove**, a

---

❶ Two hundred and eighty years ago Torbay was the home of hippopotami, mammoth, straight-tusked elephant, sabre-toothed tigers, cave bears and earliest man.

designated underwater Local Nature Reserve and the only local underwater Site of Special Scientific Interest. The **Seashore Centre** at Goodrington Sands in Paignton (T01803-528841 to check opening times, free entry) includes seawater tanks showing marine wildlife, interactive seashore displays and a video microscope for examining finds. There are regular events, or pick up a leaflet and, when the tide is out, make a DIY expedition along the **Saltern Cove Trail** to look at the teeming rock pools, honeycomb worm reefs and multi-million-year-old fossils.

Birdwatch beside the seaside

Leaving Dawlish with its villas, seafront main-line railway and quirky Victorian landscaping, it's a two-mile walk to **Dawlish Warren** on a concrete path along the sea edge, covered at high tide. Here, backed by acres of static caravans, the beach entrance offers all the conventional beach amusements. However, beyond is a 500-acre National Nature Reserve, hosting summer and winter arrivals who make a temporary home of the freshwater ponds, salt marsh, wet meadows, woodland and dunes on this long, sandy spit, extending into the Exe Estuary. You can walk along the beach with its groynes, or the more sheltered sandy paths behind. In winter there are dunlin, oystercatchers, wigeon and teal, and, in summer, sandwich terns, skylarks and linnets. Up to 8000 wading birds rest at Warren Point at high tide and the site also supports over 600 plant species (including great blackberries in late summer). The Visitor Centre (T01626-863980, teignbridge.gov.uk, Apr-Sep daily, Oct-Mar Sat and Sun) offers plenty of bird- and habitat-related things for children to fiddle with. There are also rangers year round to provide activities. More trails and birds are found at the **Exe Estuary Nature Reserve** (rspb.org.uk) further upriver at Powderham marshes.

Go wild in the country

If you want somewhere safe for children to roam, try the **Stover Country Park** north of Newton Abbot (T01626-835236, devon.gov.uk/stover_country_park). The website includes online games related to the park's Active Zone. Near the A38, the 114 acres offer a good visitor centre, large lake with path all around, other surfaced and un-surfaced paths plus several picnic areas. A 90-m wheelchair- and buggy-friendly aerial walkway takes you through the lower canopy of the woodland so visitors get a bird's eye view of the woods and ponds below, helping them understand how the average oak tree supports hundreds of different species of invertebrate and many mammals, including the elusive dormouse. You might spot a nuthatch, sparrow hawk or great-spotted woodpecker and, on summer evenings, various bats, while you hear a tawny owl hoot. The **Ted Hughes Poetry Trail** features some of the writer's best poems about the natural world with 16 'poetry posts', each displaying a poem. There is also a short **Children's Poetry Trail**, featuring poems about animals, some illustrated by Raymond Briggs. Allow two hours to complete the longer circuit.

Nod to the parson & the clerk

Between Dawlish and Teignmouth, visible from the train (running through the Parson's Tunnel) or from nearby beaches, are weathered rocks and a stack. They look vaguely like two figures facing each other, one said to be a parson, the other a clerk. There are various explanations that the parson was taken in by the devil, or that both parson and clerk got drunk, but in all events, in the words of a poem, the sea "washed the horses to Babbicombe and the Parson and Clerk away", leaving two large stones the next morning; 'The Parson is taking a service, with responses from the Clerk'. See what the kids think.

Out & about Torbay Coast

Best beaches

Bring your snorkel as the marine nature reserves are home to all kinds of creatures including sea horses.

Babbacombe Bay
This sheltered bay boasts the **Babbacombe Cliff Railway** (TQ1 3LF, T01803-328750, cliffrailway. com), opened in 1926, which carries passengers down the 73-m cliff face to family beaches at Oddicombe and Babbacombe.

Anstey's Cove
A Good Beach Guide-recommended beach of shingle and rock with steep access, including that from the coast path, plus walks leading to Hope's Nose.

Babbacombe
Getting to be something of a beach hotspot, set below the Babbacombe Downs cliffs, this shingle beach with rock pools is operated by a private company under licence by the café owner. It's the site of the Cary Arms Hotel, see page 101, and the sheltered bay also makes this a centre for diving. Reached down a steep hill with passing places, the car park is behind the beach. Neighbouring Hollicombe Beach is closed because of unstable cliffs.

Maidencombe
A Good Beach Guide recommendation, offering sand, shingle and rock pools at low tide, with access not just to the coast path but walks (some steep) along old lanes and field edges to create circular routes. There's a little café with terrace above the beautiful green-blue water by the red cliffs and, in summer, bright greenery above. Pedalos are available for hire.

Oddicombe Beach
Sitting below red cliffs, this Good Beach Guide-recommended beach offers sheltered sand and shingle with access by cliff railway, pedalo hire and other water sports, a promenade, plus café at the top.

Watcombe Beach
Marine Conservation Society-quality water in a small sandy cove, with limited parking.

Brixham

Breakwater Beach

A small shingle beach next to Brixham Harbour with good disabled access and views across the bay.

Churston Cove

Down a steep path with no nearby parking, this small sand and shingle beach, just north of Brixham, is charming and uncrowded, surrounded by cliffs and wooded hillsides.

Fishcombe Cove

Another small single beach, between Brixham and Churston Cove, reached by a steep path and surrounded by cliffs and wooded hillsides.

St Mary's Bay

A Good Beach Guide recommendation south of Brixham, operated by the Torbay Coast and Countryside Trust, long and sandy, accessed by steep steps, and backed by high, shale cliffs.

Shoalstone Beach

A Good Beach Guide recommendation, next to Brixham Harbour on the Berry Head road. A gently shelving shingle beach with an outdoor seawater pool at the eastern end, see page 94. There's a lifeguard and baby-changing facilities at the pool.

Dawlish

Boat Cove

West of Dawlish, this is another small but pleasant sandy beach, offering boat trips.

Coryton Cove

Between the fine red cliffs of Dawlish, a secluded shingle and sand south-facing suntrap beach, backed by the main-line railway and within easy walking distance from the town. There are lots of rock pools to explore and you can catch mackerel from the breakwater. Beach-hut hire is available daily or weekly (T01626-215609).

Out & about Torbay Coast

Dawlish Town Beach

Gently shelving sand and shingle, close to the town centre, with free summer entertainment in July and August.

Dawlish Warren

Sand dunes, safe, clean swimming and the usual seaside treats, including crazy golf, dodgems, Formula 1 Go-Karts, and more, make this a family-friendly beach that offers a bit of everything. Newly recreated beach huts are available for hire by the day or week (T01626-215609), or you can amble over the groynes to get away from the crowds in the sandy nature reserve, see page 87.

Paignton
Broadsands

South of Paignton, this is a gently sloping red sandy beach with Marine Conservation Society-quality water. Sheltered between rock headlands, it is backed by parkland and a long promenade lined with colourful beach huts. There's pedalo hire, crazy golf and a very modernist café (Shoreline Beach Bar & Restaurant) projecting out over the sands, or you can get snacks in a corner of Victoria Park. Reached on foot from here is the shingle **Elberry Cove**, popular with waterski boats.

Goodrington Sands

A mainly sandy beach south of Paignton that offers beach huts, a traditional municipal park, boating lake, Go-Karts and Bumper Boats (splashdown quaywest.co.uk, see page 96), as well as the slightly more peaceful Seashore Interpretation Centre, with rock pools to explore at low tide. It's divided into North Sands and South Sands; dogs are permitted on North Sands and, in season, the local steam train can be seen running along the back of South Sands.

Paignton

With Paignton Pier dividing this long stretch of red sandy and parkland behind, this is a beach for a 1950s-style holiday, complete with summer donkey rides. The shallow sea is good for paddling, there are pedalos and boats for hire and, in summer, organized family events.

Rain check

Bowling
• **AMF Bowling**, Torwood St, Torquay, TQ1 1DZ, T08448-263034, amfbowling.co.uk.

Cinemas
• **Alexandra Cinema**, Market St, Newton Abbot, TQ12 2RB, scottcinemas.co.uk.
• **Apollo Torbay**, Esplanade Rd, Paignton, TQ4 6ED, T0871-223 3467, apollocinemas.com.
• **Torquay Central Cinema**, Abbey Rd, TQ2 5NQ, T01803-380001, cromer-movieplex.com.

Indoor swimming pools
• **Brixham Indoor Swimming Pool**, Higher Ranscombe Rd, TQ5 9HF, T01803-857151.
• **Dawlish Leisure Centre**, Sandy Lane, EX7 0AF, T01626-215637, teignbridge.gov.uk.
• **Newton Abbott Leisure Centre**, Highweek Rd, TQ12 2SH, T01626-215660.
• **Plainmoor Swimming Pool**, Marnham Rd, Torquay, TQ1 3QP, T01803-323400, swimtorquay.com.
• **Waves Pool**, Riviera International Centre, Chestnut Ave, Torquay, TQ2 5LZ, T01803-299992, rivieracentre.co.uk.

Museums
• **Brixham Heritage Museum**, New Rd, TQ5 8LZ, T01803-856267, brixhamheritage.org.uk.
• **Dawlish Museum**, Knowle Barton Terrace, EX7 9QH, T01626-888557, devonmuseums.net.
• **Newton Abbot Town & GWR Museum**, St Pauls Rd, TQ12 2HP, T01626-201121, devonmuseums.net.
• **Teignmouth and Shaldon Museum**, French St, TQ14 8ST, T01626-777041, teignmuseum.co.uk.
• **Torquay Museum**, Babbacombe Rd, TQ1 1HG, T01803-293975, torquaymuseum.org.
• **Torre Abbey**, 5 Avenue Rd, TQ2 5JE, T01803-293593, torre-abbey.org.uk.

Preston Sands

A red sand beach to the north end of Paignton, lined with colourful beach huts and Preston Green, making a safe play area. At low tide there are rock pools to explore at the north end.

Teignmouth
Holocombe

Largely used by locals, a small cove at the base of the cliffs between Teignmouth and Dawlish with Marine Conservation Society-quality water. Very limited parking and steep drive.

Ness Cove

South of Shaldon, with extensive car parking behind, reached via a steep road, then accessed through a pedestrian tunnel. Backed by high cliffs with Ness Headland to the north, it can be a real suntrap, usually sheltered from strong winds, mostly shingle, with rock pools and a gentle slope into the water.

River Beach

Facing the estuary and port, a place where local fisherman mend nets, and sand eels are caught.

Shaldon

A mix of shingle and sand sloping towards the mouth of the estuary, and a place to watch the boats coming and going as container ships head towards the mouth of the River Teign. There is also the oldest passenger ferry in England, see page 93, and other facilities nearby in nearby Shaldon.

Town Beach

A long sand and shingle beach stretching from the mouth of the Teign Estuary east towards Dawlish, backed by a promenade and punctuated by a somewhat rundown Victorian pier, also including children's play area and adventure golf. Check out the ever-shifting sand bars as well.

Torquay
Beacon Cove

A small sheltered pebbled cove close to Torbay harbour and Living Coasts, with Marine Conservation Society-quality water. It offers good disabled access down to a small promenade and a warm sunny spot, even out of season.

Corbyn Head

A small sandy beach to the south of Torre Abbey Sands and close to Abbey Meadows, popular with families and offering interesting rock pools.

Meadfoot

A Good Beach Guide-recommended small beach of sand, shingle and rocks, just east of Torquay, backed by the crescent-shaped Osborne Hotel, and tree-lined hillside.

Torre Abbey Sands

One of the bay's main beaches: sandy, next to the main road, close to the resort centre and popular with visitors. Nearby is the run-around space of Torre Abbey meadow.

Take a donkey ride at the beach.

Out & about Torbay Coast

Action stations

Boat trips
See also the Exe Estuary, page 160.

Dolphin Haven
North Quay, Torquay, TQ2 5EQ, and New Pier, Brixham, TQ5 8AW, T01803-293797/852041. Apr-Nov 1000-1700 every 45 mins. Return £7 adult, £4 child.
Western Lady Ferry Service from Torquay to Brixham with a half-hour crossing where you can see the whole bay. Also look out for seatrain adventures combining a boat trip between Dartmouth and Torquay, with a return trip on the steam train.

Exe 2 Sea
T01626-774770, exe2sea.co.uk. Jun-Sep. 2-hr cruise from £10 adult, £5 child; bay trip from £5 adult, £2.50 child.
Boat trips from Dawlish seafront under the railway viaduct: half-hour trips around the bay, mackerel fishing trips (popular with dads and children) lasting 1½ hours, and two- to three-hour wildlife and coastal cruises. All trips are subject to weather and tides. They also operate the Starcross to Exmouth Ferry, see page 93.

Greenway Ferries
TQ1 2BG, T0845-489 0418, greenwayferry.co.uk. Dartmouth to Greenway Mar-Nov £7.50 adult, £5.50 child; Torquay or Brixham to Dartmouth Apr-Oct £15 adult, £8 child; Torquay or Brixham to Greenway £18 adult, £11 child (entrance extra); Torquay to Brixham £7 adult, £4 child; 2-hr fishing trips £12 adult, £7 child; 1-hr geopark cruises with commentary £7 adult, £4 child; 1½-hr seafari in conjunction with Living Coasts including information pack £12 adult combined ticket, £8 child, £38 family, under 5s free.
Ferries, fishing trips, geopark cruises and seafaris, operating from Torquay and Brixham

There is fantastic cycling around the Torbay Coast.

plus Dartmouth, Dittisham and Greenway. All boats are called *Belle* except the historic Second World War Fairmile B, the only one in the world still used as a passenger ferry, operating between Torquay and Brixham, plus trips to Slapton Sands for the Operation Tiger practice D-Day Landing story.

Starcross to Exmouth Ferry

T07974-772681/022536, exe2sea.co.uk. Mid-May to mid-Sep daily, hourly from 1010, last crossing depends on date. Return £5 adult, £3.50 child, £1 bikes.
In bad weather check website to see if operating.

Teign Ferry

T07760-240927, teignferry.com. £1.30 adult, £0.70 child (1-13). A chance to take England's oldest working ferry, crossing between Teignmouth and Shaldon 364 days of the year approximately every 20 minutes, with times of last ferry posted daily.

Cycling
Forest Cycle Hire

Haldon Forest Park, T01392-833768. Daily 0900-1700. Half day £10 adult, £7 child.
Near the forest Hub and ranger's office. A range of frame sizes for children and adults, plus tag-a-longs, child seats and buggies.

High wires
Go Ape

Haldon Forest Park, Bullers Hill, Kennford, EX6 7XR, T0845-643 9215/T01392-833437, goape.co.uk. Mar-Oct daily in school hols, Wed-Mon in term time; Nov Sat and Sun only. £25 adult, £20 child (10-17), £2 parking. Under 18s to be supervised by participating adult, minimum age 10, minimum height 1.4 m.
Climb and wobble between trees, safely harnessed on a high-wire forest adventure, suitable for anyone who can climb a rope ladder (10 m). You can stay up there for three hours and enjoy a Tarzan swing into a giant rope net, zip wires through trees, crawling through tunnels and tackling high-wire rope bridges.

Horse riding
Haldon Riding Stables

Home Farm, Dunchideock, nr Kennford, T01392-832645. £14/hr hack, £12/30-min group lesson, £18/30-min private lesson.
Right below the Haldon Belvedere, one- to two-hour hacks through Haldon Forest Park and country lanes for both beginners and experienced riders. Lessons also available, with an outdoor sand school.

Hayes Farm

Ideford, nr Chudleigh, TQ13 0BA, T01626-852941. £14/30-min lesson, £23/hr lesson, £11/30-min hack, £16/hr hack, £21/1½-hr hack.
A working 300-acre cattle and sheep farm, offering lessons for

Multi activities

Barton Hall
PGL Family Centre, T08700-551551, pgl.co.uk/PGLWeb/Families/centres/BartonHall.htm. 3 nights £185 adult, £134 child (3-18), £85 child (under 3), reductions for family rooms.

Not so much Parents Get Lost as Parents Come Too at this centre operated by the kids' activity specialists. In 46 acres with views across Torbay, there are activities on site from abseiling to zip wires. Outdoors there's a lake, heated swimming pool, dry ski slope, while indoors is a family bar, chill out/games room and play area for children under six. Family stays work as a mix of pre-planned activities and free choice, including tennis, the pool and board games, plus 'swap shop' if you want to exchange activities with another family. Accommodation is in the main house or purpose-built chalets in the grounds, with family rooms or adults with children adjacent.

Grenville House Outdoor Education Centre
Berry Head Rd, Brixham, TQ5 9AF, T01803-852797, grenvillehouse.co.uk. Year round. £76/half day.

Multi-activity centre offering kayaks, open canoes, dinghy sailing, high ropes (10 m), indoor climbing wall, caving, rock climbing, mountain biking, and many more. The cost is based on a group of up to seven people (minimum of one adult per group) to one instructor. Some activities are on site, others on Dartmoor or the River Dart.

Out & about Torbay Coast

four years and up, from slow bridle lane hacks for less-confident riders, to gallops across neighbouring Ideford Common. In school holidays there are own-a-pony days (1000-1500), where participants groom, plait and muck out a chosen horse, also feeding then riding them in a lesson and a hack, before taking home a dedicated rosette and trophy.

Karting
Churston Go-Karts
Churston track, Brixham Rd, TQ5 0HP, T01803-842779.
The complex has a junior karting track as well as senior track. Fast karts are available and some two-seaters. Beginners welcome.

Torbay Quad Centre
Moles Lane, Torquay, TQ3 1SY, T01803-615660, torbayquadcentre.co.uk. Sat, Sun and school hols 0930-1730. Single ride from £5 adult, £3 child; 30 mins £20 adult, £12 child.
Quads for five to 10 years with larger bikes for older children and adults, no experience required and training provided on a training track before tackling the main track.

Outdoor swimming
Shoalstone Outdoor Swimming Pool
Berry Head Rd, Brixham, TQ5 9AG.
No entrance fee, just a traditional pool on the rocks, where the water changes when the tide comes in.

Teignmouth Lido
Eastcliff Walk, TQ14 8TA, T01626-779063, teignbridge.gov.uk.
May to mid-Sep, adults only until 1000. £4 adult, £2.50 child (5-15), £5 family (1+1).
Just off the waterfront, a heated outdoor pool with inflatable fun sessions for strong swimmers aged eight to 14.

Sailing & boating
International Sailing School
10 Marlborough Ave, Beacon Quay, Torquay, TQ1 1TT, T01803-297800. Apr-Nov. £190/8-hr course, minimum age 5.
RYA-approved courses teaching able-bodied and disabled children from beginner to more advanced, from the marina in Torquay in easy-to-sail *Colgate 26* (colgate26.com), usually in blocks of two hours, booked to suit. Powerboat tuition also available.

Water sports
Ski West Watersports
Goodrington Sands, Paignton, TQ4 6LN, T01803-211176, skiwest.co.uk. Apr-Oct. £5/10-min speedboat ride, £30/15-min wakeboarding or waterskiing, £15/ringo rides or 2 people for £25.
Sessions of waterskiing or wakeboarding (minimum age 14), ringo rides (minimum age 10) and speedboat trips for infants up.

Torquay Kitesurfing & Kitebuggying School
55 Victoria Rd, Ellacombe, TQ1 1HX, T01803-212411, kitesurfingtorquay.co.uk. SUP £35/1½ hrs, £49/half day; powerkiting £35/2 hrs; kitebuggying £85/day; kitesurfing £180/2 days.
A range of activities suitable from seven years up, the trick being technique rather than strength. Land-based options take place in a field on top of a nearby hill including kitebuggying (in a three-wheel buggy pulled by a kite). Kitesurfing is suitable for children aged 10 or over on the water, taught from a boat, or on land for younger children, using smaller kites and sometimes a harness to reduce effort. Also stand-up paddle boarding (SUP), the origins of surfing, an easy skill to learn and good for winter days. All equipment supplied.

94

Visit Berry Head

Why? Because this National Nature Reserve is home to southern England's largest guillemot colony, part of a veritable seabird city of nesting fulmars, kittiwakes and shags, all crowded together on impressive 60-m-high limestone cliffs. Eagle-eyed visitors might also spot stonechats and the nationally rare cirl bunting. The limestone peninsula, which forms the southern arm of Tor Bay, is home to two Napoleonic-era forts, wild flowers from May to August, and caves housing horseshoe bats.

Where? Signposted from Brixham, Berry Head to Sharkham Point NNR is made up of two separate areas, separated by St Mary's Bay. There is the Berry Head promontory as far south as Durl Head, and Sharkham Point, seven miles south of Durl Head. There's parking on Berry Head Common and at Sharkham Point. Drive past Landscove Holiday Village up a single-track road and you'll find the car park and visitor centre (T01803-882619, berryhead.org.uk).

How? The Countryside Trust (T01803-882619) operates a free watch point from March to August. Staff are on hand from Sunday to Thursday plus bank holidays from 1000 to 1600, to help visitors use telescopes and binoculars to identify the birds. For fair-weather twitchers, there's also a CCTV link between the guillemot colony and visitor centre.

Guillemots at Berry Head.

Out & about Torbay Coast

Big days out

Living Coasts
Torquay, T01803-202470, livingcoasts.org.uk. Mar-Oct daily from 1000. £9.20 adult, £6.90 child (3-15), £28.90 family; joint admission with Paignton Zoo £19.55 adult, £14.15 child (3-15), £61.35 family.
Part of Paignton Zoo on the Torquay Harbour front, focusing on coastal habitats and wildlife, and successfully breeding penguins, inca terns and even seal pups. There's an underwater-viewing gallery, or watch the penguins on the beach (a group of young ones is called a hoodlum). Imaginative displays recreate the habitats of a South African penguin rookery, an Atlantic sea cliff with crashing waves and tufted puffins, an estuary teeming with rare waders and a mangrove swamp squirming with upside-down jellyfish, stingrays and fiddler crabs. Don't miss Seal Cove where the three resident fur seals are fed daily at 1230 and 1630. The café overlooking the bay is open to all, whether visiting Living Coasts or not.

Paignton & Dartmouth Steam Railway
Steam trains run for seven miles in Great Western tradition along the fine Torbay Coast to Churston, and through the wooded slopes bordering the Dart Estuary to Kingswear, see page 66.

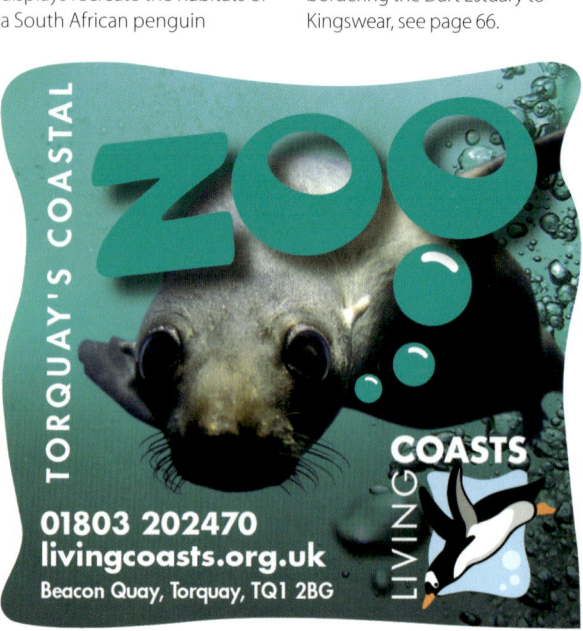

Paignton Zoo
Totnes Rd, Paignton, TQ4 7EU, T01803-697500, paigntonzoo.org.uk. Daily from 1000. £12.50 adult, £8.80 child (3-15), £39.30 family, see Living Coasts for combined entry rates.
Track down the wild things at Lemur Wood, Monkey Heights, Crocodile Swamp and other skillfully recreated habitats arranged in 'Primley' (the oldest part of the zoo), savannah, forest, wetland, tropical forest and desert. There are plenty of shows (check out feeding times) and special events.

Powderham Castle
EX6 8JQ, T01626-890243, powderham.co.uk. Apr-Oct. £9.50 adult, £7.50 child (5-14), £26.50 family.
The Earl of Devon's magnificent home features a deer park, secret garden, archery, birds of prey, play castle, tractor/trailer rides, a House of Marbles shop and local food shop. A guided tour takes you through the house and Victorian kitchen, and there are lovely walks and picnic spots in the park and gardens, or visit the Animal Park, where there are regular animal-handling sessions. In high season there are also regular events like teddy bear picnics.

Splashdown@Quaywest
Goodrington Sands, Paignton, TQ4 6LN, T01803-555550, quaywest.co.uk. £9 adult, £4 child (under 5), £34 family.
Pools and flumes for toddlers to teens and up, outdoors with heated water and wetsuits for

hire. The shop sells buckets, spades, surf wear, boogie boards and more.

More family favourites

Babbacombe Model Village
Hampton Ave, Babbacombe, TQ1 3LA, T01803-315315, model-village.co.uk. £8.25 adult, £5.95 child (3-14), £25.95 family.

Thousands of model buildings in scenes ranging from a fire-breathing dragon and castle to a house on fire. There are Georgian towns, thatched cottages, miniature lakes, a railway with 1930s layout, plus landscaping. There are illuminations for evening openings, a 4D theatre and, for little ones, a Letterland phonics trail. And, as well as a café, you can patronize the ice-cream cabin, or enjoy burgers and fries on the terrace.

Berry Pomeroy Castle
Nr Berry Pomeroy, TQ9 6LJ, T01803-866618, english-heritage.org.uk/berrypomeroy. Apr-Nov from 1000. £4.50 adult, £2.30 child.

In a steep wooded valley, a family castle with 15th-century defences, planned to be one of the most spectacular houses in the country. Never finished, it's the subject of several ghost stories, some recounted on the recorded guide. There are woodland walks from the car park (including steep tracks). with views of the ruins, plus the Castle Café.

Bradley
Newton Abbot, TQ12 6BN, nationaltrust.org.uk.

A National Trust-owned medieval manor house, still lived in by the family that gifted it and little changed, with decoration dating back to the 13th century. There's a children's quiz/trail and, surrounding the house, are meadows and woodland.

Bygones
Fore St, St Marychurch, TQ1 4PR, T01803-316874, bygones.co.uk. Apr-Oct 1000-1800, Nov-Feb 1000-1600, Mar 1000-1700. £6.50 adult, £4.50 child, £20 family, under 4s free.

Recreations of Victorian shops, an amusement arcade, 1940s and 1950s shopping arcade, period rooms, model railway and a chance to climb into a loco cab and take hold of the controls.

Coleton Fishacre
Brownstone Rd, Kingswear, TQ6 0EQ, T01803-752466, nationaltrust.org.uk. Mar-Nov Wed-Sun 1030-1700. £7 adult, £3.50 child, £17.50 family.

The lovely, protected gardens of this Arts and Crafts house reach down to a little cove and there's a children's quiz and family trail to help you explore them. There's also an award-winning tea room for refuelling.

Compton Castle
Marldon, nr Paignton, TQ3 1TA, T01803-843235, nationaltrust.org.uk. Apr-Nov Mon, Wed, Thu. £7.45 adult, £3.75 child, £18.65 family.

Once home to Sir Walter Raleigh's half brother, this rare fortified manor house in a dip in the Devon hills has towers, buttresses, a portcullis and battlements for children to revel in. There is a family guide and quiz trail.

Greenway Estate
Galmpton, nr Brixham, TQ5 0ES, nationaltrust.org.uk, Mar-Sep Wed-Sun 1000-1730, spaces limited so booking required for a timed ticket. £7.45 adult, £3.75 child, £18.65 family.

In contrast to her grisly tales, Agatha Christie chose to holiday in the peaceful seclusion of this elegant. Teenagers can enjoy one of her books set locally, some at her house, see page 23. There are walled gardens (often steeply sloping), fernery, farm, woodland and river frontage, with walks overlooking the Dart. It's reachable by foot ferry from Dartmouth to Dittisham (see page 60) and cream teas are served in these most appropriate surroundings.

HiFlyer
Torquay, T01803-298550, theHiFlyer.com. £14 adult, £8 child (5+), £35 family.

A tethered balloon on the sea front offers 15-minute rides, rising 400 m to admire the Devon coast and countryside.

Out & about Torbay Coast

Kents Cavern
89/91 Ilsham Rd, Torquay, TQ1 2JF, T01803-215136, kents-cavern.co.uk. Open from 0900. £8.50 adult, £7 child (3-15), £29 family.
There's a chance to experience the Ice Age home of Britain's earliest humans in this National Protected Monument and prehistoric show cave. Trained guides lead hour-long tours to see stalagmites and stalactites, along with prehistoric remains of cave bears, sabre-toothed tigers, woolly mammoths plus flint face marking. Along the woodland trail also check out Stone Age Shopping and Animal Hunt. All paths are concrete, with nine shallow steps halfway around, so it should be suitable with a buggy, although there are some steep slopes in both the caves and woodland trail. The cave temperature is 14°C. Stone Age activities for children to try afterwards include a Fun Dig, Tribal Cave Painting and more. This is a popular attraction with tours leaving every 10 minutes in high season, and waits of up to an hour on wet days, so pick your time to visit.

Prickly Ball Farm
Denbury Rd, nr Newton Abbot, T01626-362319, pricklyballfarm.co.uk. Mar-Nov daily 1000-1700. £5.95 adult, £5.25 child (3-14), £21 family.
Farm parks are not a rare breed in Devon but this one, although small, stands out from the herd with its hedgehog hospital, including a chance to meet the patients, plus a growing range of hands-on activities, from petting lop-eared rabbits to bottle-feeding lambs, collecting eggs to walking the goats. When that palls, there's a wildlife trail, mini adventure playground, undercover play area plus café.

Shaldon Wildlife Trust
Ness Drive, Shaldon, TQ14 0HP, T01626-872234, shaldonwildlifetrust.org.uk. Apr-Sep 1000-1800, Oct-Mar 1000-1600. £5.75 adult, £3.25 child (3-15), £14.75 family.
In just one acre (although due to expand) is the smallest member of the Zoo Association, with only three paid staff but 40 volunteers. The zoo focuses on smaller animals like marmosets, tamarins, ocelots and lemurs, plus butterflies, bugs and birds, and because there are breeding programmes, there's a good chance of finding babies.

Taverner's Farm Shop/ Orange Elephant Ice Cream Parlour
Lower Brenton, Kennford, EX6 7YL, T01392-833776, tavernersfarm.co.uk. Tue-Sat 1000-1700, Sun 1100-1600. Ice cream scoop £1.20, sundaes £1.75, quiche and salad £6.25.
Just off the end of the M5, the converted barn serving 25 flavours of organic ice cream also provides cream teas, hot meals and snacks. There are viewing areas to watch activities such as ice cream being made. The courtyard has sandpits, mini tractors in a straw-bale circuit, and there's a play barn with children's diggers and sandpit for children under eight, plus swings and slides outdoors. There's also a farm trail with a summer-meadow walk, passing a bridge to play Pooh sticks, 'elephants' (big orange cattle), the chooks who produce the eggs and a vegetable garden. There's also a farm shop with ready-made dishes, home-produced meat, home-made sausages, burgers, vegetables and groceries.

Kents Cavern – a glimpse into how our ancestors lived.

Don't miss Haldon Forest Park

Haldon – where they actively encourage den building.

Kennford, near Exeter, EX6 7XR, T01392-832262, forest park 834251, haldonforestpark.org.uk. Summer 0830-1900, winter 0830-1700. £1.50 parking.

This is a 3500-acre forest spanning both the A38 and the A380. The rangers positively encourage children to go a little wild, building dens and creating new worlds for themselves. You can explore on foot, bike, or even horseback with more than 10 miles of off-road tracks, a dedicated equestrian area and half-mile gallop stretch (for riding, see page 93).

There are two easy family cycle routes, as well as a more demanding track down steep, wooded valleys for those who want a technical mountain bike trail. Forest Cycle Hire (see page 93) is near the Hub and ranger's office.

Miles of walking paths include the 1½-mile buggy-friendly Play Trail for all abilities, with viewpoints and regular stops for features such as hidden dens and climbing frames. However, with a wooden play area at the start, including activities like rustic musical instruments, you could find it difficult to get the kids down the trail. The Mamhead Sensory Trail is another 1½-mile easy walk, rewarded with views over the Exe Estuary. Alternatively, journey deeper into the forest on the Butterfly Trail and see how many different butterflies, moths, dragonflies and damselflies you can spot, or else try the 2½-mile Tree Trail.

There's a bird hide where you might see rare goshawks along with sparrowhawks. The 18th-century **Belvedere** (haldonbelvedere.co.uk) on Haldon Hill near the Kings Ridge and carriage drive has a panoramic walk, visitor centre, regular events and the **Centre for Contemporary Art & the Natural World** (T01392-832277, ccanw.co.uk) with exhibitions, live events and activities. Right by the play area the **Ridge Café** (T01392-833268, summer 0900-1700, winter 1000-1600, weekends from 0930) serves local, organic, Fairtrade food and drink for breakfast, lunch and snacks. If all that isn't enough, check out the Go Ape! high wire adventure course, see page 93.

Sleeping Torbay Coast

Pick of the pitches

Cofton Country Holidays
Starcross, nr Dawlish, EX6 8RP, T0800-085 8649, coftonholidays.co.uk. Year round. £13-28/pitch + 2 people, £2.50 additional person.

A smart four-star family-run park on sloping fields in a stunning 80-acre setting with a heated outdoor pool, children's play area, Wi-Fi, five coarse fishing lakes, donkeys and a David Bellamy Award. Static caravans, cottages and apartments are also available.

Dornafield
Two Mile Oak, nr Newton Abbot, TQ12 6DD, T01803-812732, dornafield.com. Mar-Jan. £5-11/pitch, £3.50-7 adult, from £1.50 child (5-16).

Luxury site based around a 14th-century farmhouse once besieged by Roundheads, with underfloor-heated shower block, games room with TV, pool and table tennis, freezer pack facilitiy, free Wi-Fi, orchard site for camping, adventure area and fort in the woods for children with Wendy house and sandpit. De-luxe caravan pitches have their own adventure play area with swings.

Galmpton Touring Park
Greenway Rd, Galmpton, nr Brixham, TQ5 0EP, T01803-842066, galmptontouringpark.co.uk. Apr-Oct. £11.70-16/pitch + 2 people, £2.50 child (5-16).

An award-winning family park in a delightful location above the Dart, looking towards Dittisham, with pitches arranged for maximum views and with plenty of open grass space, including a children's play area. Cottages and studios are also available.

Leadstone Camping
Warren Rd, Dawlish, EX7 0NG, T01626-864411, leadstonecamping.co.uk. Mid Jun-Sep. £6.50 adult, £2.50 child (3+).

Family-run for 30 years, an uncommercial site in seven acres, with sheltered fields just half a mile from the sea, and including a children's adventure playground plus ice packs to rent.

Widend Touring Park
Berry Pomeroy Rd, Marldon, TQ3 1RT, T01803-550116, devon-connect.co.uk/camping-touring/widend. Apr-Oct. £7-15/pitch + 2 people, £1 child (3-14).

A family-friendly four-star site inland from Paignton with views over the country, just three miles from the beach. Landscaped with shrubs and trees, heated outdoor pool, children's entertainment in the bar most nights in high season.

The rooms at the Cary Arms look right out on to the waterfront.

The Langstone Cliff Hotel pool.

Also recommended
Beverley Park
Goodrington Rd, Paignton, TQ4 7JE, T01803-661976, beverley-holidays.co.uk. There are four sections to this multi-facility park overlooking Torbay, one offering touring pitches.

Ross Park
Park Hill Farm, Ipplepen, Newton Abbot, TQ12 5TT, T01803-812983, rossparkcaravanpark.co.uk. An inland site in 26 acres with barn restaurant and bar, tropical conservatory and playground.

Splashing out

The Cary Arms
Babbacombe Beach, TQ1 3LX, T01803-327110, caryarms.co.uk. From £195 B&B, £35 extra child bed. Newly refurbished and describing itself as The Inn on the Beach, it aims to combine the best of an English pub with the style and comfort of a boutique hotel. Lots of good food and accommodation (all sea-facing), including luxury fishermen's cottages with terraces. There's a wood-fired pizza oven and a barbecue in the summer to cook local sausages. The sea and beach are right in front, and children get their own fishing net, bucket and spade for days by the rock pools.

The Langstone Cliff Hotel
Dawlish, EX7 0NA, T01626-868000/0845-458 8077, langstone-hotel.co.uk. Family rooms from £74 person, under 10s free including food, over 10s half price. The family who have run this waterfront hotel since 1946 are hands on in welcoming visitors and creating improvements. In 20 acres there's tennis, indoor and outdoor pools, relaxation treatments, dinner dances and cabaret weekends. A direct footpath leads to Warren Beach, 500 m from the hotel. There is an outdoor play unit and toddler room, children's entertainers and more. As the brochure puts it, 'Children are fun, nasty, dirty, disobedient and good business, children are very, very welcome!'

Eating Torbay Coast

Local goodies

Delis
Brixham Deli
68a Fore St, TQ5 1WE, T01803-859585, thebrixhamdeli.co.uk. Groceries, plus cooked meats, pies, cheeses and cakes, also served in the café.

Browse Brothers
Torquay Harbour, T01803-559267. A seafood stall selling cockles, mussels, brown crab, lobster pinks and sandwiches made from Dartmouth- and Brixham-caught crab.

Nourish Café & Deli
Fore St, St Marychurch, TQ1 4PR, T01803-311314. Offering home-made food from the deli and bakery, including home-cooked meats, pies and takeaway meals. The café specializes in cooking with local, seasonal produce.

Farm shops
Boyces
New Barn Farm, Manstree Rd, Shillingford St George, EX2 9QR, T01392-832218, boyces-manstree.co.uk. Tue-Sun 1000-1700. Pick-your-own and shop for fruit and berries.

Farmers' markets
Dawlish, second Friday.
Torquay, Friday.
Newton Abbot, Tuesday.

Getting to know the Ruby Red cows at Occombe Farm.

Cherston Traditional Farm Shop
Brockenbury Quarry, Dartmouth Rd, Churston, nr Brixham, TQ5 0LL, T01803-845837, churstontraditionalfarmshop.org.uk. Mon-Sat 0900-1700, Sun 1000-1600. Beef butchered on site, local fish, cooked crab, vegetables, home-baked pasties and cakes, preserves and chutneys, cheeses, wines, plus staples like fresh bread and milk. Will deliver locally.

Occombe Farm
Preston Down Rd, Paignton, TQ3 1RN, T01803-520022, occombe.org.uk. Mon-Sat 0900-1730, Sun 0930-1630. Inspired organic farm with award-winning farm shop, bakery, butchers, deli and nature trail, plus a chance to meet Ruby Red cows, sheep, pigs, hens and ducks, and take part in family events. Profits go towards the conservation work of the Torbay Coast & Countryside Trust. There's also a café, see page 103.

Powderham Country Store
South Town, Kenton, EX6 8JE, T01626-891883, powderham.co.uk/extras/countrystore.ashx. Mon-Sat 0900-1700, Sun 1000-1600. The store includes a food hall with deli, butchery, bakery and West Country produce.

Shute Fruit & Produce
Newton Rd, Bishopsteignton, nr Teignmouth, TQ14 9PN, T01626-777570, shutefruit.co.uk. Pick-your-own from June to October, plus farm stall selling ready-picked fruit, vegetables, ice cream, cordial and more. You can also order ready-picked in advance. See website for what's available on the day.

Quick & simple

The Breakwater Bistro
Berry Head Rd, Brixham, TQ5 9AF, T01803-856738, thebreakwater.co.uk. May-Oct daily 0900-2130; Nov-Apr Sun-Wed 1000-1600, Fri and Sat 1000-2100.

A popular spot for fresh-cooked local food, served almost on top of the water, around the corner from Brixham Harbour. Sandwiches, salads, jacket potatoes and light lunches served from 1200 to 1730. Fish and chips £7.95 or lunch £10.

Gays Creamery
20 Brunswick Place, Dawlish, EX7 9PD, T01626-863341, gayscreamery.co.uk.
Famous for the ice creams but also selling baked goods like quiches and pasties, cooked on the premises, plus fudge and toffees. Also own the Monkey House play space in the old post office (child entry £3) with a café serving food to the waiting adults.

The Ness
Ness Drive, Shaldon, TQ14 0HP, T01626-873480, innforanight.co.uk.
Tucked down below the smugglers' tunnel, an attractively refurbished pub with terrace, next to a big field with picnic tables for watching the comings-and-goings in the estuary. The food is mainstream: fish and chips, pies, pasta and other mains from £9. The children's menu is £6. There are also nine bedrooms at £110 per night B&B, including two rooms with sofabeds.

The Nobody Inn
Doddiscombesleigh, nr Exeter, EX6 7PS, T01647-252394, nobodyinn.co.uk.
Three miles north of the A38, to the east of Dartmoor, this traditional inn has a cottage garden for families and serves food made with fresh, local ingredients.

Occombe Farm
Preston Down Rd, Paignton, TQ3 1RN, T01803-520022, occombe.org.uk. Mon-Sat 0900-1730, Sun 0930-1630.
There's a board of daily specials at the Bakehouse Cafe above the Farm Shop (see page 102), serving fresh home-made dishes, based on the shop produce. Enjoy it on sofas with views across the farm and nature reserve.

Posh nosh

Burton Farmhouse & Garden Restuarant
Galmpton, nr Kingsbridge, TQ7 3EY, T01548-561210, burtonfarmhouse.co.uk.
This 325-acre working farm with pedigree sheep has turned itself into something of a visitor hotspot, offering not just B&B and self-catering cottages but cream teas and a large children's playing field, as well as traditional three-course meals, complete with coffee at £23.95.

Fish & chips

Hanbury's
Princes St, Babbacombe, TQ1 3LW, T01803-414616, hanburys.net.
Reclaimed railway timber adorns the restaurant of this popular fish and chip outlet, which also does takeaway. Waiting customers have daily papers to read and historic photos to admire and can sit on stools by a retired Lotus car designer. Medium cod and chips £4.15.

Jolly Good Fish Café
6 Teign St, Teignmouth, T01626-779020. Tue-Sat 1200-1400 & 1730-2100; Fri, Sat from 1700.
Small dining room or takeaway from this bijou outfit which offers high-quality fresh fish.

The London Fryer
6 Seaway Rd, Paignton, TQ3 2NY, T01803-552939.
Takeaway queues build up in the eating area especially for the fish, which is what they're best at.

Ode Restaurant
21 Fore St, Shaldon, TQ14 ODE, T01626-873977, odetruefood.co.uk.
Main courses from £16 in a three-storey Georgian house with a highly experienced and well-travelled chef, a Best Organic Restaurant finalist serving modern British-style dishes using local produce. With just 24 seats, booking is essential. There's a high chair if required, and, although there's no children's menu, smaller portions are possible with advance notice.

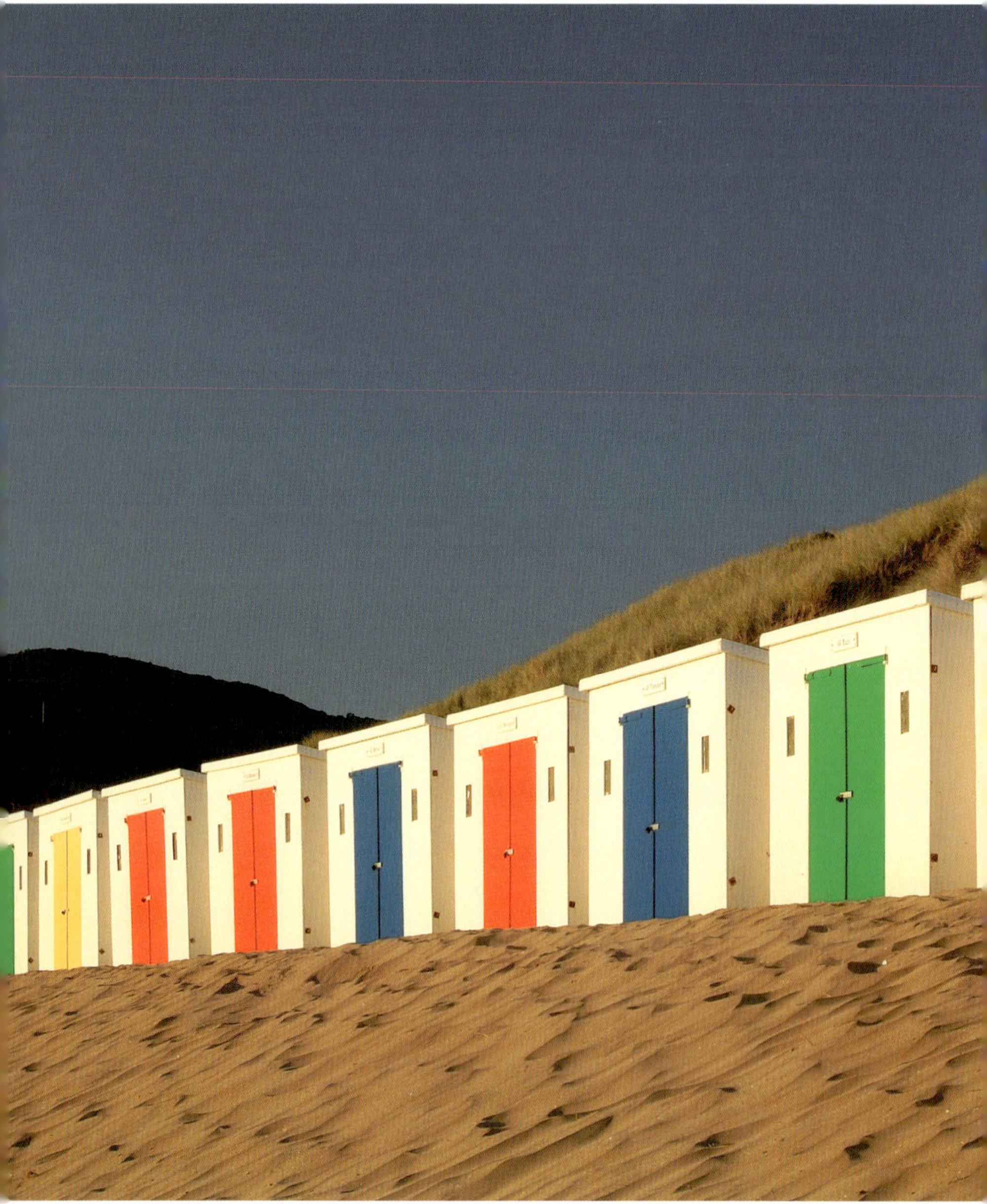

Contents

106 Map
110 Fun & free
114 Best beaches
118 Exmoor National Park
120 Action stations
128 Big days out
130 More family favourites
134 Lundy Island
136 Sleeping
142 Eating

North Devon

Colourful North Devon beach huts.

N
2 km
2 miles
Ilfraco
Aquar
Walkers
Chocolate
Emporium
Ferry to Lundy
9
Ilfracombe
2
Bull Point
Lee
Mortehoe
Borough
Farm
Morte Point
Trimston
Woolacombe
B3343
Morte Bay
3
Dean
Woolacombe Sand
North
Buckland
A361
Pickwell
Baggy Point
Georgeham
Croyde Bay
Croyde
Saunton
Knowle
Braunton
10
Marwood
Saunton
Sands
Wrafton
Braunton
Burrows
5
Bideford Bay
Yelland
Fremington
Instow
A39
Appledore
Tapeley Park
7
Westward Ho!
Northam
Horwood
Hartland
Point
1
Windbury
Point
Titchbury
Orchard Hill
Abbotsham
Big Sheep
6
Bideford
Newton
Tracey
Stoke
Clovelly
10
Fairy
Cross
Handy
Cross
Alverdiscott
Hartland
B3248
Bucks
Mills
Horns
Cross
A39
Woodtown
Philham
Higher
Clovelly
A386
Weare
Giffard
Milford
Goldsworthy
Milky Way
Bucks
Cross
Elmscott
Parkham
Monkleigh
Tosberry
Woolfardisworthy
Dartington
Crystal
South Hole
Hartland
Forest
Alminstone
Cross
Buckland
Brewer
Great
Torrington
Welcombe
Ashmansworthy
Frithelstock
Stone
Meddon
Little Torrington
East Putford
Gooseham
Eastcott
Youlstone
West Putford
B3227
RHS Garden
Rosemoor
Morwenstow
Shop
Dinworthy
Gnome
Reserve
Langtree
Bradworthy
A39
A388
Stibb Cross
Woodford
Winswell
Abbotts
Bickington
Woollaton
Merton
Coombe
Kilkhampton
Alfardisworthy
Bradworthy
Cross
Torridge
Soldon
Cross
Venn Green
Stibb
Shebbear
Petrockstow
Poughill
Hersham
Holsworthy
Beacon
Sheepwash
Bude
Stratton
Grimscott
Pancrasweek
Chilsworthy
Holemoor
Upton
Launcells
A3072
Highhampton
A3254
Holsworthy
A3072
Brandis
Corner
A3072
Bude Bay
Marhamchurch
Bridgerule
Widemouth Bay
Pyworthy
Derriton
Hollacombe
A388
Budd's
Titson
Leworthy
Claw
Tamar
Halwill
Junction
Millook
Coppathorne
Deer
Carey
Northlew
Treskinnick
Cross
Clawton
Halwill
Patchacott
Tregole
Whitstone
A3079
Ashbur

You must

1. **Spot** seals – and dolphins and porpoises – from Hartland Point.
2. **Leap** into the tidal pool at Tunnels Beaches.
3. **Take** to the waves at Woolacombe.
4. **Seek** the deer on Exmoor.
5. **Cycle** the Tarka Trail.
6. **Back** the winning woolly in the Big Sheep sheepstakes.
7. **Go** alternative at eco Tapely Park Gardens.
8. **Discover** the Doone Valley.
9. **Board** a boat to Lundy.
10. **Fetch** fish and chips from Squires.

Learn to surf in North Devon.

This is deep, green Devon, where the farms are gentle but the wildness of Exmoor tumbles into the sea, and the sand runs for miles. The North Devon biosphere (northdevonbiosphere.org.uk) follows the coast from Lynton to south of Hartland, and reaches inland as far as Okehampton. This is Tarka country and, after years without them, otters are now back on every major river.

Coast by Valley of Rocks overlooking Lee Bay.

Along the wild and windy coast the Atlantic makes its mark and surfing is the high-profile reason to take to the waves. **Woolacombe**, **Croyde** and **Westward Ho!** are the places to find the rollers, and the lifestyle to match: this is surely home to the highest number of campervans per capita in the UK. Salt-bleached surfies drive the less fashionable, rusty ones; visitors can hire immaculate alternatives, see page 17.

If the van seems a step too far, no centre is without its surf shops, selling clothing and accessories, and, although October to Easter remains quieter, nowadays you're likely to find activity year round. If you don't fancy the big waves, there are other options. The small town of **Barnstaple** is the largest centre, and **Ilfracombe**, the biggest of the resorts, is based around a sheltered harbour between rocks. However, none of the resorts is large and the lack of development has left plenty of space for a culture of coastal campsites and holiday parks, offering priceless views for a fraction of the cost elsewhere.

Inland you'll find gentle, agricultural Mid Devon, known as Ruby Country after the Ruby Red cattle. It includes towns with prosperous pasts, rebuilding themselves in a new world of 'think local' around the thatch and cob of **Hatherleigh**, the history of **Torrington**, and the busy livestock market at **Holsworthy**.

Out & about North Devon

Fun & free

Admire the sand castles
As part of the **Gold Coast Ocean Fest** during July each year, Woolacombe hosts an annual charity competition on the beach. Competitors have just three hours to produce a fabulous sandcastle, although entries include not just castles but anything from daleks to crocodiles (more details from T01271-344248). Teams of six are welcome and it costs £100 per entry. Alternatively, you can get help from the Northam Burrows' rangers on one of their Sand Castles and Sculptures events (check details at torridge.gov.uk under Leisure, Northam Burrows).

Go rock pooling
This is a great coast for finding aquatic animals, and Devon Wildlife Trust's North Devon VCMA publishes a guide you can download (devonwildlifetrust.org) telling you what you might find on each beach, from blue-rayed limpets and bladder wrack to strawberry anemones (see page 20). You might catch a blenny by drawing your net slowly over seaweed at the side of a pool. But take care as they can nip. Other nippers are the crabs that hide in crevices between rocks, where you can find them looking out at you. Also look for dog whelks that look like snails, some of them stripy but mostly off white. They use their tongue to drill into the shells of barnacles and mussels, which you might also spot. Harder to find but fascinating is a shanny, a fish chameleon, able to change colour to match its surroundings. Beadlet anemones, glued to the side of rocks, are a waving mass of tentacles under water, but shrink to a jelly blob when the tide goes out.

Places to find these creatures include the north end of **Saunton Sands**, the north end of **Croyde** beach, **Barricane** beach at the north end of Woolacombe, **Rockham Bay**, **Lee Bay** west of Ilfracombe, the privately owned and operated **Tunnels Beach** in Ilfracombe, **Hele Bay** east of Ilfracombe, and **Combe Martin Bay**. If you'd like some guidance try the Northam **Burrows Country Park** summer programme (T01237-479708, torridge.gov.uk, under Leisure), which includes free rock-pool rambles.

Rock up
There are fabulous rock formations to be seen around **Hartland**, where the land has been folded into some spectacular geology. Hartland Quay was lost long ago in storms; the twisted and broken shards out in the water support a long history of shipwrecks, detailed at the Hartland Quay Museum. The lighthouse on the 100-m cliffs at Hartland Point continues to emit the strongest light of any on the British coast, keeping passing ships safely away. You can walk up to it while watching for dolphins and seals, just a five-minute walk from the Hartland Point car park (£1.50), where there is a nice summer café. To reach sea level, drive down to the quay (£2.50) and, at low tide, explore the neighbouring beach, rock ridges and dips, loomed over by impressive cliffs. The waterfall at **Speke's Mill Mouth** is considered the most spectacular of the coastal falls, but the 20-minute walk might be too much with younger children.

Rugged, spectacular coastline.

❷ Blennies are little fish that change colour with their surroundings, often spotted as they dart for cover.

Seek shells
If you're serious about shell collecting, there's one Devon beach you must not miss. Known locally as Shell Beach, **Barricane**, see page 114, is between Woolacombe and Mortehoe and has as many as 40 different shell varieties. These include blue-rayed limpets, cockles, necklace shells, netted dog whelks, painted topshells, periwinkles, razor shells, sand dollars, scallops, tellins and, the jackpot for most shell seekers, the tiny cowrie shells that are no larger than your little fingernail, and said to have been carried from the Caribbean on the Gulf Stream.

Walk the coast
Although there are attractions like spotting seals, dolphins and porpoises, not all the South West Coast Path in this part of Devon is good walking for children (southwestcoastpath.com). Even on the road, the coastal drop on the A39 driving west into Lynton is a little unnerving. However, **Baggy Point** near Croyde is a National Trust site with an upgraded path. The second half of the mile-long route can be a bit strenuous but gives views of the cliff-nesting seabirds. You'll pass a memorial to Henry Williamson of *Tarka the Otter* fame before reaching the tip of the headland where there's a viewing area.

Alternatively, take the kids on a walk to the beach, some only

Retro resorts

The dramatic gorges, steep cliffs and sheltered valleys of parts of North Devon were admired by the Victorians, who developed resorts, often in a rather bombastic style, that can be better appreciated now that it has softened with age. These are resorts where you can slow your pace, following in the footsteps of earlier visitors.

Ilfracombe boomed when the Victorians built the railway. Victorian week in June celebrates the history. Today, activities include rock pooling on Tunnels Beach (see page 116), watching the boats in the sheltered harbour, visiting the aquarium (see page 131), watching a show at the Landmark Theatre and strolling past the traditional shops, cafés and amusements.

Nearby are **Lynton** and **Lynmouth**, cleverly located to shield them from sea winds and much of Exmoor's rain. They are approximately 150 m apart at the top and bottom of the cliff, and linked by a dizzying Victorian Cliff Railway (T01598-753908, £2.85 adult return), once the steepest funicular in the world, driven by water from the Lyn River. At the bottom, next to the parish church is the Lyn Model Railway, free but donations gratefully accepted.

For real scenic drama visit the **Valley of the Rocks** half a mile west of Lynton, where moor plunges to the sea. Dubbed 'Little Switzerland' in the 19th century, when it was described as 'rock reeling upon rock', it's not much of an exaggeration. You can walk up it for between one and five miles, starting from the centre of Lynton, along a paved and fairly level route, with views of the sea and, beyond that, Wales (devon.gov.uk/walk37.pd).

The West Lyn River tumbles down waterfalls in the wooded **Glen Lyn Gorge**, where hydroelectric turbines (T01598-753207, theglenlyngorge.co.uk/Power-Of-Water-Attraction.htm, Easter-Oct; £4 adult, £3 child), operate water wheels, make electricity and fire water canons. A gentle walk leads up to Moses' Pool in the wooded gorge. Walking further along a steep path to the upper gorge reaches the intake for the turbine houses 75 m below.

East of Lynton is **Watersmeet**, the valley meeting point of Hoar Oak Water and the East Lyn River. See page 118.

Take a step back to the days of good old-fashioned seaside holidays.

Out & about North Devon

reachable on foot, including **Rockham Bay**, see page 116, near Mortehoe, **Peppercombe** to the west, see page 115, a pretty wooded valley off the A39 leading down to the sea, and **Bucks Mill**, see page 114, with a walk down from the car park through the village to a small, rocky beach.

Make an estuary expedition

On the north side of the Taw-Torridge Estuary are **Braunton Burrows**, an extraordinary and massive dune system supporting all kinds of rare plants like sea stock, with the core area a Special Area of Conservation. Here, birds feed on the mudflats and, although it's a long hike from the car park to the water, it's a great space for running, hiding and playing.

On the south side are **Northam Burrows**, a Site of Special Scientific Interest, much flatter than Braunton Burrows but the water is closer. The Blue Flag-rated beach of **Sandymere**, see page 116, reaches for three miles down to the less-than-inspiring Westward Ho!, giving way to rocks at one end and backed by an enormous pebble ridge. East of the Burrows is the salt marsh known as the **Skern**, visited by more waders and migrating birds. There's a hide to view them, a summer programme run by rangers (details at torridge.gov.uk under Leisure, Northam Burrows) and an activity centre open from May to September with hands-on activities for children, including puzzles, a rock pool complete with wildlife, and

Braunton Burrows.

Off the beaten track North Devon

Inland, North Devon isn't as packed with visitors as the coast, but there's plenty to explore. Three hundred and sixty-five acres of common land were given to the town of **Great Torrington** in the 12th century and they remain a habitat for flora and fauna along with 20 miles of footpaths. The Ruby Trail is a four-mile circular walk from the market town of Hatherleigh, also on the Tarka Trail. Alternatively, try a half-day walk along the Tarka Trail north of Great Torrington, starting with a short bus ride and walking back.

Eggesford Forest (forestry. gov.uk) near Chulmleigh includes Hilltown Wood on the A377 offering a picnic area, information point and level, circular walks plus off-road cycle routes. A walk taking approximately 2½ hours passes the remains of a Norman castle and trees planted almost 100 years ago.

Eggesford Country Centre, with a licensed restaurant, plus art and craft gallery, is based in Eggesford Gardens, and provides visitor information on the history and places to visit.

The Devon Wildlife Trust also has a growing number of reserves. Halsdon, just outside the village of **Dolton** south of Great Torrington, offers an hour's walk exploring oak woodland on the River Torridge and the surrounding water meadows. There's a hide on the river (look out for kingfishers and even otters), and the route passes the ruins of a Victorian corn mill and a point called Top of the World with views to Dartmoor.

You could explore the 'culm', the local name for moor grass and rush pasture, a kind of traditional boggy grassland heath and woodland fringes. You can see the culm at

Dunsdon Farm (devonwildlifetrust. org) between Holsworthy and Kilkhampton, four miles south of Tamar Lakes and close to the village of Lana. Farmed by the same family since 1927, the DWT bought the site to keep the tradition of light summer grazing and winter 'swaling' (burning). There's an easy-access boardwalk along an old track through wet woodland, and you might hear the harsh 'frarnk' calls from the old heronry nearby. There's also an old canal with surviving towpath, which was used 100 years ago to carry lime-rich sea sand to the acid farmland here. To see the whole area would take two hours or more and you need to watch out for boggy ground. It's at its best between May and September, when it's a haven for wildflowers, butterflies and insects.

information about rubbish and how long it takes to decay in the sea. A £3 parking fee applies in the summer.

If, in your book, it's four wheels bad, two wheels good, then head to the other side of the Torridge Estuary, north of Instow, to the **Isley Marsh RSPB Reserve**, where visitor access is restricted to paths largely outside the reserve, but with views into it to see the wintering ducks and waders including curlew. There's no public parking for two miles but the reserve is passed by the **Tarka Trail**, see page 126, along a former rail track. The route skirts the water from east of Braunton, in to Barnstaple, continuing to Instow.

Alternatively, for really easy bird viewing, hang out along the frontages of **Appledore** or **Instow** (in summer a ferry runs between them, bikes carried) and watch the seabirds at low tide, searching for titbits. Appledore is a particularly attractive spot, with cobbled streets, quay, Georgian houses and cottages. Look out for the Hoskings ice cream van. Or there's the old port of **Bideford**, with 17th-century merchant houses and a mile-long, tree-lined quay, now popular with amateur sailors.

Sunset at Crow Point.

Out & about North Devon

Best beaches

Barricane Bay
Half a mile towards Mortehoe from the main beach at Woolacombe, this Good Beach Guide-recommended shingle/sand bay offers excellent shell collecting, as well as body surfing, rock pooling, safe swimming and even a small island to climb. Sandy Combesgate comes next, while Grunta beach next along got its name from a cargo of pigs that was washed up there.

Broadsands
A sandy cove surrounded by high cliffs close to Berrynarbour, with a climb down of 220 steps, and then back up.

Bucks Mills
A secluded north-facing rocky beach, Bucks Mill is sheltered from the prevailing wind and swell, and situated below the village that sits half way up the cliff. Parking is approximately half a mile away, so limited access means it's quiet. It's also great for rock pooling. If energetic, you could walk the couple of miles to Clovelly.

Combe Martin Bay
This sandy beach has only achieved minimum water-quality standards in recent years and the Good Beach Guide still advises against swimming, but it remains a popular spot for families: sheltered, close to the shops and cafés, with plenty of rock pools, and sand at low tide.

Croyde Bay
Much smaller than the other surf meccas of Woolacombe and Saunton, Croyde Bay can get crowded, but there's no denying the huge appeal of this beautiful sandy beach backed by dunes, with its easy access, gently shelving sand, plus lifeguards between May and September. It's a surfing beach but the surf can be hazardous, especially at low tide.

Hartland Quay
A backdrop of spectacular cliff scenery gives way to pebbles and rocks with sand exposed by the retreating tide on this Good Beach Guide-recommended spot with nearby coves and waterfalls.

Hele Bay
A sheltered cove in an Area of Outstanding Natural Beauty between Ilfracombe and Combe Martin, Hele Bay has sand and rock pools, and is close to Hillsborough Nature Reserve. Free parking in easy reach, the beach is accessed by a slipway.

Ilfracombe Capstone (Wildersmouth)
A sheltered sand and shingle bay surrounded by rocks, this is close to the centre of the resort.

Beaches next to open land is one of North Devon's big draws.

Instow
🌊 ♿ 🐕 🅿 ⚠

Sand without the surf, Instow's beach is snug in the Torridge Estuary, where the river joins the Taw. It's become something of a hotspot for the local fishing and sailing crowd and is wheelchair-accessible too. However, poor water quality means swimming is not advised.

Lee Bay & Woody Bay
🌊 🐕 🅿

West of Lynmouth, the Valley of the Rocks forms a rugged gateway to the most dramatic section of the North Devon coast. Here crumbling rock spires inhabited by wild goats loom above cliffs draped with ancient oak. Lee Bay (rocky with sand at low tide) is tucked away, while further west a toll road (£1 per car) twists and turns through the woodland, offering dizzying views of the sea below. Secluded Woody Bay, backed by steep cliffs covered in woodland, can only be reached by a steep hike that zig-zags down to the rocky pebble and shingle beach. For an easier sea-level perspective, join a tour boat from Lynmouth, see page 120.

Lynmouth
🌊 ♿ 🐕 🅿

You can run the gauntlet of shops selling fudge, ice cream and sticks of rock to reach the seafront at picture-perfect Lynmouth, but the small shingle beach is Good Beach Guide-recommended and has great skimming stones and rock pools. It's also a fine spot to eat fish and chips from Esplanade Fish Bar (see page 143) or catch crabs from the harbour wall.

Peppercombe
🐕

Red cliffs form the backdrop to pebbles over rock plus a sandy 'Gut', created when the rock was blasted by an Elizabethan landowner to build the harbour; the boulders seen at low tide are the remains of the Old Quay. The beach extends along the cliffs in either direction on this undeveloped section of coast.

Out & about North Devon

Putsborough Sands

Another family favourite, Good Beach Guide-recommended and located at the southern end of Woolacombe Sands, near Croyde, it's good for both swimming and surfing with surf gear for hire. With little more than a beach car park and shop, it offers a more tranquil alternative to Woolacombe, although there is a lost-child centre and first-aid post.

Rockham Bay

North of Woolacombe, this small, secluded bay is reached by a walk including three flights of steep steps down to a beach that is largely covered at high tide, although otherwise offering plenty of rock pools, deep rock formations and sand. From the camping fields above you can see the green phosphorescence when the plankton glows at night.

Sandymere

On the south of the Taw-Torridge Estuary, reached through the Northam Burrows Country Park, this is more than two miles of sandy beach, backed by a distinctive pebble ridge, running down to the less attractive Westward Ho! Popular with families, surfers, watersports enthusiasts and sand yachters, the surf isn't as good here as on beaches further up the coast, but being on the southern side of the estuary does put you within easy reach of highlights like Clovelly (see page 130) and Hartland Point (see page 110).

Saunton Sands

Wrapping its tail end around the combined estuary of the Taw and Torridge rivers, the four miles of Saunton Sands stretch north in a long swathe of sand, sandwiched between impressive dunes and some of North Devon's most renowned surfing waters. Saunton Break at the Saunton beach car park uses local suppliers for hot and cold snacks; the takeaway shop is open year round. The smarter Sands Café, below the Saunton Sands Hotel, has a raised balcony and serves salads, steaks, pasta and panini.

Tunnels Beaches

No matter how galling you may find the prospect of paying to visit a beach (Easter-Nov £1.95 adult, £1.50 child, £6.50 family), this privately owned stretch of rocky shoreline on the western outskirts of Ilfracombe is not to be missed. The approach is supercharged with mystery and anticipation as you walk through tunnels, hand-carved in the 1820s, to emerge next to a sheltered cove dominated by a huge tidal pool that's visible by the grey sands for three hours either side of low tide. Kids love swimming, snorkelling or mucking about on inflatables in this stunning Victorian bathing lagoon, but don't overlook the natural rock pools dotted around, as they're some of the best in the UK and are often the focus of rock-pool rambles run by the Devon Wildlife Trust.

Saunton Sands stretches for miles.

Kayaks are available for hire (£10/hr), while the Café Blue Bar is a top spot for family meals (see page 143). In bad weather the Play Hut in the same building offers soft indoor play space.

Woolacombe Sands

This is the big one – more than two miles of surf-strafed, squeaky-clean sand. Woolacombe is beach heaven whether you're a bucket-toting toddler or wave-riding teen – watched over by lifeguards from May to September. At first glance it seems rather swamped by modern facilities: you'll pay around £5.50 to park in the field behind the beach, then it's a short walk down a slipway crammed with beach shops, cafés and surf-school kiosks (see page 125). You may also find a bouncy castle, swing boats and other beach entertainments. If it's summer, the northern part of the beach is likely to be staked out by a maze of windbreaks but, even when Woolacombe is heaving, you can always find space for your picnic rug and a game of beach cricket, and dunes shield the development if you walk along the flat, wide sand. Wave-jumping and body boarding or surfing are compulsory, as is building a sandy rampart to hold back the tide, the seawater warming as it slides in over those acres of sun-baked sand.

Wringcliff

Half way between Lynton and Woody Bay, this is a secluded bay surrounded by high cliffs with a steep access path. Not suitable for disabled visitors or young children. Parking is in the Valley of the Rocks.

Woolacombe is a great place for gentle seaside activity.

Off the beaten track

Exmoor National Park

Exmoor offers a bit of everything, from wild open moors to deep lush valleys and, at the coast, steep, ragged cliffs looming over the sea, all accessible on more than 700 miles of footpaths and bridleways. Quieter than Dartmoor, it's a place to luxuriate in astonishingly beautiful scenery, punctuated by little hamlets.

As you explore you might find the remains of prehistoric earthworks, mounds, standing stones and barrows. The deep combes are where furze and scrub provide cover for red deer, descendants of Britain's prehistoric wild deer and the largest group in England. They're spotted at dawn or at dusk, like badgers and bats. If you want help finding them, try one of the organized trips, see page 124.

There's also the rare but hardy Exmoor pony, a breed dating back thousands of years, rounded up only for checking at Bampton in late October, when the ancient Bampton Charter Fair has been revived. The **Exmoor Pony Society** (Moorland Mousie Trust, Ashwick, nr Dulverton, TA22 9QE, T01398-323093, exmoorponysociety.org.uk) gives confident riders aged 10 years and over a chance to roam on one for 2½ hours from January to October for £40.

Ditch the car
The **National Park** (exmoor-nationalpark.gov.uk) offers maps of paths on the website, organizes regular events including guided walks from Dulverton year round (T01398-323841), and Lynmouth Harbour boat trips with commentary from a park ranger from Easter to November (T01598-752509). Alternatively, for DIY rambles see exmoorwalks.co.uk, or *Exmoor: Leisure Walks for All Ages* (Short Walks Guides, Pathfinder Short Walks, Crimson Publishing, £6.99), which includes ideas for half-day family walks, avoiding the bogs.

The **National Trust** centre at Heddon Valley (Parracombe, EX31 4PY, T01598-763402, Mar-Nov daily 1100-1700) offers a shop and ice creams at a point where you can set off on cliff and woodland walks. **Watersmeet** (Watersmeet Rd, Lynmouth, EX35 6NT, T01598-753348, Mar-Nov daily from 1030) is a romantic 19th-century fishing lodge and historic tea garden on the banks where the East

Lyn River meets Hoar Oak Water, offering more refreshments, a shop and information centre in a deep wooded valley.

Follow the novel
From Watersmeet you could walk or drive up the East Lyn into **Doone Country**, made famous by the Victorian novel *Lorna Doone* by RD Blackmore. Based on Devon folklore, it's about forbidden love, Exmoor highwaymen, fights to the death and a villain who nearly triumphs. Many of the locations are real places, based around four villages on or near the river, with Oare the furthest, five miles upstream.

The dramatic steep-sided, heavily wooded valley passes the **Rockford Inn & Brewery** (T01598-741214, therockfordinn.co.uk), overlooking the river and serving restaurant-style pub food, including meals for kids, and offering accommodation. Beyond is Malmsmead, where a 17th-century packhorse bridge (narrow with bulges for the packhorses to pass each other) crosses the river. From here you can walk up Badgworthy Valley, also known as **Doone Valley**. Footpaths and footbridges are generally good and well marked, although they can be muddy. After a steep climb up, on top of the moor are fantastic views to the coast and, on a clear day, South Wales.

In Oare village, **Lorna Doone Farm** is perhaps the model for Jan Ridd's farm in the tale, although further along is another candidate, **Oare House**. There is also **Oare Church**, where the story reaches its high Victorian climax; even now it's small, dark and atmospheric. Up the valley, along Badgworthy Water through Badgworthy Wood, is the waterslide where **Lank Combe Water** rushes down over huge rocks and where, in the story, Jan almost drowns and meets Lorna.

Alternatively, if you're not interested in the Doones' exploits, the streams and countryside offer lots of open space to run and play, with shallows at Badgworthy Water suitable for paddling, stone skimming or searching for fish and water bugs. You can also look out for herons, dippers, buzzards, deer, plus the wild Exmoor ponies. Take a picnic or there's food on offer at the Doone Valley stables, see page 121.

Out & about North Devon

Action stations

Archery
Dragon Archery
Holsworthy, EX22 7YQ, T0800-037 2466, dragonarcherycentre.co.uk. £29 adult, £18 child (under 17) or £14 with adult, minimum age 8. Down a National Trust track. Not just bows and arrows but a chance to hunt dinosaurs, defend against orcs, win at Agincourt and, of course, be Robin Hood over a morning or afternoon. Booking is required.

Take the Ilfracombe Princess to spot seals or seabirds.

Boat trips
Devon Duck Tours
The Quay, Appledore, EX39 1QS, T01271-861077, devonducktours. co.uk. Apr-Oct 0900-2000. Single £3 adult, £2.50 child, £1 bike; round trip £5 adult, £4 child, £15 family. Amphibious tours cover a triangular route on the Torridge Estuary available as a round trip, one way, or stepping off at Instow, Crow Point at the south of Saunton Sands/edge of Braunton Burrows, or Appledore.

Exmoor Boat Trips
The Quay, Lynmouth, T01598-753207, theglenlyngorge.co.uk. Daily, times depending on tides, from £10 person.
The latest boatmen from a family of Lynmouth sailors will take you out in parties as small as 12, past the Valley of the Rocks or visiting Woody Bay, past the ruins of the limestone trade and Victorian pier, telling stories of paddle steamers and the Lynmouth Lifeboat. Fishing trips for mackerel are also available.

Ilfracombe Princess
Pier Kiosk, Ilfracombe Harbour, T01271-879727, ilfracombeprincess. co.uk. Easter-Oct. 90-min cruise £12 adult, £6 child (5-15). Carrying up to 100 passengers, this is the largest and, being twin-hulled, the most stable cruise boat operating along the North Devon coast. Two cruises are available, either head west towards Morte Point in search of seals and porpoises, or east towards the soaring cliffs at Hangman Point to spot nesting seabirds and peregrine falcons.

Independent Charters
Bucks Mill, nr Bideford, T01237-431374, independentcharters.co.uk. Charter rates vary.
Sailing from Clovelly Harbour, trips feature fishing, wildlife watching and drop-offs/pickups at Lundy Island.

Kingfisher Boat Charters
Ilfracombe Harbour, T0796-919 8429. Easter-Oct. Mackerel fishing £15 person, half day £25 person.
One-and-a-half-hour mackerel fishing and half-day deep-sea fishing trips, suitable for families with children aged six or over for up to 12 passengers; everything supplied.

Climbing
The Mill Adventure Centre
Hacche Mill, South Molton, EX36 3NA, T01769-579600, milladventure. co.uk. Mon-Fri 1000-2200, Sat and Sun 1000-1800. £12.50/1-hr taster session with instruction.
The biggest indoor climbing wall in Devon offers courses from beginners to advanced, including taster sessions for children aged seven and over, plus indoor high ropes

adventure, outdoor zip wire, climbing and coasteering. Families are welcome.

Cycling
Bideford Cycle Hire
Torrington St, East-the-Water, Bideford, T01237-424123, bidefordbicyclehire.co.uk. Daily 0900-1700. Adult bike £8/half day, £10.50/day; child bike £6/half day, £7.50/day; child seat £4, tag-a-longs and buggies £14/half day; £18.50/day, discounts for return visits; also surf and kayak hire.
Offering a wide range including tandems, trailers, trikes and a wheelchair tandem.

Biketrail
Fremington Quay, EX31 2NH, T01271-372586, biketrail.co.uk. Daily during holidays 1000-1800. Adult bike £5.50/hr, £10/day; child bike £4/hr, £7.50/day; £32 family.
Rates include helmets, panniers, locks and tool kits. Bikes on offer include tandems, choppers and go-karts.

Otter Cycle Hire
Station Rd, Braunton, EX33 3AQ, T01271-813339. Mar-Nov daily 0900-1700. Adult bike £9/half day, £12/day; child bike £6/half day, £9/day.
Bikes for all ages, less than 20 m from the Tarka Trail. Buggies, tag-a-longs, child seats and specialist buggies with harnesses for tiny ones.

Tarka Trail Cycle Hire
Barnstaple Station, EX31 2AU, T01271-324202, tarkabikes.co.uk. Mar-Nov daily 0915-1700. Adult bike £8/half day, £10.50/day; child bike £5.50/half day, £7.50/day; child seat £3/half or full day; tag-a-long £5/half day, £7.50/day; rail passengers receive £2 discount.
Offering evening pickups and drop-offs by special arrangement.

Torrington Cycle Hire
Old Town Station, Station Hill, EX38 8JD, T01805-622633, torringtoncyclehire.co.uk. Feb-Nov Mon-Fri 0930-1700, Sat and Sun 1000-1600, weather permitting, or book in advance. Adult bike £8/half day, £10.50/day; child bike £6/half day, £7.50/day; tag-a-longs and buggies £6/half day, £8/day; child seat £2, adult helmet/£2; child helmet/free.
On the Tarka Trail, offering tag-a-longs, buggies, adult trikes and tandems.

Falconry
Exmoor Forest Birds of Prey
T01643-831458, exmoorforestbirdsofprey.co.uk. Hawk walk £15, half-day basic falconry experiences £60, hunting day £45.
Have a bird of prey fly to your hand on an hour-long hawk walk, or even a half-day basic falconry session, suitable for children aged seven and over accompanied by an adult. The session teaches you how to handle the birds, including Harry Potter-style owls and Harris hawks, before taking them out flying. You can also watch the birds in action on hunting trips.

Fishing
Blakewell Family Fishing & Trout Farm
Muddiford, Barnstaple, EX31 4PJ, T01271-344533, blakewell.co.uk. Daily 0900-1700. £2.50 person fishing, £5.80/kg for your catch.
Blakewell provides the fishing tackle and tips to ensure you catch your own supper. Once you've hooked your trout, they'll prepare and pack it ready for you to cook, along with other (limited) farm shop provisions.

Horse riding
Dean Riding Stables
Lower Dean Farm, Dean, Trentishoe, nr Parracombe, EX31 4PJ, T01598-763565, deanridingstables.co.uk. £15/pony ride (minimum age 4), £26/1-hr lesson, £40/2-hr hack, £58/half-day course including lesson, stable management and hack.
Full-specification stables within Exmoor National Park offering options from a half-hour taster on a pony to a living-and-breathing-horses holiday, with self-catering in the farmhouse.

Doone Valley Trekking
Cloud Farm, Oare, EX35 6NU, T01598-741234, doonevalleytrekking.co.uk. £20/1-hr starter ride, £37.50/2-hr trek, £97.50/day ride (minimum age 12).
Daily horse rides in this lovely valley for complete novices,

Out & about North Devon

as well as longer treks for the more competent rider. Even little ones can saddle up on the farm's miniature ponies and there are huge horses for any larger dads who want to join them. Accommodation is available in cottages or at Cloud Farm campsite (see page 136) and a cream tea at the café overlooking Badgworthy Water is a must. Alternatively, stay for an evening barbecue.

Outovercott Riding Stables
Nr Barbrook, Lynton, EX35 6JR, T01598-753341, outovercott.co.uk. Year round. £20/hr.
Accompanied rides for children aged five and over with instruction as you go. Offering rides along the Lyn Valley, over the moor or around the coast, plus horses and ponies for all abilities. Families are welcome, and children can help in getting the horses ready.

Roylands Riding Stables
Moor Lane, Croyde, EX33 1NU, T01271-890898, roylands-stables. co.uk. From £25/trekking, from £14/lessons, from £90/Own a Pony.
Family-run stables offering woodland rides, sand-dune rides, trekking, lessons and Own-a-Pony days: catching a pony from the field, grooming and setting up, followed by a lesson and ride. Complete riding holidays are also available.

Woolacombe Riding Stables
Eastacott Farm, EX34 7AE, T01271-870260, woolacombe-ridingstables. co.uk. £12/half hr, £20/1 hr, £50/day with pony (minimum age 7).
By Woolacombe Sands Park, riding for children aged four and over with lessons, hacks, plus Pony-for-a-Day and Pony Club tests. For little ones and non-riders half-hour lessons and half-hour rides are offered, also beach rides for children aged 12 and over plus experienced riders.

Kayaking
Tunnels Beaches
Bath Place, Ilfracombe, EX34 8AN, T01271-879123, tunnelsbeaches. co.uk/kayaking.html. Easter-Nov. Single kayak £10/hr, £30/half day; double £15/hr, £45/half day.
See also Bideford Cycle Hire, page 121.

Take to the water on sea kayaks.

Multi activities

H2Outdoor
Unit 5B, Mullacott Ind Est, Ilfracombe, EX34 8PL, T01271-863777, h2outdoor.co.uk. From £25-35 person depending on activity, treasure hunts/£5.
This is your chance to pick just one activity, or make up a week-long package, choosing from kayaking, canoeing, high ropes, surfing, coasteering, mountain biking, horse riding, pony trekking, rock climbing and abseiling around the coast and Exmoor. More land-based activities are recommended in winter. Families are welcome with children as young as eight, or you can book 30-minute sessions for younger children. If all that sounds too much for your crew, try one of the self-guided treasure hunts and orienteering days around Woolacombe.

Keypitts Stables n Quads
Oxen Park Lane, Ilfracombe, EX34 9RW, T01271-862247, keypitts.com. Easter-Oct 1000-1800, Nov-Easter 1000-1500. Quads £10/15 mins, paint balling from £15, riding £20/hr.
Quad biking from six years up with a cushioned track for little ones, wind-powered electric quads, paint balling from 13 years up, and riding stables.

Skern Lodge Activity Centre
Bideford, nr Appledore, EX39 1NG, T01237-475992, skernlodge.com. Family activities during school holidays Easter-Oct. £30/adventure day, discounts for 3 people or more.
Right on the coast, this highly regarded centre welcomes families

H2Outdoor offers many activities including sea kayaking.

for half- and full-day courses in a mind-boggling range of options, such as abseiling, zip-wiring, kayaking and surfing, plus adventure weeks packing in no fewer than 17 activities. There are residential options too, including accommodation and a heated pool outdoors.

Southdown Adventure
Southdown, Yarnscombe, nr Barnstaple, EX31 3LZ, T01271-858791, southdownadventure.com. Jun-Sep Mon-Sat 1000-1730, Sun 1000-1600, bookings only Oct-May. £30 person (16+), £20 child (12-15), £15 child (6-11).
Offering quad biking (minimum age six) and buggy racing (minimum age 16). Kids can rev up after proving themselves in the training paddock, using Madtrax buggies powered by 400cc engines. Also a Zorb ball where two people are strapped in and pushed down a field for approximately £15 each (minimum height 1.5 m) and archery at £3 for 12 shots. Booking is required.

The Ultimate High
Abbotsham Rd, Abbotsham, EX39 5AP, T01237-471010/07779-639793, theultimatehigh.com. Summer daily 1000-1800, winter Sat 1030-1630. Climbing from £5, surfing lesson £25.
One of the cheapest providers in North Devon but AALA- and Devon County Council-approved. Offers high ropes, zip wire, climbing wall, Jacob's ladder, teen tasks, leap of faith, plus off-site coasteering, kayaking, climbing and surfing. Activities are suitable for children aged five and over; the focus is on personal development through the great outdoors.

Out & about North Devon

Llama walks
Exmoor Llamas
Oakford, between South Molton and Bamford, EX16 9JY, T07902-936120, exmoorllamas.co.uk. £75 for 1-2 people and 1 llama, £95 for 2-4 people and 2 llamas, £110 for 3-6 people and 3 llamas.
Treks around Dunster Forest, with the route customized to the walkers and weather conditions, but lasting approximately two to three hours with a stop for light refreshments.

Water sports
Wimbleball Lake
Nr Dulverton, TA22 9NW, T01398-371460, swlakestrust.org.uk. Year round. Taster sessions from £22/1 hr, Wet and Active Days 1000-1600 with 3 activities including raft building £40+VAT/person.
The Exmoor reservoir offers water sports such as sailing, windsurfing, kayaking, canoeing, rowing, plus fishing and equipment hire. There's a tea room for refreshments and campsite open from March to October, see page 138.

Wildlife
Devon Badger Watch
Nr Cove, north of Tiverton, T01398-351506, devonbadgerwatch.co.uk. Apr-Oct Mon-Sat from 1930. £10 adult, £7 child (7-15).
Not one for fidgets, Devon Badger Watch promises spine-tingling encounters with Brock and his buddies. There's a talk, then walk to the hide and up to 90 minutes spent in the hide, a few feet from where the badgers emerge, with live commentary.

Devon & Somerset Wildlife Discovery
T01884-881284, devonandsomersetwildlifediscovery.co.uk. £30 adult, £25 child (under 15).
You need to keep quiet but children who manage that can track deer, and watch the wild ponies, foxes, hares and buzzards on the moor. Experienced guides lead tailor-made tours of around three hours on foot or by Land Rover, year round at dawn or dusk. Within a 10-mile radius, they'll even collect you, so you don't have to navigate the narrow moorland lanes.

National Park Centre
Dulverton, T01398 323841, exmoor-nationalpark.gov.uk. £3/up to 4 hrs, under 16s free.
Park rangers run evening deer-spotting outings from start points like Anstey Gate, fortnightly in July and August, less regularly the rest of year (see Enjoying section on the website) covering around three miles over two hours. Booking not required.

Surf schools

North Devon sees the full force of the Atlantic waves, making it a great centre for surfing. Croyde's combination of waves and village make it a big surfie hang out – see the wetsuits drying outside cottages. Saunton Sands' slower waves are better for beginners, with slightly calmer waters around Morte Bay and Woolacombe.

Especially with children, the larger rollers may make this more of a spectator than participation sport, but it can be fun to watch the experts braving the waves.

Nick Thorn Surf School
Woolacombe, T01271-871337, nickthorn.com. Year round. £30/2-hr lesson, £55/full day (2 lessons), £90/1:1.
Set up by the UK Iron Man champion and boasting a beachfront location at Woolacombe, Nick Thorn lessons teach you how to paddle a surfboard, choose your waves and get to your feet, as well as progressing to intermediate and advanced skills. There's a minimum age of eight years for group lessons, although younger ones can be taught privately. If you've got a group of five children you can even organize a surf party.

North Devon Surf School
Pebbleridge Rd, Westward Ho! EX39 1HN, T01237-474663, northdevonsurfschool.co.uk. Year round. £28/2-hr lesson, £50/full day (2 lessons), minimum age 8.
At the south entrance to Northam Burrows close to Westward Ho! beach, away from the big waves and experienced surfers. Private tuition is available for children under eight.

Point Breaks
Croyde, T07776-148679, pointbreaks.com. £35/3-hr lesson, minimum age 8.
Croyde Bay's original surf school, also offering wakeboarding and waterskiing if the sea is flat.

Surfing Croyde Bay
Croyde, T01271-891200, surfingcroydebay.co.uk. Mar-Dec. £35 adult, £25 child (8-16).
Established surf school with a beach café, solar-powered showers, plus sandpit training area. Surfing lessons have a 5:1 student to instructor ratio.

Surf South West
Moor Lane, Croyde Bay, EX33 1NZ, and Saunton Beach, EX33 1LG, T01271-890400, surfsouthwest.com. Mar-Nov. £25-30/lesson, £95/5 midweek sessions, £25-72/1:1.
The first UK school awarded Level 4 status by the British Surfing Association, offers tuition at both Croyde and Saunton, with all beginner courses in shallow water. Private sessions are available for children under eight, alone or with the rest of the family.

Learn to surf in North Devon.

Don't miss
Biking the Tarka Trail

Looping for 180 miles across North Devon, the Tarka Trail (devon.gov.uk/tarkatrail.htm) offers traffic-free cycling and walking through countryside that inspired Henry Williamson's *Tarka the Otter*. The most family-friendly sections are between Braunton and Meeth.

Braunton to Barnstaple (six miles) is a flat, easy ride along the River Taw, linking Braunton Burrows with Barnstaple, where you can find out about river life at the museum (see page 134). Three miles west the Ashford Bird Hide is a great spot to watch wading birds and wildfowl on the mudflats, with picnicking nearby.

Barnstaple to Bideford (nine miles) has more twitching at RSPB Isley Marsh, see page 113, but the highlight is the former china clay port of Fremington Quay with glorious views of the estuary and superb café (see page 144). Further south Instow has a sheltered beach and ferry to Appledore, while Bideford has a pannier market and 13th-century bridge.

Bideford to Great Torrington (six miles) is where the trail crosses the Torridge at the Landcross Viaduct, setting for the Pool of Six Herons from *Tarka the Otter*. Then it's four miles of beautiful riverside scenery, including near Beam Aqueduct, described as Tarka's birthplace.

Great Torrington to Meeth (10 miles) offers views of Dartmoor, with Dartington Crystal, see page 130, and RHS Garden Rosemoor, see page 131, tempting diversions in Torrington. Dotted along the Trail are 21 discovery posts with history and wildlife information. And the Tarka Audio Trail (northdevonbiosphere.org.uk) can be downloaded to your MP3 player or mobile phone. Bike hire outlets all along the trail offer children's seats and buggies, see page 121.

127

Out & about North Devon

Big days out

The Big Sheep
Abbotsham, nr Bideford, EX39 5AP, T01237-472366, thebigsheep.co.uk. Apr-Nov daily 1000-1800. £9.95 person, £9.45 person for groups of 4 or more, children under 90 cm free, reduced prices and facilities during winter.

Farm diversification gone mad, the Big Sheep is utterly *baa*-rmy with an indoor and outdoor mixture of sheep-themed attractions that is certainly Devon's most original day out, and possibly the most fun; and with modest admission prices you won't feel fleeced either. The highlight is the sheep racing at Ewe-toxeter where you can place bets using Ewe-ros, the park's ubiquitous currency, before cheering on Red Ram, Sheargar and other favourites down the 230-m course. If you think that's bizarre, brace yourself for the sheep-duck trials where border collies round up gaggles of woolly-headed runner ducks. There are also traditional sheepdog trials, shearing demos, horse-whispering demos, pony rides, a farm safari, pedal go-karts, ride-on tractors and a train ride departing from – you guessed it – Eweston Station. You'll find all the cute-and-fluffies in the Nursery Barn, where puppies are available for regular cuddling sessions and newborn lambs can be bottle-fed. Other barns house soft-play areas, a sheep-shearing arena, restaurant and the all-important Sheepy Shop.

Something of a contrast to the main attraction, the Big Sheep is also the venue for Battlefield Live, offering war games using state-of-the-art 'eye-safe' laser guns (minimum age eight) and, if teenagers find the whole thing too silly, they can check out the neighbouring Ultimate High, see page 123.

The Big Sheep offers more than just woolly fun.

Sand dunes at Braunton Burrows.

Out & about North Devon

The Milky Way
Nr Clovelly, EX39 5RY, T01237-431255, themilkyway.co.uk. Easter-Oct daily 1030-1800, winter 1100-1700. £6.50-11 adult, under 3s free.
When it rains, many families set warp drive for this park where a good number of the attractions, such as the Clone Zone Alien Interactive Ride and the huge adventure play area for adults and children, are all under cover. Pray for a dry spell though, so you can escape the indoor mayhem and visit the birds of prey, where falcons demonstrate speeds of over 100 miles per hour (you can book bird of prey experiences from £60 for half a day); a darkened theatre allows the owls to show off their night-time skills. The park is also home to Devon's biggest roller coaster, the Cosmic Typhoon (minimum height 1.2 m) and there's a pets' corner and a special area for children under five, plus five live shows daily.

More family favourites

Arlington Court
Arlington, nr Barnstaple, EX31 4LP, T01271-850296, nationaltrust.org.uk. Mar-Oct daily 1030-1700. £8.20 adult, £4.10 child (5-17), £20.50 family.
There's something for everyone at this 2700-acre estate on the edge of Exmoor. The Regency house in a wooded valley contains the souvenir haul of globetrotter Rosalie Chichester, so you can see cabinets of stuffed birds, seashells, silver spoons and model ships. In the nursery there's a Victorian trapeze artist in a glass case, and a clockwork tortoise. In the carriage museum there are almost 50 horse-drawn carriages (rides available) and one designed to be pulled by a dog, while an interactive bat-cam allows you to spy on a colony of lesser horseshoe bats. In addition, the animal-loving Miss Chichester left Shetland ponies and wiry Jacob sheep, descended from those she brought back from Australia and New Zealand.

Borough Farm
Nr Mortehoe, EX34 7HE, T01271-870056, boroughfarm.co.uk, experiencefalconry.co.uk. Jul-Aug Wed eve 1800. £4 adult, £2 child.
The farm where David Kennard filmed his sheepdog DVDs and wrote the Mist sheepdog stories offers live shows. Along with a falconry display, you can marvel at the intelligence and enthusiasm of these bright dogs rounding up not just sheep but also the farm's ducks.

Clovelly
Clovelly Visitor Centre, T01237-431781, clovelly.co.uk. Daily from 0900. £5.75 adult, £3.65 child (7-16), £15.50 family.
Owned by the same family since 1738, Clovelly is an old fishing village, complete with (buggy-unfriendly) steep cobbled High Street, lined by whitewashed cottages dripping with geraniums leading to a harbour with its own lifeboat ramp. Something of coach-tour heaven, the visitor centre sets the scene with an informative film, while the adjacent donkey stables are an essential distraction for kids before beginning the walk down. For an extra fee you can catch a Land Rover back up.

Combe Martin Museum
Eberliegh House, Cross St, EX34 0DH, T01271-889031, combemartinmuseum.org. Easter-Oct 1030-1730, Nov-Easter 1030-1300. £2.75 adult, accompanied children free.
This new and attractive hands-on experience is for all ages but especially children, with a bit of everything including microscopes to examine sea life, a chance to learn how to load a ship, some dressing up, information on how fast materials decay in the sea, and more.

Dartington Crystal
Torrington, EX38 7AN, T01805-626242, dartington.co.uk. Mon-Fri 0930-1700, Sat 1000-1700, Sun 1000-1600. Factory tour £5 adult (Mon-Fri only).
This is a rare chance for kids to watch skilled artisans at work, some engraving, but most blowing glass. You can also try yourself (£5 to blow, £20 to buy the result, £7 to post if you can't collect the next day). Hand or foot casts are from £15.

Hit or miss?

The Gnome Reserve
Bradworthy, T01409-241435, gnomereserve.co.uk. Mar-Oct daily 1000-1800. £2.95 adult, £2.50 child.

Cynics may scoff, but where else can you take a family of four for under £12 *and* get free use of gnome hats and fishing rods into the bargain? So forget your inhibitions, puff out your cheeks and enjoy an hour or two at this four-acre reserve, populated by over 1000 gnomes. You'll find the chirpy chappies up to all sorts of fun and games, including a motorbike scramble.

Exmoor Zoo
Bratton Fleming, Barnstaple, by the A399, T01598-763352, exmoorzoo.co.uk. Daily from 1000. £8.25 adult, £6 child (3-15), £26.50 family.
All zoos need crowd pullers and at Exmoor Zoo that role falls to the 'Beast of Exmoor' or, to be more specific, a black leopard called Ebony. Wolves and cheetah also vie for attention but it's the smaller creatures (wallabies, spiders, otters and meerkats) that steal the show, thanks partly to the zoo's programme of talks and feeding sessions.

Ilfracombe Aquarium
The Pier, Ilfracombe, T01271-864533, ilfracombeaquarium.co.uk. Daily from 1000. £3.50 adult, £2.50 child (3-15), £11.50 family.
This isn't the most dramatic aquarium, so don't expect shark tunnels and penguin pools. Instead you'll be taken on a fascinating journey from an Exmoor stream to Lundy Island, passing estuary, rock pool and harbour habitats teeming with native marine life. There's a children's quiz, café and gift shop.

Lynton & Barnstaple Railway
Woody Bay Station, Martinhoe Cross, nr Parracombe, EX31 4RA, T01598-763487, lynton-rail.co.uk. Mar-Dec. £6 adult, £3 child (under 14), £15 family.
Once 19 miles long, this Victorian route is now being restored, with the first mile opened, operating steam and diesel services eight times a day.

The Old Corn Mill
Hele Bay, EX34 9QY, T01271-863185, helecornmill.com. Apr-Jun, Sep-Oct, Fri-Sun 1100-1700, Jul-Aug daily 1100-1700.
The engineering marvels of previous centuries are on show in this 16th-century watermill with working water wheel and other milling engines that the owners are happy to explain. The children's trail involves spotting the five little mice, and there's a café offering pottery painting along with cream teas.

Quince Honey Farm
North Rd, South Molton, EX36 3AZ, T01769-572401, quincehoney.co.uk. £5 adult, £3.95 child (5-16).
There's a real buzz about the largest honey farm in the country! It not only offers a finger-licking opportunity to sample the sweet stuff (you must try the honey ice cream) but also a chance to see processing in late summer and a fascinating exhibition about the lives of honey-bees with buttons to press to open different hives.

RHS Garden Rosemoor
Great Torrington, EX38 8PH, T01805-624067, rhs.org.uk. Oct-Mar daily 1000-1700, Apr-Sep daily 1000-1800. £6.50 adult, £2 child (6-16).

Watch the bees at the Quince Honey Farm.

Out & about North Devon

The perfect antidote to North Devon's surf-n-sand scene, this tranquil oasis consists of 65 acres of gardens and woodland, including a new eco family picnic and play area, along with a programme of family events, plus a quality organic, sustainable café.

Tapeley Park
Instow, EX39 4NT, off the B3233, T01271-860897, tapeleypark.com. Mid Mar-Nov. £4/adult, £2.50/child.
A stately home with a difference, with solar panels heating the water for showers, washing machine and the public loos; a demonstration straw-bale house, plus sheep as mowers for the front lawn. It's also almost self sufficient in providing meat, vegetables, eggs and water. Run by a member of the Christie family (others own the Glyndbourne Opera House), Tapeley is home to the Save Our World Trust. There's a permaculture garden, a heat sink, and the Victorian kitchen garden is back in action. If this all seems too worthy, it is beautiful too, offering a labyrinth walk with estuary views, Italian terraces and a lake surrounded by trees. The Dairy Tea Room, Tapeley Tea Room and Tapelia Restaurant serve breakfast, lunch, picnics, cream teas and evening meals. There are regular health and harmony weekends, plus in mid-July and end August are two annual Save Our World Charity Festivals with quality bands, speakers, alternative film shows, renewable energy displays and family entertainment.

Torrington 1646
Castle Hill, South St, Great Torrington, EX38 8AA, T01805-626146, torrington-1646.co.uk. Apr-Jun and Sep Mon-Fri 1000-1500, July-Aug Mon-Fri 1000-1500, Sat 1000-1300. £7.95 adult, £5.50 child, £23 family.
Folk in 17th-century garb are de riguer in Torrington, site of the last big battle of the English Civil War and a popular venue for re-enactments. Here, visitors can join in, with tours that focus on the winter night of the battle and all its mess and chaos. Costumed interpreters speak the language of the time to tell the story, while you can dress in the kit, see the church blow up, try out pikestaffs, check sword etiquette, find out about herbs in the physic garden, or watch the gruesome barber surgeon's work. You can even see musket balls being cast. The café serves local food including pasties and cream teas.

Walkers Chocolate Emporium
6 High St, Ilfracombe, EX34 9DF, T01271-867193, chocolate-emporium.co.uk.
A shop with a museum and a film, chance to see chocolate being made, then enjoy one of 12 hot chocolate drinks in the Café Cocoa.

Watermouth Castle
Berrynarbor, nr Ilfracombe, EX34 9SL, T01271-867474, watermouthcastle.com. Apr-Oct. £12 adult, £10 child (under 10), children under 92 cm free.
Castle fairy tales and more in a family theme park. There are gentle rides in Merrygoland, Gnome Land, the rather wetter slides and rides of Adventure Land and, under the Victorian castle, Dungeon Labyrinths, which also amuse with traditional hall of mirrors, model railway, mechanical music and vintage items.

Wildlife & Dinosaur Park
Combe Martin, T01271-882486, dinosaur-park.com. Mar-Nov daily from 1000. £12 adult, £7.50 child (3-15), £34 family.
Life-size animatronic dinosaurs headline the attractions at this eclectic theme park, where one moment you'll be cowering beneath a T-rex or ducking to avoid a spitting dilophosaurus, and the next you'll be clinging to a Wild West runaway train as it lurches into a simulated earthquake. The park's snow leopards, lions, lemurs, gibbons, meerkats and other exotic creatures have no need for special effects, although the daily howling shows by wolf expert Shaun Ellis certainly add an extra dimension to the wolf exhibit. You can also watch falconry displays, swim with sea lions, or take refuge from the wild things in the lovely gardens.

Rain check

Cinemas
• **The Central**, Barnstable, scottcinemas.co.uk.
• **Deckchair Cinema**, Croyde, T07970-051058, croydedeckchaircinema.co.uk. Sun.
• **The Embassy Cinema**, Ilfracombe, cromer-movieplex.com.
• **Lynton Cinema**, Lynton, lyntoncinema.co.uk.
• **Plough Arts Centre**, Torrington, plough-arts.org.
• **Vintage Mobile Cinema Company**, T01271-346747, vintagemobilecinema.co.uk.

Indoor activities
• **Atlantis Adventure Park**, Atlantic Village shopping mall, Bideford, EX39 3QU, T01237-478888, atlanticvillage.co.uk. Mon-Sat 1000-1800, Sun 1030-1630.
• **Burton Art Gallery and Museum**, Kingsley Rd, Bideford, EX39 2QQ, T01237-471455, burtonartgallery.co.uk.
• **Crazy Cabin**, Castle St, Combe Martin, EX34 OHT, T01271-883474. Mon, Wed, Fri, Sat 1000-1800. £2.50 child (under 10).
• **Funder Zone**, Barnstaple Trade Centre, Whiddon Drive, Barnstaple, EX32 8RY, T01271-328328, funderzonebarnstaple.com. Daily 1000-1830. £1 adults, £3.95 child (5-12), £3.55 child (1-4), under 1s free.
• **Glaze Craze**, 12 Grenville St, Bideford, EX39 2EA, T01237-420330, glazecraze-bideford.co.uk.
• **Higher Meadow**, Northleigh House, Goodleigh, Barnstaple, EX32 7NR, T01271-321502, highermeadowfarm.co.uk.
• **Paint a Pot**, 5 Exeter Rd, Braunton, EX33 2JL, T01271-813999. Year round except Jan.
• **Pots 'n' Paints**, Glebe Farmhouse, Little Torrington, EX38 8PS, T01805-625577, postnpaintsonline.co.uk. Daily 1000-late (phone to book).
• **Play Hut**, Tunnels Beaches, Bath Place, Ilfracombe, EX34 8AN, T01271-879882, tunnelsbeaches.co.uk/playhut.html. £2/hr child (under 10).
• **Waves Ceramic Studio**, Golden Coast Holiday Park, nr Woolacombe, EX34 7HW, T01271-871360, woolacombe.com/waves.

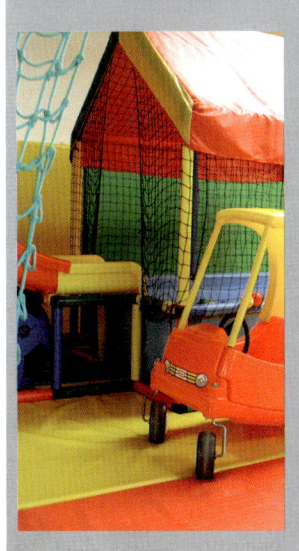

Indoor swimming pools
• **The Cascades**, Ruda Bay Park, Croyde, EX33 1NY, T01271-890671.
• **Holsworthy Leisure Centre**, Well Park, EX22 6DH, T01409-254013.
• **Ilfracombe Swimming Pools**, Hillsborough Rd, EX34 9QG, T01271-864480.
• **North Devon Leisure Centre**, Seven Brethren Bank, Barnstaple, EX31 2AP, T01271-373361.
• **South Molton Swimming Pool**, Mill St, EX36 4AS, T01769-572522, southmoltonpool.org.uk.
• **Torridge Leisure Centre**, Churchill Way, Northam, nr Bideford, EX39 1SU, T01237-471794.
• **Torrington Swimming Pool**, School Lane, EX38 7AJ, T01805-623085.

Museums
• **Museum of Barnstaple & North Devon**, EX32 8LN, T01271-346747, devonmuseums.net/barnstaple.
• **Bideford Railway Museum**, 28 Stanbridge Park, EX39 3RS, T01237-476769.
• **Bradworthy Transport Museum**, T01409-241597, bradworthy-transport-museum.co.uk.
• **Braunton & District Museum**, EX33 1AA, devonmuseums.net/braunton.net.
• **Holsworthy Museum**, EX22 6DJ, devonmuseums.net/holsworthy.
• **Ilfracombe Museum**, EX34 8AF, T01271-863541, devonmuseums.net/ilfracombe.
• **Lyn & Exmoor Museum**, EX35 6AF, devonmuseums.net/lynton.
• **Mortehoe Heritage Centre**, EX34 7DT, T01271-870028.
• **North Devon Maritime Museum**, Appledore, EX39 1PT, T01237-422064, devonmuseums.net/appledore.
• **South Molton & District Museum**, EX36 3AB, southmoltonmuseum.org.

Off the beaten track

Lundy Island

Sailing from Bideford or Ilfracombe (Apr-Oct, Tue, Thu, Sat plus Jul and Aug, Wed, sailing times vary. £32.50 adult, £17 child (4-16), £5 infant (under 4), £75 family day return), the 267-passenger *MS Oldenburg* takes under two hours to reach Lundy Island, a three-mile-long chunk of granite rising from the Bristol Channel, 11 miles north of Hartland Point as the gull flies.

The only Marine Nature Reserve in England, Lundy has a chequered history. After prehistoric inhabitants, Vikings may well have used the island as a base for raiding Britain – 'Lund-ey' is Norse for Puffin Island. In the Middle Ages, Lundy was a popular lair for pirates, including a gang of Turks who threatened to burn Ilfracombe. This was followed by a pillaging band of Spaniards and, finally, by the French who hurled the islanders' livestock over the cliffs.

As you'd expect from such a turbulent past, a map of Lundy is littered with wicked place names, like Dead Cow Point, Devil's Kitchen and Brazen Ward. Making landfall at the island's jetty feels like you have been transported into the pages of a Famous Five novel and there are no worries about cars and traffic.

It's a short walk to the Marisco Tavern, an atmospheric inn at the heart of Lundy's tiny settlement, where you will also find a shop, church, old lighthouse and a 13th-century castle, originally paid for by the sale of rabbits when Lundy was a royal warren; along with other buildings from a hostel dormitory to a lighthouse, it's been restored by the Landmark Trust as holiday accommodation (see page 19). Limited camping is also available. There are Lundy ponies, sika deer, wild goats and local sheep (also available to eat), but this is mostly about the wild. One of the best places to spot wildlife is on the west side of the island. Follow the track from the settlement to South West Point, then head north along the cliff tops towards Jenny's Cove, keeping an eye out for basking sharks, seals and seabirds. At the southern end you can spot guillemots, razorbills and fulmars diving for fish, plus the black-legged kittiwake, herring gulls, lesser black-backed gulls, shags, oystercatchers, skylarks, meadow pipits, linnets, plus the occasional peregrine falcon. You might even hear sea lions barking. Warden-led events on the island include rock-pool rambles at Devil's Kitchen and snorkelling safaris from June to September where you can glide through forests of kelp in search of Montagu's blennies and rare corals. The puffins only arrive to nest April to June, and hang out at the opposite end of the island from where you disembark, so on a day trip you have to walk fast to see them.

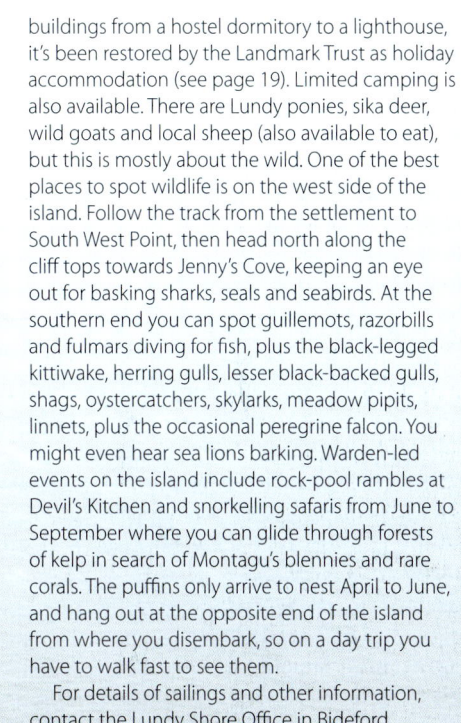

For details of sailings and other information, contact the Lundy Shore Office in Bideford (T01271-863636, lundyisland.co.uk). Out of season, a scheduled helicopter service flies from Hartland Point (Nov-Mar Mon and Fri 1200).

Sleeping North Devon

Pick of the pitches

Bay View Farm Camping
Croyde, EX33 1PN, T01271-890501, bayviewfarm.co.uk. Easter-Oct. Pitches from £29/week.

So popular are these fields on the edge of Croyde, with views across to Lundy, that bookings are taken just Saturday to Saturday, and only families and couples are welcomed. There is a safe play area for children, a shop and an on-site fish and chips outlet.

Cloud Farm Campsite
Oare, T01598-741234, doonevalleyholidays.co.uk. Year round. £5.50-7.50 adult, £4-5.50 child (5-12).

Doone Valley is quintessential Exmoor and Cloud Farm is sitting pretty in the middle with heather-blushed moor, a stream tumbling over rocks into cool dark pools shaded by trees, grey wagtails fussing over moss-covered boulders and ponies grazing in riverside meadows. More than a farm with a camping field, this lovely old whitewashed property has three self-catering cottages, a tea room and horse-riding stable (see page 121). You can pitch your tent next to the effervescent Badgworthy Water, where kids will happily while away an afternoon netting water bugs, racing sticks through the rapids or taking a dip in one of the natural pools. Walk or ride a horse out of the campsite and you'll find you are in the wilds of Exmoor National Park. And, what better way to round off a day's hike than by sipping hot chocolate and toasting marshmallows around your own campfire?

Doone Valley Campsite
Oare, T01598-741267, brendonvalley.co.uk. Year round. £5 adult, £3 child.

Almost opposite the track leading to Cloud Farm (above), Doone Valley is a larger campsite with riverside fields, so offering more space for frisbee and football, and excellent toilet facilities. It's not as pretty as Cloud Farm, but having the Buttery next door is a definite bonus. This riverside bar and café serves cream teas, light lunches and stone-baked pizzas.

Goulds Farm
Nethercott, nr Braunton, EX33 1HT, T01271-815074, gfea.co.uk. Easter-Oct. £8/pitch.

Camping is in a flat field next to a stream and woodland, with plenty of space in woods and fields. Fires permitted when the site is not busy. Showers available for five electric hook-up spaces in a separate area; toilets and basins for the rest.

Hidden Valley Touring Park
West Down, nr Ilfracombe, EX34 8NU, T01271-813837, hiddenvalleypark.com. Year round. £15-25/pitch.

Inland from Ilfracombe, a five-star option offering a long narrow site with pine trees above, also home to a farm shop and eco shop. The site has free solar-powered showers, adventure play parks, woodland walks and a café serving breakfast, lunch and cream teas, plus adult therapy suite. Also own Newberry Valley Park near Combe Martin (T01271-882334, newberryvalleypark.co.uk).

Hole Station Campsite
Highampton, Beaworthy, EX21 5JH, T01409-231266, freewebs.com/holestationcampsite. Apr-Sep. £12/pitch, £5/firepit including kindling and firewood, Rent-a-Tent £21/night.

Wood shavings from the coppicing is used to keep the 12 pitches dry in these 23 acres of woodland, open to all those staying at this eco site, with benches and chairs dotted about for the best views of the tors of Dartmoor. There are compost toilets, a fire pit with each tent including wood from the site, plus Rent-a-Tent super pitches, provided with own toilet, air mattresses, cool box and dining shelter with full kitchen. No cars are allowed next to the tents, but

Enjoy the simple life at Cloud Farm.

wheelbarrows are provided for use on planked walkways. The owner has kids, horses, a friendly cat and Crash and Burn the goats, who join in the fun.

Little Meadow
Watermouth, Ilfracombe, North Devon, T01217-866862, littlemeadow.co.uk. Apr-Oct. From £7 person, £1 extra person, under 3s free.

A chance to camp on an organic working farm (recycling is compulsory) on a quiet hillside above Watermouth Bay with views from the grass terraces to the sea. Although there are just 50 pitches, the shop sells items including home-made cakes and there's Wi-Fi. The notice on arrival advises that children must be supervised but a traffic-free play area is provided for them.

Lobb Fields
Saunton Rd, Braunton, EX33 1HG, T01271-812090, lobbfields.com. Mar-Nov. £9-15/pitch, £2-3 child (5-14).

A four-star site on the road from Braunton to Saunton, set on flattish fields with hills behind; easy access, with a surf-hire outlet.

Millslade Camping
Brendon, Lynton, EX35 6PS, T01598-741322, £4.50 adult, £1.50 child (5-14).

In the Doone Valley, here is a very simple site with no showers and just 20 pitches. No bookings taken, although with families coming back generation after generation, it is worth phoning ahead. Food is available from the local pub if you don't feel like cooking over the fire.

North Morte Farm Caravan & Camping
Mortehoe, Woolacombe, EX34 7EG, T01271-870381, northortefarm.co.uk. Easter-Nov. £6-8.50 adult, £2.50-3 child (2-15).

Location, location, location… on gently sloping National Trust land just 450 m from Rockham Bay and the coast path, this family-run four-star site has welcoming staff and a children's play area. The camping fields offer both level and sloping pitches – first-come-first-served – along with lovely views. The

Sleeping North Devon

village has shops, including a good deli, post office, restaurants, pub (with family room) and takeaway. Static caravans are also available.

Over Weir Camp Site
Umberleigh, EX37 9DU, T01769-560009, umberleigh-camping-caravaning-devon.co.uk. Apr-Nov. £5.65-8.35 adult, £2.50-2.60 child, £6.60 non-member fee.

A quiet four-star touring park on a grassy site run by the Camping and Caravanning Club on behalf of the owners, inland from the coast in the Taw Valley. There are 60 pitches, a pond for fishing, woodland walk, two tennis courts (a charge applies), with free coaching for children aged eight and over in school holidays, plus a games barn with table tennis, table football, skittles, pool, Wendy house, plus TV room. Fish and chips are available on Tuesdays.

Parkhill Farm
Shirwell, Barnstaple, EX31 4JN, T01271-850323, parkhillfarmcamping.co.uk. Apr-Oct. £8/pitch.

A low-tech site on a working organic farm with sheep, cows, free-range chooks, a sheepdog and cats. There are just five caravan pitches but lots of room for tents. A freezer service is available.

Steart Farm Touring Park
Bucks Cross, Bideford, EX39 5DW, T01237-431836, steartfarmtouringpark.co.uk. Apr-Sep. £8.50-10/pitch, £1 person, £2.50/hook-up.

A particularly quiet site (no radios, etc between 2300 and 0700) with 70 pitches across seven acres, including two acres for exercising dogs, a two-acre recreation area and some secluded terraces for tents only. One of the few camping options at the westerly end of the north coast, there's a footpath to the coast approximately one mile away. There's an order service for milk, bread, eggs and papers, plus ice pack-freezing service and battery charging.

Stoke Barton Farm Camp Site
Stoke, Hartland Quay, EX39 6DU, T01237-441238, westcountry-camping.co.uk. Easter-Oct. £5.50 adult, £3 child (under 16), £1 child (under 5).

Situated on a slope behind Hartland Quay; some fields have sea views. The farm is complete with working dogs and battered barns. There's a children's play area, rides for kids behind the quad bikes and breakfast is served daily excluding Monday plus cream teas on Saturdays, Sundays and bank holidays.

Stowford Farm Meadows
Berry Down, Combe Martin, T01271-882476, stowford.co.uk. Year round. £9.20-28/pitch (2 people), £1.50-4.50/extra person.

On the northern fringe of Exmoor, this 500-acre site offers an impressive range of facilities and activities, including an indoor heated swimming pool, horse-riding centre, cycle hire, mini zoo, Kiddies' Car and crazy golf. Far from being brash, Stowford retains a tranquil atmosphere, particularly in the adjacent oak woodland that can be explored on a network of trails directly from the campsite.

Warcombe Farm
Camping Park, Station Rd, Mortehoe, EX34 7EJ, T01271-870690, warcombefarm.co.uk. Mar-Oct. £12-33/pitch + 2, free-£2.20 child.

A David Bellamy gold award-winning site with 15 acres of developing woodland, pitches in tree groves, a dog walk, fishing lake, with all the wildlife that attracts.

Wimbleball Lake
Nr Dulverton, T01398-371257, swlakestrust.org.uk. £6 person, £3 child (5-14), £14 family.

A three-star site a short walk from the water-sports centre (see page 124), also with access to fishing and walking trails.

138

Best of the rest

Hill Farm
Weare Trees Hill, Great Torrington, EX38 7EZ, T01805-622432, hillfarmcottages.co.uk.
£331-995/week.
Five neat properties around a courtyard, almost Mediterranean-style, with lots of flowerbeds and a shared laundry room. All cottages have cots, stair-gates, high chairs and babysitting is offered. There's also a games room with table tennis, pool table and toys, plus the seven acres of grounds include a children's play area, indoor heated pool and lots of animals.

Newhouse Farm Cottages
Newhouse Farm, Witheridge, EX16 8QB, T01884-860266, newhousecottages.com.
£250-1650/week.
Lots of family facilities, including indoor pool, 23 acres of grounds and woodland with lake and stream, children's wooden play area, trampoline with safety net, toddler soft-play room, golf-practice area, field for ball games, badminton, basketball net, table tennis, football tables, and communal gardens.

North Hayne Farm & Holiday Cottages
Bishops Nympton, South Molton, EX36 3QR, T01769-550807, northhaynefarmcottages.co.uk.
£271-1077/week.

Devon Holiday Homes
T01271-376322, devonandexmoor.co.uk.
Offering 400 properties in North Devon and along Exmoor's National Trust coastline, from beachside homes to country cottages.

Cottages named after Beatrix Potter characters in 10 acres with views of Exmoor. There are eggs to collect, animals to feed, including goats, ducks, sheep and pigs, plus donkeys to be ridden, a play barn, games room and outdoor play equipment. Qualified babysitting can be booked, together with treatments like aromatherapy, Indian head massage and reflexology.

Torridge House Cottages
Torridge House, Little Torrington, EX38 8PS, T01805-622542, torridgehouse.co.uk.
£342-1434/week.
Set in farmland near the Tarka Trail, slightly ramshackle but lots of space and really geared to children. There are cows, pigs, rabbits, turkeys, ducks and hens to feed plus lambs in spring and early summer. Also a heated pool including baby pool in a walled area from May to September, a grass tennis area, table tennis, small playroom; cots and high chairs can be supplied.

Park life

Woolacombe Bay Holiday Parcs T01271-870343, woolacombe.co.uk. Apartments £195-650, pitch £5-18.30 adult, £2.50-9.15 child.

If you want a good-value base on the North Devon coast that's hassle-free and rainproof, this group of four different parks around Woolacombe is ideal. Stay at one and you can use all the facilities at the others, most of them free, including evening entertainment. Also free are the kids' clubs for children age five to 12 plus a play zone for children under five.

Easewell Farm is the main camping site but also offers holiday cottages plus facilities including an indoor pool, bowls, snooker, restaurant and bar, plus golf course.

Golden Coast is the largest and open year round with accommodation in lodges plus neighbouring Cleavewood House, indoor and outdoor pools, restaurant, tennis courts, supermarket, pitch-n-putt, 10-pin bowling, cinema, plus Wave Ceramics Studio, see page 133.

Twitchen House, based round the Victorian manor and with a footpath to the sea, has accommodation in caravan holiday homes plus camping options, and there are indoor and outdoor pools, adventure playground and restaurant.

Woolacombe Bay is 15 minutes' walk from the beach with views to the sea and offers caravan holiday homes plus camping. There's an outdoor fun and toddler pool, golf, pitch-n-putt, bowls, tennis, spa and restaurant.

Sleeping North Devon

YHA Elmscott
Hartland, EX39 6ES, T0845-371 9736, yha.org.uk. From £15 adult, £10.50 child (under 18).
On the Hartland peninsula, a converted old school house and school barn with a walled garden, picnic tables, views to Lundy and rooms sleeping two to six.

Cool & quirky

Broomhill Sculpture Gardens
Muddiford, nr Barnstaple, EX31 4EX, T01271-850262, broomhillart.co.uk. £75/double B&B, £15 child sharing (under 13). Gardens daily 1100-1600, gallery Wed-Sun 1100-1600, closed mid-Dec to mid-Jan. £4.50 adult, £1.50 child (under 13), £10 family.
This Edwardian house, once an uninspiring hotel, has been given a new lease of life by a Dutch couple; comfortable accommodation at the heart of a sculpture park, with 300 works, some monumental, in eight acres of a green, wooded valley, plus an indoor gallery if the weather is bad. The gardens, woods and small river, make a place to splash, explore and marvel before unwinding over an organic meal with home-made bread and cheese in the Slow Food Terra Madre restaurant, open for lunch from Wednesday to Sunday, dinner on Friday and Saturday, or teas all week. Two of the rooms are family rooms and there's a jazz evening once a month.

Happy Tipi Holidays
Southdown Woods, Yarnscombe, EX31 3LZ, T01271-858279, happytipi.co.uk. £350-600/week.
Just three tipi sleeping three to eight people and, although this is about getting back to a simple life, they come furnished with comfortable mattresses and seating, plus pans, crockery, cutlery, a bag of smokeless charcoal for cooking, picnic tables; there are toilets and showers 200 m away. There's also an open fire (wood an extra cost). Survival Paintball is also on site (T01271-858279).

The Yarner Trust
Welcombe Barton, Welcombe, Bideford, EX39 6HF, T01288-331692, yarnertrust.org. Courses from £40/day, summer camp £195 adult, £115 child (6-18), £40 child (under 6).
This small charity promoting sustainable and creative living offers courses and workshop-based holidays, including activities such as pottery, drumming, block printing or willow sculpture, plus Summer Camp with activities for children and entertainment like a barn dance or puppet show, a safe play area for children under six, and 'spoil yourself' sessions for adults. Accommodation is available in the rustic house or yurts. More family-friendly activities are planned, particularly around school holidays.

Saunton Sands with Saunton Sands Hotel in the background.

Splashing out

Heasley House
Heasley Mill, North Molton, EX36 3LE, T01598-740213, heasley-house.co.uk. £60/adult B&B.
Inland, the old copper mine captain's house has been lovingly restored to offer an attractive sloping garden, eight rooms, two lounges and a friendly welcome. Children can eat at 1800 or later with parents.

Saunton Sands Hotel
Nr Braunton, EX33 1LQ, T01271-890212, sauntonsands.com. £85 adult, child 40% of adult price, £190/apartment, £217-686/2-bedroom beach villa.
The white mass of this Art Deco hotel stands over one

end of Saunton Sands, hosting weddings and conferences as well as families who return year-after-year for facilities, including children's play area, nursery from 1000 to 1800, indoor and outdoor pools, and access to the acres of sand below. There's self-catering from three to five stars, including beach villas (upmarket huts), and most hotel rooms take a third bed or cot; some offer single- or twin-bedded rooms en suite. If the price seems too high, drop in for a drink, as the views are great. Down on the beach, the hotel runs the Sands Café serving snacks, cappuccinos and more, and, in the evening, it becomes an informal bistro.

Woolacombe Bay Hotel

Woolacombe, EX34 7BN, T01271-870388, woolacombe-bay-hotel.co.uk. £80 adult B&B, £15 child (2-16), £210-1155/flat for 4.
Lots of polished brass sums up this Victorian hotel aiming to be the best three-star in the country. There are six acres of gardens, outdoor pool (heated June to September), indoor heated pool, tennis, squash, nine-hole approach golf, billiard room, table tennis, dance studio, classes, a boat you can charter for a trip to Lundy… and the list goes on. For families there are holiday clubs, early suppers and more. As well as hotel rooms there's associated self-catering nearby.

Farm favourites

Beer Mill Farm
Clawton, nr Holsworthy, EX22 6PF, T01409-253093, selfcateringcottagesdevon.co.uk/hillcottage.html. £630-2050/week.
Roam your own 45-acre nature reserve on this organic farm, including three properties sleeping up to 10, with cots and high chairs available and children and pets welcomed, plus cats, dogs, horses and more. The Beer Mill reserve includes pasture, scrub, broad-leaved woodland, areas of new woodland planting, quarry and wetland habitats including ponds and a stream, so you could while away whole days there.

Huxtable Farm
West Buckland, Barnstaple, EX32 0SR, T01598-760254, huxtablefarm.co.uk. Feb-Nov. £36 adult B&B, £10-17 child, £25 adult dinner, £12 child (under 15), £10/high tea.
Down a half-mile private lane in restored buildings dating back to 1520, facilities at this very comfortable B&B include a sauna, fitness room, tennis, games room, library and selection of board games, children's outside play area with swings, sandpit, Wendy house, plus friendly dogs, sheep (lambing in April), rabbits and more. Early teas available, and adults eat together around a large table.

North Devon Farm Holidays
B&B T01288-341215, self-catering T01769-560796, north-devon-farm-holidays.co.uk.
Association for farms offering accommodation in the area.

Widmouth Farm Cottages
Watermouth, nr Ilfracombe, EX34 9RX, T01271-863743, widmouthfarmcottages.co.uk. £345-1560/week.
Offering B&B and self-catering, the excellent location is the big draw at this higgledy-piggledy, family- and dog-friendly 35 acres on the heritage coast, close to a private beach. It also offers a chance to meet the alpacas and feed the animals.

141

Eating North Devon

Local goodies

If self-catering, you can order fruit, vegetable, meat and dairy from local farms using **Local Farmbox** (T01271-869191, localfarmbox.co.uk).

Delis

Challacombe Post Office & Stores
T01598-763229.
Fresh pasties, pies, local cheese, ham, milk and cream.

Crescent Foods
3 The Crescent, Mortehoe, EX34 7DX, T01271-870688.
Deli and café serving cream teas.

Dunstaple Farm Dairy
Holsworthy Beacon, Holsworthy, T01409-261106.
Different varieties of ice cream, including bubblegum, coconut and lemongrass, liquorice or curry flavours, plus a shop on Mill Street, Bideford.

Ethel Brathwaite's
T01598-753721 & Trim Greengrocers, 1 Castle Hill, Lynton, EX35 6JA, T01598-752488.
Selling pasties, sandwiches, local ice cream, fudge, chocolate, jam, preserves and marmalades, plus fruit and vegetables.

Johns of Appledore
6-7 The Quay, Appledore, EX39 1QS, T01237-425870.
A post office and deli offering local cheese, fresh-made baguettes, cakes and hot pasties.

Johns of Instow
Marine Parade, Instow, EX39 4HY, T01271-860310, johnsofinstow.co.uk.
Supermarket and deli.

Marshford Organic
Churchill Way, Northam, EX39 1NS, T01237-477160, marshford.co.uk.
Stocking a wide range of organic goods and there's a café serving cream teas.

The Westcountry Cheese Co
10 Butchers Row, Barnstaple, T01271-379944, westcountrycheese.co.uk.
Specialist shop offering 100 cheeses, organic olives, antipasti, local jams, honey and chutneys, clotted cream and more.

Whitstone Village Stores & Post Office
Nr Holsworthy, EX22 6TX, T01288-341444.
Encompassing a farm shop, and member of Taste of the West.

Farm shops

Besshill Farm Shop
Arlington, nr Barnstaple, EX31 4SW, T01271-850311. Tue-Sat 0930-1700.
Not far from Arlington Court, sells own eggs, beef and lamb, local pork, chicken and duck, bacon, sausages, apple juice, ice cream, clotted cream, seasonal vegetables and spring water.

Heal Farm
Kings Nympton, Umberleigh, EX37 9TB, T01769-574341, healfarm.co.uk.
Fresh bacon, ham, sausages, meat pies, deli products and baked goods, such as flans and cakes, plus ready meals.

Hidden Valley Farm Shop West
Down, nr Ilfracombe, EX34 8NU, T01271-813837.
Campsite shop, see page 136.

Higher Hacknell
Burrington, nr Umberleigh, EX37 9LX, T01769-560909, higherhacknell.co.uk.
High-quality organic meat (Soil Association award-winners) plus prepared dishes, from lemon chicken to smoked trout flan.

Lizzy's Larder
Blackberry Farm, Milton Damerel, nr Holsworthy, EX22 7NP, T01409-261440, lizzyslarder.co.uk.
Just off the A388, offering a meat section with buttery service, deli with local cheese and cold meats, preserves, pickles, cakes and ready meals, eggs, pasties and other local treats, plus a tea room for organic cream teas, and petting area for children to bottle-feed the lambs.

Orchards Farm Shop
St Johns Garden Centre, St Johns Lane, Barnstaple, EX32 9DD, T01271-324294. Open daily.
On the edge of Barnstaple, selling local meat, vegetables,

dairy (including eggs and yoghurt), bread, plus jams and other local dry goods.

Quick & simple

Beaver Inn
2 Irsha St, Appledore, EX39 1RY, T01237-474822, beaverinn.co.uk.
A real-ale pub on the waterfront with a single bar where children are welcome, and also dogs, for whom they have a biscuit barrel. Well-priced food in the bar, or pricier in the restaurant; fish is a speciality, followed by home-made desserts. Folk and fiddle groups play on Mondays.

Black Venus
Challacombe, nr Barnstaple, EX31 4TT, T01598-763251, blackvenusinn.co.uk.
North Devon pub of the year, largely traditional but with good food using local produce. Sandwiches include ham £4.75, hot-ciabatta Exmoor steak burger £7.25, or lamb shank £12.50. There's a grassy outside area with children's play space.

The Buttery
Malmsmead Riverside Bar and Café, Malmsmead, Oare, Lynton, EX35 6NU, T01598-741106, brendonvalley.co.uk/Malmsmead.htm. Mon-Tue 1000-1800, Wed-Sun 1000-2000.
A licensed café in the Doone Valley serving light lunches, cream teas and cakes, plus home-made pizzas from 1700.

Café Blue Bar
Bath Place, Ilfracombe, T01271-879882, tunnelsbeaches.co.uk/cafebluebar. Easter-Oct Mon-Thu 0900-2100, Fri-Sun 0900-2300, Nov-Easter weekends only, closed Dec.
Located at the entrance to Tunnels Beaches (see page 116), this courtyard café has an outdoor pirate play ship and indoor Play Hut (see page 133). Cream teas at £3.50 and snacks are served all day, while lunches from £2.75 include ploughman's, tortilla wraps, jacket potatoes, salads, burgers and kids' sarnies at £1.75. For dinner choose from old favourites like rump steak £10.95, whole-tail scampi £7.95, or go for one of the daily specials that often includes an excellent seafood platter. The puddings at £3.95 are delicious, so try the Eton Mess or fruit crumble with clotted cream. Kids' meals (pizza, spaghetti bolognaise, etc) cost from £4.50.

Cheristow Lavender Farm
Hartland, EX39 6DA, T01237-440101, cheristow.co.uk. Mar-Oct 1100-1800.
A member of the Tea Guild, this is the place to try lemon and lavender or cherry and lavender cake, or the more conventional coffee and walnut or fruit cake, as well as baguettes £5.50, or soup £3.90. Lavender ice cream is £3.75. There's a farm walk taking 45 minutes to one hour, with children's quiz, and they can also learn about growing vegetables as well as the lavender.

Fish & chips

For fish check out fisherman Mick Hook at Instow, where a beach board details his 'due-in' times.

The Esplanade Fish Bar
2 The Esplanade, Lynmouth, EX35 6EQ, T01598-753798.
Runners up in the Fish and Chip Shop of the Year, with the option to eat in or takeaway, £4.95 for cod and chips.

Squires Fish Restaurant
Braunton, T01271-815533.
Winner of the Best Fish and Chip Shop around these parts, year after year, with good reason. Get there early as both the elegant restaurant and the takeaway see queues build up fast.

Croyde Ice Cream Parlour
6 Hobbs Hill, Croyde, EX33 1LZ, T01271-891003.
Ice cream in all tastes and sizes sold from a tiny shop that sees queues in summer.

Docton Mill
Lymebridge, nr Hartland, EX39 6EA, T01237-441369, doctonmill.co.uk. Gardens Apr-Oct Sun-Fri 1200-1700. House Apr-May Wed, Thu, Sun and bank hols; Jun-Oct Sun-Thu 1400-1700. £4 adult, under 17s free, café entry free.
Off-the-beaten-track but winner of the best cream tea in North Devon and the site of an old working water mill, offering options such as soup £3.75, cream tea £3.95, salad £7. Nearby is Hartland Abbey

Eating North Devon

Market days

Farmers' markets
Barnstaple, Tuesday, Friday.
Bideford, Easter-September, second and fourth Saturday.
Bratton Fleming, fourth Saturday.
Braunton, fourth Saturday.
Bude Parkhouse Centre, Saturday.
Combe Martin, third Saturday.
Croyde, January-November, third Saturday.
Eggesford, Fox & Hounds Hotel, second Sunday.
Hartland, April-October, first Sunday.
Heanton, second Saturday.
Holsworthy, third Friday.
Ilfracombe, second and fourth Saturday.
Lynton, first Saturday.
South Molton, fourth Saturday.

General markets
Barnstaple, Tuesday, Friday, Saturday.
Bideford, Tuesday, Saturday (June-September only) and Wednesday at the football ground.
Holsworthy, Wednesday.
South Molton, Thursday, Saturday.
Torrington, Thursday, Saturday.

Cattle markets
Bideford, Tuesday.
Holsworthy, Wednesday, Thursday (the southwest's biggest livestock market).
South Molton, Thursday.

Pannier markets
Check out these covered markets at Great Torrington, Bideford, South Molton and Barnstaple (panniers were the baskets farmers' wives used to carry goods).

(hartlandabbey.com); it's a 20-minute walk down to the coast or you can explore the lovely gardens leading through woodland and past peacocks and donkeys.

GJ's Dutch Pancake Bar
3 South St, Woolacombe, EX34 7BB, T01271-870 992, gjpancakes.co.uk. Great for after the beach: pancakes with fresh fruit, sweet and savoury filings such as cheese and tomato, bacon and brie, plus kids' specialities. Pancake sundae with ice cream, marshmallows, cream and wafers anyone?

The King's Arms
Fore St, Winkleigh, EX19 8HQ, T01837-83384, thekingsarmwinkleigh.co.uk. A thatched old and friendly country pub with pine tables, wall settles, plus an old mine shaft visible through a glass cover. As well as real ale, it serves pub meals like sandwiches, jacket potatoes, prawn or crab salads, plus ham, eggs and chips. The only downside is the lack of outdoor space.

Lee Cottage
Lee Abbey, Lynton, EX35 6JJ, T01598-752621, leeabbey.org.uk. May-Sep Tue-Sun 1030-1700. Cream teas, home-made cakes, drinks, ice creams and light lunches from the abbey community, served in a tea garden next to one of the estate's streams but with limited indoor space.

The Poltimore Arms
Yarde Down, Brayford, nr South Molton, EX36 3HA, T01598-710381. No credit cards, no mains electricity and right on the edge of Exmoor, but so busy you have to book, especially weekends, at this family-run operation. Food is good pub grub like ham, eggs and chips £6.25, lasagne or steak and kidney pie £8.25, and fish pie £8.95. The children's menu includes egg, beans and chips, and fish fingers and chips from £3.50, or you could choose child portions of main courses.

The Quay Café
Fremington Quay, T01271-378783, fremingtonquaycafe.co.uk. Term time, Tue-Sun 1030-1700, lunch 1200-1500. A prime refuelling spot for cyclists on the Tarka Trail, see page 126, this excellent family-run café overlooks the Taw Estuary and uses local, mostly organic ingredients. The cream

Head to a North Devon pannier market to pick up some quality local produce.

teas at £3.60 are legendary, using freshly baked scones, Tiverton strawberry jam and Torrington clotted cream. For savouries there are home-made soups and baguettes, both £5, plus a small selection of light lunches from £8.50, like smoked salmon pâté and quiche, or specials like fresh-caught sea bass £10.50. Kids' meals at £4.50 include veggie bites and plaice goujons served with sauté potatoes. Wash it all down with a Luscombe organic soft drink £2.25, and don't forget the Loxingtons/Dunstaple Farm ice cream at £1.60 a scoop.

Tarr Farm Inn
Dulverton, TA22 9PY, T01643-851507, tarrfarm.co.uk.
At Tarr Steps in the Barle Valley on Exmoor. Families are welcomed for tea (cream teas £5.45) and lunches (main courses from £12.95; children are probably best with a starter like cod fish fingers some of the best food on the moor). Also own the Royal Oak at Winsford.

Tordown Farm
Swimbridge, EX32 0QY, T01271-830265. Easter-Oct 1330-1700.
Cream teas (£3.75), including scones and cake, are served in a traditional farmhouse with a nature trail, tawny owl, Red Ruby cattle, lambs, goat and rabbits.

Posh nosh

The Grove Inn
The Grove Inn, Kings Nympton, EX37 9ST, T01769-580406, thegroveinn.co.uk.
London refugees from advertising and publishing, now with their own small boys, have taken over this admired free house and offer high chairs and a safe courtyard plus children's board with locally sourced food like sausage with mash and onion gravy, fish and chips, ham, egg and chips, even steak and chips and child-size roast dinners on Sundays, from £4. Or, for the more adventurous, small portions are available from the adult menu (adults from £9.50). If children eat their entire main course they get an ice cream made in the village.

The Masons Arms
Knowstone, EX36 4RY, T01398-341231, masonsarmsdevon.co.uk. No under 5s in evenings.
In a 13th-century thatched inn, award-winning cooking by an ex-head chef of the Waterside Inn at Bray, father of three and holder of a Michelin Star. There's a small garden to play in and high chairs and booster seats for children. Pasta and fresh sauces are available for those who don't want the fancier food.

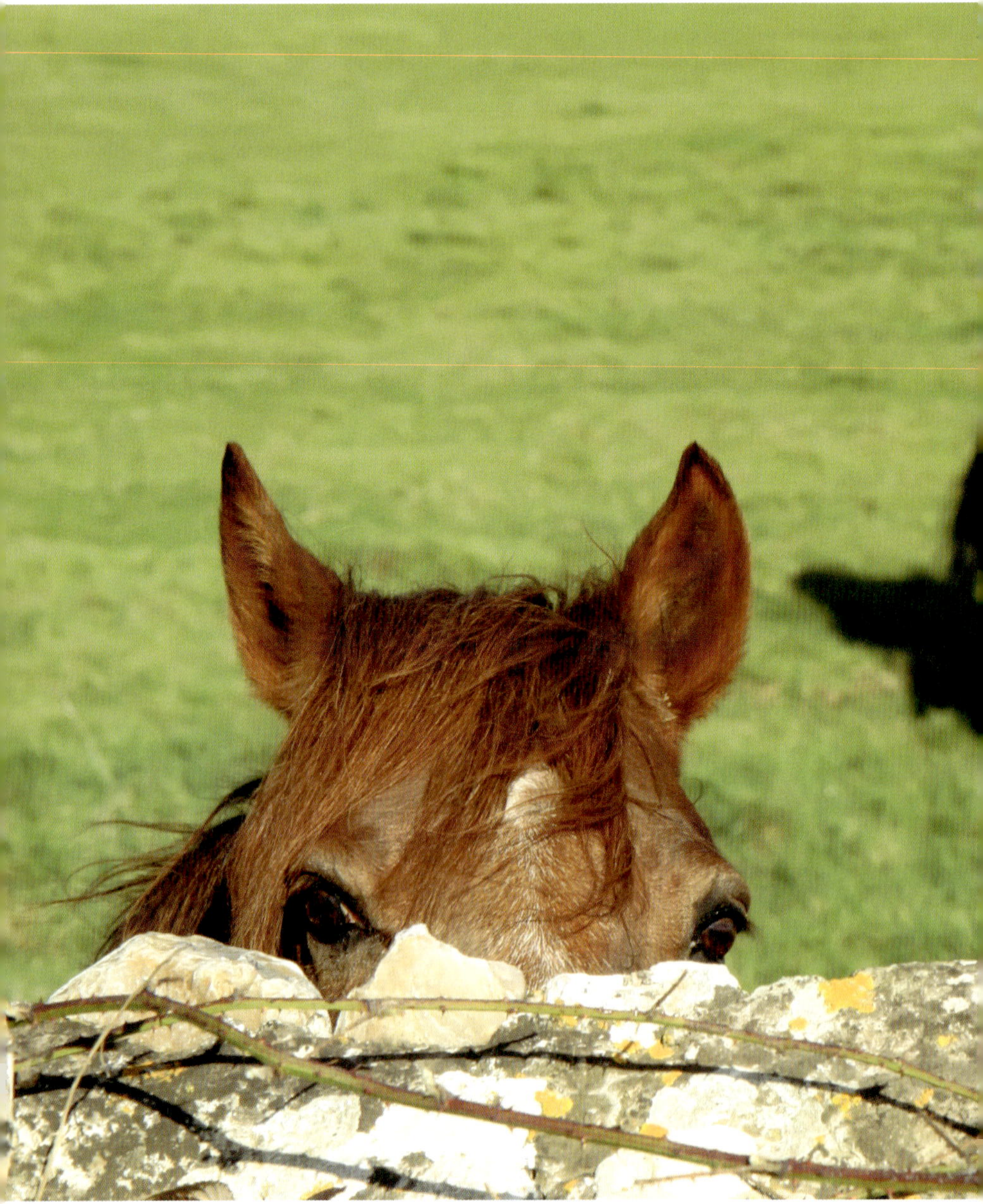

Contents

148 Map
152 Fun & free
156 Exeter
158 Best beaches
162 Action stations
164 Big days out
167 More family favourites
169 The Blackdown Hills
170 Sleeping
174 Eating

Exeter & East Devon

Grazing horses in a field near Sidmouth.

You must

❶ **Admire** the desert-red rocks of the Jurassic Coast.

❷ **Beat** the bounds of Blackbury Camp fortifications.

❸ **Explore** the Exeter Ship Canal.

❹ **Scrunch** through the pebbles at Beer.

❺ **Fly** a kite on the cliffs above Sidmouth.

❻ **Find** the exit to the Escot maze.

❼ **Trundle** the tram from Colyton to Seaton.

❽ **Listen** out for the birds on the Exe Estuary.

❾ **Tread** the ancient paths of the Blackdown Hills.

❿ **Savour** the River Cottage Canteen chips.

Taunton
Bathealton
Langford Budville
Kittisford
Nynehead
Bradford on Tone
Appley
Thorne St Margaret
Wellington
West Buckland
Staplehay
Rockwell Green
Holcombe Rogus
Sampford Arundel
Wrangway
Ford Street
Westleigh
Burlescombe
Nicholashayne
Blackdown Hills
Clayhidon
Appledore
Culmstock
Rosemary Lane
Hemyock
Uffculme
Coldharbour Mill
Craddock
Stapley
Churchinford
Bolham Water
Abbey
Smeatharpe
Blackborough
Sheldon
Dunkeswell
Kentisbeare
Upottery
Kerswel
Dulford
Luppitt
Rawridge
Beacon
Broadhembury
Wick
Monkton
Combe Raleigh
Payhembury
Awliscombe
Tale
Buckerell
Colestocks
Talaton
Feniton
Honiton
Fenny Bridges
Gittisham
Escot
Alfington
Fairmile
Ottery St Mary
West Hill
Otter
Ark Pottery
Wiggaton
Tipton St John
Sidbury
Venn Ottery
Harpford
Newton Poppleford
Bowd
Sidford
Colaton Raleigh
Sidmouth
Salcombe Regis
Cotmaton
Norman Lockyer Observatory
Bicton Park
Otterton
East Budleigh
Budleigh Salterton
Henlade
Thornfalcon
Stoke St Mary
Orchard Portman
Thurlbear
Pitminster
Corfe
Angersleigh
Staple Fitzpaine
West Hatch
Hatch Beauchamp
Hatch Green
Bickenhall
Windmill Hill
Fyfett
Bishopswood
Whitestaunton
Combe St Nicholas
Howley
Wadeford
Newcott
Yarcombe
Wambrook
Tatworth
Stockland
Furley
Chardstock
Millhayes
Membury
Heathstock
Alston
Churchill
Cotleigh
Ham
Smallridge
Dalwood
Weycroft
Offwell
Kilmington
Axminster
Shute
Church Green
Farway
Whitford
Colyton
Musbury
Broad Down
Colyford
Axmouth
Harcombe
Weston
Branscombe
Beer
Seaton
Branscombe Bakery, Mill & Forge
Pecorama Pleasure Gardens
Wrantage
Fivehead
Curry Mallet
Isle Abbots
Hambridge
Westport
Puckington
Stocklinch
Shepton Beauchamp
Ashill
Broadway
Horton
Ashwell
Ilminster
Seavington St Michael
Donyatt
Kingstone
Crock Street
Dowlish Wake
Chillington
Chaffcombe
Cudworth
Chard
Cricket St Thomas
Forton
Whatley
Winsham
Axe
Holditch
Thorncombe
Hawkchurch
Birdsmoor Gate
Marshalsea
Marshwood
Wootton Fitzpaine
Whitchurch Canonicorum
Char
Morcombelake
Uplyme
Charmouth
Combpyne
Rousdon
Lyme Regis
Lyme Bay
Isle
M5
A38
A30
A35
A303
A358
A373
A378
A3052
B3187
B3391
B3177
B3174
B3178
B3168
B3162
B3167
B3165
B3261
B3172
N
2 km
2 miles

**Branscombe Beach
after the day's fishing.**

Mazzard Farm.

If you want to tread in the footsteps of visitors past, then East Devon is the place to do it; centres like Sidmouth still offer a certain Georgian gentility; perhaps it's the decorum passed down from Queen Victoria's visits as a child. Although there are resorts, this is one of the least touristy parts of the county. Go to one of the many carnivals and parades and you'll see locals waving to friends as they pass. It's as much fun as any foreign fiesta.

Exmouth, the oldest resort, was where Lady Nelson took refuge while Nelson was making whoopee with Emma Hamilton. However, today, with the Imperial Recreation Ground behind the beach, the narrow-gauge Exmouth Express, swan boats on the lake and crazy golf, it offers something more akin to a 1930s holiday experience. It's all fairly low-key, as is neighbouring **Budleigh Salterton**, once popular with visitors like PG Wodehouse and Noel Coward.

The coast is magnificently wild, and the estuaries of the Exe, Culm, Otter, Sid and Axe rivers are home to myriad flocks of resident and over-wintering birds, protected by growing nature reserves, many just a short walk from small centres, notably foodie **Topsham**.

The fine landscape is recognized in the designated Area of Outstanding Natural Beauty extending along the coast from Lyme Regis – beyond the Devon border but well worth a trip for its beach and harbour – almost to **Exeter** and inland to **Honiton**. Further north are the **Blackdown Hills**, another AONB with little-known upland plateaus and deep cutting valleys, a place to change down a gear. And, beyond, is the rural activity of **Mid Devon**.

Out & about Exeter & East Devon

Fun & free

In the footsteps of dinosaurs
The coast here is the only place in the world where you can see unbroken evidence of 185 million years of evolution. That's why UNESCO declared the **Jurassic Coast** (jurassiccoast.com) a World Heritage Site in 2001, putting it on a par with the likes of the Great Barrier Reef in Australia. You can see evidence not just of the Jurassic but also the older Triassic and relatively more recent Cretaceous periods. The coast stretches from the conical 'geoneedle' at Orcombe Point, Exmouth, to Old Harry Rocks at Studland in Dorset.

The reds and oranges of Exmouth's Triassic cliffs, also found at Seaton and the striking **Ladram Bay**, were formed in scorching desert conditions. At **Budleigh Salterton** are unique and protected quartzite pebbles carried here from Brittany by a river flowing into the Triassic desert approximately 240 million years ago.

East of Sidmouth is the Cretaceous Upper Greensand layer, and the small inlet of **Weston Mouth** is the place to see veins of gypsum. At **Beer** there are visible folds in the soft chalk and, in the **Quarry Caves** (EX12 3AS, T01297-680282, beerquarry.caves.fsnet.co.uk), a layer of densely packed shell fragments. Guided one-hour tours tell the story of this vast complex of caverns where the stone has been quarried since Romans times.

For information on fossils see discoveringfossils.co.uk, 'a practical guide to palaeontology', or the *Jurassic Fossil Map*, by Nigel J Clarke, sold locally or from nigelclarkepublications.co.uk. You can collect fossils from fallen or beach material, but should leave some for others.

Go prehistoric
Among the most striking evidence of previous residents is **Blackbury Camp**, an Iron-Age fort, where majestic trees stand in late spring above a carpet of bluebells. North of the A3052, inland from Branscombe, it was the fort of cattle-keeping folk around 100-200 BC who defended themselves with earthworks that kids love to circuit; there are more walks nearby when they tire of that.

Woodbury Castle is also heavily wooded; here the earthworks are best avoided as they are beginning to erode but there's plenty of alternative running-around space. It's easy to find as the road between West Hill and Budleigh Salterton passes straight through the north and south 'gates'.

Fly a kite
The name **Windgate** for the cliffs just west of Sidmouth suggests they're going to be good for kite flying. They're just in front of Mutter's Moor, named after a famous smuggling family. Equally satisfying can be the heights of **South Down Common** behind Beer Head, east of Branscombe. There's also **Exmouth and Harpford Common**, a good spot just

Let them go wild in the country.

below Fire Beacon Hill, see page 154. Alternatively, watch the professionals at the **Exmouth Kite Festival** on the Imperial Recreation Ground in June; there are kite-making workshops for kids too.

Stroke the donkeys
The Donkey Sanctuary, nr Sidmouth, EX10 0NU, T01395-578222, thedonkeysanctuary.org.uk. Daily 0900-dusk. Free to visit, although contributions are welcome.
The focus here is on the animals, so there are no rides or play parks, but approximately 500 rescued donkeys to see and stroke, some older and quieter ones wandering free in the main yard. There's a small maze, nature trail, picnic area, activity days in school holidays; it's also a good place for walks, including down to Branscombe beach.

Channel your energies
The five-mile **Exeter Ship Canal**, west of the River Exe, is the oldest pound canal in the country, accessible along the Exeter towpath and ending south of the Exminster Marshes RSPB reserve. Both canalside pubs (the Double Locks, between Exeter and Topsham, and the Turf Locks Hotel at Exminster) are family friendly. There's canoe and bike rental at the Exeter quayside, see page 162, windsurfing opportunities, see page 163, and cruises, see page 161.

Fossil find.

The **Grand Western Canal** (devon.gov.uk/grand_western_canal) runs for 11 miles from the southeast of Tiverton, where the little Ducks' Ditty café bobs on the water. Designed to link the Bristol and English Channels, but never completed, it's now a linear nature reserve with wide green verges lining the towpath, a good place to spot wildflowers, dragonflies, coot, mallard, swans and even a kingfisher. Abbotshood Cycle Hire, see page 162, is happy to deliver or collect anywhere along the canal. Or cycle from Abbotshood to Sampford Peverell, stopping at the Globe Inn, or continuing to the end and the Prince of Wales at Holcombe Rogus (both with child facilities).

On the water are the shire-horse-drawn painted barges of the Tiverton Canal Company (tivertoncanal.co.uk), which offers trips and also hires rowing boats and electric launches. Alternatively, Mid Devon Hire Boats and Moorings has a narrow boat for hire, see page 173.

Coast along the coast
The best cycling route with kids is the **Southern Coast Route NCN2 Exe Cycle**, an easy six miles from Exmouth Station via Littleham to Budleigh Salterton, following the path of a former railway. You could also walk it, possibly as a circular route taking the cycle path inland and walking back via the coast, perhaps stopping off en route at the World of Country Life, see page 166, above Sandy Bay,

Out & about Exeter & East Devon

or exploring the Maer Local Nature Reserve at Exmouth. Take a magnifying glass or insect inspection kit to these sand dunes, now cut off from the beach by the road, and watch out for the unusual solitary bee nest tunnels in the sand, plus the little ones flying out of holes in the ground (harmless to humans). Watch too for the skylarks that, when disturbed, fly up singing loudly.

Potter about

The village of **Ottery St Mary**, reportedly the fictional Ottery St Catchpole in the Harry Potter stories, home of the Weasley family, nowadays seems fairly fictional itself, with real butchers, bakers, homeware and hardware stores, plus a good bookshop (The Curious Otter) and nearby small toyshop. Catch it now before the threatened superstore gets the go-ahead. After the kids have admired the village stocks by the church gate, you can visit the magnificent scaled-down version of Exeter Cathedral, including a minstrel gallery on pillars, and admire its attractive Elizabethan astronomical clock. At the other end of the High Street, there's a tumbling weir on the River Otter, featuring a water-down-the-plughole effect, created to serve the world's first water-powered factory, currently disused. Starting from the weir you can walk south for two miles along the river to the French-run Golden Lion pub at Tipton St John.

The river runs through

Running past Ottery St Mary and Newton Poppleford, the River Otter reaches the thatched village of **Otterton** where the restored Otterton Mill (EX9 7HG, T01395-568521, ottertonmill.com, daily 1000-1700) offers a bakery, working flour mill (check website for milling dates), resident artists' studios, gallery and evening musical events, as well as occasional arty initiatives to encourage wildlife in the surroundings – check out the grass sofa. Food is organic or near, with cream teas at £4.50, quiche or pâté at £4.95, and while you finish your meal you could let the children lean over the courtyard millstream to look for eels. Afterwards there are level riverside walks, maybe spotting marsh marigolds, kingfishers and dippers as well as grey heron and egret. Or a three-mile circular route will take you to the sea at Budleigh Salterton, named after the old saltpans once owned by the Otterton Priory. The **Otter Estuary Nature Reserve** (clintondevon.com) includes the estuary reed beds and grazing marsh, with a buggy-friendly footpath to spot redshank, greenshank, dunlin, ringed plover and grey plover, and there's also free river fishing here, if that takes your fancy.

Fires for London

Fire Beacon Hill is named after the signal used to warn Elizabethan London of the arrival of the Armada. You'll find it east of Tipton St John and the Ark Pottery at Wiggaton, see page 167, and north of the A3052, on heathland with views across Lyme Bay. It's home to grayling butterflies, yellowhammers and the nationally scarce Dartford warbler with its grating call. To find them look for the stonechats that sit in clear sight on trees and shrubs, making the sound of two stones hitting together. The Dartfords lurk on the ground below, using this as a sentry service. There are a variety of paths, so you can use a three-wheeler buggy, and it's a good spot for a picnic. Start from the White Cross car park and it should take about an hour to complete a circuit. For details download the leaflet at eastdevon.gov.uk/cs-firebeaconhillleaflet.pdf.

It's a beaut

Omitting only the built-up areas of Seaton and Sidmouth, and stretching inland as far as Honiton, is a fine landscape of outstanding coastline plus wooded coombes, heathland, open river valleys, cliffs and hilltops that form the **East Devon Area of Outstanding Natural Beauty** (eastdevonaonb.org.uk). From Sidmouth as far as

West Bay in Dorset there is also a Special Area of Conservation, best seen in spring for flowers and nesting birds, edged by the coast path. Branscombe to Beer also makes a good section to walk, with cliff-top views as far as Portland Bill to the east and Torbay to the west. However, there are steep drops so, with younger ones, you might like to stick to Branscombe at beach level, strolling east or west along it, or parking at Salcombe Regis National Trust car park (opposite Norman Lockyer Observatory, see page 168), and walking to and along the coast from there.

This coast is a designated Area of Outstanding Natural Beauty.

Rain check

Arts & crafts
- **MakeArt**, 126 Fore St, Exeter, EX4 3JQ, T01392-437167, makeartexeter.com.

Cinemas
- **Exeter Odeon**, Sidwell St, T0871-224 4007, odeon.co.uk.
- **Exeter Picturehouse**, Bartholomew St West, T08707-551238, picturehouses.co.uk.
- **Exeter Vue**, Summerland Gate, T0871-224 0240, myvue.co.uk.
- **The Savoy Cinema**, Rolle St, Exmouth, EX1 1HP, T0871-230 3200, scottcinemas.co.uk.
- **Sidmouth Radway Cinema**, Radway Place, EX10 8TL, T0871-230 3200, scottcinemas.co.uk.
- **The Tivoli Cinema**, Fore St, Tiverton, EX16 6LD, T01884-255554, cromer-movieplex.com.

Indoor play
- **Playdome**, Honiton, EX14 1DB, T01404- 47007, theplaydome.com. £12.

Indoor swimming pools
- **Exeter Northbrook Swimming Pool**, Beacon Lane, EX4 8LZ, T01392-667020, dcleisure.co.uk.
- **Exeter Pyramids Swimming and Leisure Centre**, Heavitree Rd, EX1 2LA, T01392-253553, dcleisure.co.uk.
- **Exeter Riverside Leisure Centre**, Cowick St, EX4 1AF, T01392-221771, leisure-centre.com.
- **Exmouth Sports Centre**, 1 Royal Ave, EX8 1EN, T01395-266381, ledleisure.co.uk.
- **Honiton Leisure Centre**, School Lane, EX14 1QW, T01404-42325, ledleisure.co.uk.
- **Sidmouth Swimming Pool**, Ham Lane, Sidmouth, EX10 8XR, T01395-577057, ledleisure.co.uk.

Museums
- **Allhallows Museum of Lace and Local Antiquities**, High St, Honiton, EX14 1PG, T01404-44966, honitonmuseum.co.uk.
- **Axe Valley Heritage Museum**, Town Hall, Seaton, EX12 2LD, T01297-242227, seatonmuseum.co.uk.
- **Axminster Museum**, The Old Courthouse, Church St, EX13 5AQ, T01297-34137, devonmuseums.net/axminster.
- **Exmouth Museum**, Sheppards Row, off Exeter Rd, EX8 1PW, T01395-263785, devonmuseums.net/exmouth.
- **Fairlynch Museum and Arts Centre**, 27 Fore St, Budleigh Salterton, EX9 6NP, T01395-442666, devonmuseums.net/fairlynch.
- **Royal Albert Memorial Museum**, exeter.gov.uk/RAMM. Temporary RAMM exhibition at the library until the museum reopens in 2011.
- **Sidmouth Museum**, Sid Vale Heritage Centre, Church St, Sidmouth, EX10 8LY, T01395-516139, devonmuseums.net/sidmouth. Open Apr-Oct.
- **Tiverton Museum of Mid Devon Life**, Beck's Square, Tiverton, EX16 6PJ, T01884-256295, tivertonmuseum.org.uk.
- **Topsham Museum**, 25 Strand, EX3 0AX, T01392-873244, devonmuseums.net/topsham.
- **Whimple Heritage Centre**, Lockyers Linhay, Church Rd, Whimple, EX5 2TA, T01404-822499, whimple.org.

Let's go to…

Exeter

The war did little for modern Exeter and, although the cathedral quarter around the twin-towered St Peter's Cathedral offers a glimpse of how it must have been, it is mostly a place to shop today: the attractive new Princesshay centre is a place to find names from Apple to Zara, while Fore Street hosts the weekly farmers' market.

The lazy way to tour the city is with the **Big Red Bus Company** (T01404-831045, thebigredbuscompany.com, Jul, Aug and Sep daily, Jun and Oct Sat and Sun, from 1000, £8 adult, £4 child). Alternatively, free daily **Red Coat**-guided walking tours are led by 30-plus volunteers, on 15 different themes including a summer Saturday one for children aged five to 10, although guides are well used to tailoring all talks for families. Meet on Cathedral Green outside Abode, Royal Clarence Hotel (T01392-265203, exeter.gov.uk/guidedtours), no booking required. Look out for the Gothic façade of the Norman **cathedral** (exeter-cathedral.org.uk), where rows of figures include kings Alfred, Athelstan, Canute, William the Conqueror and Richard II. Inside is reputedly the longest Gothic ceiling in the world. You can admire the atmosphere from the entrance but stepping further incurs a charge of £4 per adult to see the 18-m bishop's throne, and misericords. These were folding seats on which tired monks could perch, but they would fall with a clatter if they dozed off.

The 14th-century **Guildhall** on the pedestrian High Street, complete with carved bears, is reckoned to be England's oldest municipal building still in regular use. Probably more memorable though are the **Underground**

Passages (2 Paris St, EX1 1GA, T01392-665887, exeter.gov.uk/passages, Jun-Sep Mon-Sat 0930-1730, Sun 1030-1600, shorter hours Oct-May, £4.90 adult, £3.40 child, £14.65 family), excavated from the 14th century to carry water. There is a 35-minute guided tour but no under fives, and it's not recommended for claustrophobics. The **Royal Albert Memorial Museum**, due to reopen in 2011, will be a gleaming new option, offering a bit of everything, from watches and clocks, to stuffed animals plus café.

St Nicholas Priory (The Mint, off Fore St, EX4 3BL, T01392-665858, exeter.gov.uk/priory) is a former Benedictine priory, currently presented as a home of 1602, complete with dressing-up clothes and lots of items to handle. There are more old buildings down by quayside, where the **Quay House Visitor Centre** (T01392-271611) is free and gives an audio-visual display of the city's 2000-year history. On the way there you will pass **Cricklepit Mill** (Commercial Rd, EX2 4AB, T01392-279244, devonwildlifetrst.org), a working watermill, home to Devon Wildlife Trust with its eco green-roofed offices and good hands-on activities for kids.

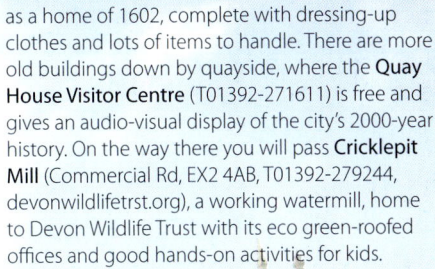

Part of the university is the exhibition and research **Bill Douglas Centre for the History of Cinema and Popular Culture** (Old Library, Prince of Wales Rd, EX4 4SB, T01392-264321, billdouglas. org, Mon-Fri 1000-1600, free), offering a collection including Disney memorabilia as well as early entertainment like magic lanterns. For art and culture check out **Spacex** (T01392-431786, spacex. co.uk), a contemporary art space, or **Phoenix Arts and Media** (T01392-667080, exeterphoenix.org. uk), for performance, music, film and family events, with family-friendly café bar and outside terrace.

Parking in Exeter is difficult so use the Park and Ride at £4 per family, or take the train, refuelling at Juice Moose (1b Central Station Buildings, Queen St, EX4 3SB, T01392-215756, juicemoose.com), which offers locally sourced, organic sandwiches, tapas and cakes.

Grab a bite

Enjoy a snack on the Cathedral Green. Perhaps buy from nearby **Warrens** (corner of High St and North St), baking since 1860, or try a café with a view such as **Tea on the Green** (2 Cathedral Close, T01392-276913) in an Elizabethan building offering bangers and mash for £7.50. For a slap up meal there's **Michael Caine's Abode**, see page 177. Or nearby is the vegetarian **Herbie's** (15 North St, EX4 3QS, T01392-258473), with snacks from £2.50 and mains up to £9.50. **Shaker Maker** (122 Fore St, EX4 3JQ, T01392-436717, shakermaker.biz) offers snacks and smoothies.

Out & about Exeter & East Devon

Best beaches

Beer
A steeply shelving suntrap pebble beach with deep water, which is small enough to be described by some as a cove, between cliffs. You can watch the fishing boats being pulled up the shingle and make your way through nets and pots to buy the catch from the stall, filleted if you prefer. There are all-day breakfasts and ice cream in the village (at Styles), and there's the option of fishing trips or coastal cruises from this one-time smuggling base. Street parking is limited with more on the cliff top a steep walk away.

Branscombe
A Good Beach Guide-recommended beach of approximately two miles of sloping pebbles, backed by coastal huts under striking cliffs on a 300-acre estate owned by the National Trust. Boat hire is available.

Budleigh Salterton
This Good Beach Guide-recommended 1¼-mile stretch is known for its smooth, protected pebbles, with a steep shelf into deep water, backed by red sandstone cliffs at the western end and the Otter Estuary at the east. There's an esplanade and cafés in town.

Exmouth
At the mouth of the River Exe, this is a traditional, spacious, bucket-and-spade resort backed by pleasant houses, parks and gardens, and offering two miles of flat, gently shelving sandy beach, popular for water sports (zone for jetskis) and, at the east end, rock pooling at low tide. The beach is backed by a sea wall and wide promenade lined with shops and eating places and, in summer, there are amusements like donkey rides and swing boats for that old-fashioned holiday experience. Attractive for sports like kitesurfing, it is dangerous for swimming along some stretches because of tidal and river currents, so follow advice on signs.

Exmouth beach.

Ladram Bay

Good Beach Guide-recommended, near Budleigh Salterton, sheer, red sandstone cliffs surround this pebbly but popular beach, good for rock pooling at low tide. Reached through the Ladram Bay Holiday Park, see page 170, where parking is £2 and you can also pick up a cream tea and snacks.

Salcombe Regis

A pebble beach, part National Trust-owned, this is reached by a mile of footpath through fields from Salcombe Regis village or along the beach from Sidmouth.

Sandy Bay

Just around the corner from Orcombe Point, a heritage site good for fossil hunting, Sandy Bay is privately owned by the Devon Cliffs Holiday Park behind, see page 172. It's a real suntrap, backed by high cliffs and, at low tide, connected all the way to Exmouth, so it can get crowded in summer. There's the Beach Shack on the beach and, above, the Beachcomber Café Bar plus shop and playground. A webcam in the park shows the kittiwakes nesting on Straight Point to the east, reserved for military use.

Seaton

Commended by the Good Beach Guide, Seaton offers a mile of legally protected pebble beach with a wide esplanade (look out for the plaques showing the different planets to scale) providing easy access, backed by steep cliffs to the western end with café, plus nearby shops.

Shelly Beach

At the start of the Exe Estuary, a large expanse of sand and mud stretches around to the docks. It's very tidal with a gentle shelf, sometimes completely covered by water at high tide. It's good for windsurfing and sailing, but there's a strong tidal rush, isolating whole areas of sand, so, even if walking, crossing creeks can be dangerous.

Sidmouth

Two beaches are separated by a rock known on maps as Chit Rocks, although called Jacob's Ladder by locals after the original form of access to one of the two beaches. The various walled sections of Connaught Gardens are a place to sit in the sun at the top, perhaps furnished with refreshments from the excellent, if pricey, Clock Tower Café (Apr-Oct daily 1000-1700, Nov-Mar daily 1000-1500) with an upstairs room as well as outdoor tables, serving cream tea £4.95, lovely cakes £2.70 and breakfast until noon, £6.45.

Town Beach

Backed by largely 18th-century seafront buildings, this is formed by an expanse of legally protected pebbles with sand at low tide. At its western end the beach has some lovely rock pools, while cliffs overhang the beach at the eastern end. An esplanade runs along the entire length, with cafés, shops and amusements nearby.

Jacob's Ladder

A few minutes' walk away and backed by steep cliffs, this offers shingle and more legally protected pebbles at high tide, with lots of sand when the water is out, now reached by a white-painted wooden flight of steps, steep driveway or level walkway around the point from the Town Beach.

Weston Mouth

Part National Trust-owned, a quiet, sloping pebbly beach that shelves under the water, backed by cliffs. Access is by a steep mile-long footpath from Weston.

Don't miss the Exe Estuary

The mud flats and salt marshes of the River Exe are bird heaven, a Site of Special Scientific Interest and home to birds, including egrets. In winter there are up to 25,000 waders and ducks, including curlew, oystercatcher, teal, widgeon, mallard and more, best spotted at high water when they roost on the drier ground in the reserves. Print off or pick up a copy of the *Exe Wildlife* information leaflet (exe-estuary.org) and look out for everything from cormorants to cockles in an area where birds find as many calories in a metre of mud as we do in a Mars bar. Here you see gulls and crows dropping mussels from a height to get at the tasty meal inside, and black-headed gulls jigging on the spot to make the worms think it's raining and come to the surface.

The sands at the mouth of the river – Dawlish Warren and Exmouth – include habitats of mud, salt marsh, grazing flats and sand, while the 26-mile walking and cycling **Exe Estuary Trail** (T0845-155 1004, devon.gov.uk/exeestuarytrail), due for completion in 2011, helps explore further. Exmouth to Lympstone, alongside the railway, includes a boardwalk over marshy ground and raised sections for better views. Also open is the part from Exeter city centre to Topsham. On the south side is access from the canal, see page 153, and an onward route being created past **Exminster Marshes RSPB Reserve**. You can also check out the reed beds of the **Old Sludge Beds Nature Reserve**, between the River Exe and Exeter Ship Canal (T01392-279244, devonwildlifetrust.org), and the **Bowling Green Reserve** (T01392-824614, rspb.org.uk) on the edge of Topsham, the largest roost north of the estuary, easily reached from the town along The Strand and then Goat Walk.

Exmouth Local Nature Reserve Education Rangers provide free seashore safaris and birdwatching (T01395-517557, eastdevon.gov.uk, search for 'countryside'). Or **RSPB Exe Avocet cruises** leave from Topsham, Exmouth and Starcross (T01392-432691, rspb.org.uk/datewithnature, Nov-Feb), with commentary suitable for beginners up. Download the information leaflet at devon.gov.uk/exeexplorer07.pdf, see exe-estuary.org, or contact the **RSPB** (T01392-879438) at Darts Farm, see page 174, which also runs family events.

Grab a bite
Foodie **Topsham**, once a bigger centre than Exeter, makes a good stop, full of delightful old houses and accommodation. The Globe, see page 177, also owns the new **Route 2 Café** (1-2 Monmouth Rd, EX3 0JQ, T01392-875085, route2cafe.co.uk, open 0800-2000), plus self-catering apartments from £495 per week and bike hire. Alternatively, try the **Avocet Café** (86 Fore St, EX3 0HQ, T01392-877887) a place for cream tea.

Getting around

Bike
For cycling details see exeterandessentialdevon.com/ste/cycling, and for bike hire, see page 162.

Boat
Exe 2 Sea Cruises, see page 92.

Exeter Cruises and White Heather Ferry, Historic Quayside, Exeter, T07806-554093, exetercruises.com. July and August daily, April to June and September weekends. £4. Cruises to Double Locks or Turf Locks on the river or Exeter Canal. Pedalo hire also available in summer.

Stuart Line Cruises, Exmouth Marina, EX8 1DS, T01395-222144, stuartlinecruises.co.uk. Year round, timetable depending on weather and tides, sea trips Easter to October, ring for details or check website. River cruise £5 adult, £3 child, birdwatching £9 adult, £5 child, Jurassic Coast £7 adult, £5 child, day trip to Torquay or Brixham £12 adult, £6 child, Sidmouth £10 adult, £5 child. Winter birdwatching cruises, river cruises from Exmouth, trips along the Jurassic Coast to Sidmouth, or west to Torquay or Brixham, plus occasional Exeter Canal cruises.

Topsham Ferry, Trout's Boatyard, Ferry Rd, Topsham, T07778-370582, topshamtoturfferry.co.uk. Easter to October weekends, June to September daily 1100-1600. Return £4.50 adult, £3 child, £1/bike, dogs free. Trips from Topsham to Turf Locks, 15 minutes up the Waterway, £4.50. Tides affect the timetable so just wave when you need it. A water taxi service is also available.

Water Taxi, Exmouth Docks, T07970-918418. April to September 0900-1700. Return £4 adult, £2 child, discounts for groups. From Exmouth to Dawlish Warren, drop-off on the beach. To get back, return to drop-off point, booking a time, or phone from there when ready.

Train
The **Avocet Line** (First Great Western) runs from Exeter to Exmouth via Lympstone and Topsham, and the Riviera Line from Starcross to Exeter links with an hourly ferry. The **Exe Estuary Circular** (T08457-484950, nationalrail.co.uk) is a combined train and ferry ticket, £7 per adult, £4 per child for Exeter–Starcross–Exmouth–Exeter, ask for Round Robin tickets.

Out & about Exeter & East Devon

Action stations

Bush craft
Wildside Education
4 Abbey Rd, Dunkeswell, Honiton, EX14 4RL, T01404-892771, wildsideeducation.co.uk. £5 person, £200 family overnight camp.
Go blindfold in the wild on this 50-acre farm with woods, bog and meadow, learning nature awareness and bushcraft, with overnight camps that include other types of field games and activities like marshmallow toasting. There are also one-day courses, with activities like bow-making, for all ages but especially five to 15 years. Yurt accommodation is available March to November with other shelters year round.

Cycling
Abbotshood Cycle Hire
Abbotshood Farm, Greenway, Halberton, EX16 7AE, T01884-820728, abbotshoodcyclehire.co.uk. Daily dawn to dusk. £9.50 adult per day, £6.50 child bike, trailer, tag-a-long.
Approximately five miles from Tiverton. Offers trailers, tag-a-longs, baby seats, Duet (wheelchair) bikes and even adult trikes. Will deliver in the area.

Exmouth Cycle Hire
1 Victoria Rd, EX8 1DL, T01395-225656, exmouthcycle.com. Mon-Sat 0900-1745. Per day £10 adult, £7 child, £6/tag-a-long, trailer, £5 child seat, £10/trikes, £18/tandem.

Knobblies Bikes
107 Exeter Rd, Exmouth, EX8 1QE, T01395-270182, knobbliesbikes.co.uk. Mon-Sat 0900-1730. Per day £10 adult, £7.50 child, £5/tag-a-long, child seat free.

Saddles & Paddles
4 Kings Wharf, The Quay, Exeter, EX2 4AP, T01392-424241, sadpad.com. Daily 0930-1730. £9/half day, £25 family.
Including tag-a-longs for children under seven, child seats, trailers for children under five, plus small bikes without stabilizers. Also canoe and kayak hire with access to the Riverside Valley Park and canal.

Horse riding
Budleigh Riding School
Heatherways Stables, Dalditch Lane, Budleigh Salterton, EX9 7AS, T01395-442035, devonriding.co.uk. £25/1½-hr hack, £30/2 hrs, £11/30-min group lesson, £21/hr, £43/Pony Day, £120/3 days.
On the edge of Woodbury Common, a very flexible centre offering lessons and hacks to suit each child, half-and-half school session and walk out, plus Pony Days of up to four days with two hours of riding per day, practical experience plus talks on stable-management.

Devenish Pitt Stables
Faraway, nr Colyton, EX24 6EG, T01404-871355, devenishpitt.co.uk. £22.50/1 hr, £14.50/half hr, £34/half day.
A 260-acre farm with riding stables offering hacks over the farm and lessons in the indoor riding school and outdoor menage (half and half for those they haven't seen ride before). For seven years plus there are morning and afternoon sessions at the stables, including a one-hour ride, mucking out, grooming, stable management and BHS test practice on handling a horse. Hats to hire.

Sidmouth Riding
Saltwynds Farm, nr Sidmouth, off the A3052, T01395-579441, sidmouthriding.co.uk. £30/hr for riding hire and lessons.

Live the outdoor life with Wildside Education.

A centre with high standards, minimum age six for lessons and 12 years for riding out, as you are expected to be able to rise to the trot and go without a lead rein. Also riding holidays with B&B accommodation.

Llama walks
Walking with Llamas
Pinn, nr Otterton, T01395-578697, walkingwithllamas.co.uk. 2-hr summer walks £25 for 1 person and 1 llama, £20 for 2 people and 1 llama, £60 for a family and 2 llamas, 1-hr winter walks £20 for 1 person and 1 llama, £15 for 2 people and 1 llama, £50 for a family and 2 llamas. Morning, afternoon and summer evening strolls on the Jurassic Coast.

Outdoor swimming
Topsham Pool
Fore St, EX3 0HF, T01392-874477, topsham.org/pool.html. Open-air heated pool open from mid-May to mid-September.

Paintballing
Skirmish Paintball & Laser Games
Stoke Woods, nr Exeter, EX4 5BW, T01548-580025, skirmishexeter.com. From £15/half day, £19.50/day including barbecue lunch and all equipment.
Adults and children play together on this 100-acre woodland site with different arenas. Paintballing, for children 11 years and over, is run in half-day sessions (four to six games) or full days (10 to 12 games), with five to 15 minutes per game. Laser tag (for eight years plus) is run in three two-hour sessions per day for groups of six or more (you might be able to join another group) and costs £18.50 per person.

Quad biking
Quad World
Nr Cullompton, EX5 4LB, on B3181, T01392-881313, quadworld.co.uk. Mar-Oct 1000-1800, Nov-Feb 1000-1600. £25 adult, £20 child (13-18), £15 child (6-12).
Beginners' one-to-one tuition, with quads suitable for children aged six years plus, with 12 laps over half an hour, parent sometimes riding too. The child practises with a trainer on a larger bike and, when ready (perhaps after two or three laps), moves on to an age-appropriate bike of their own.

Raceworld
Unit 3, Greendale Business Park, Sidmouth Rd, Aylesbeare, EX5 2JJ. Arrive & Drive Mon-Fri 1400-2100, Sun 1400-1700. £10/10 mins, minimum age 12.

Water sports
Edge Watersports
The Royal Ave, Exmouth, EX8 1EN, T01395-222551, edgewatersports.com. Mon-Sat 0900-1730, Sun 1000-1600. £20/powerkite lesson, £100/day on water, £60/half day, £10/kayak hire.

Zorbing South
Come Zorbing! Go head over heels
Harness Zorbing or try Hydro Zorbing
cross between a waterslide and a rollercoaster at speeds of 25mph down our man made run

Website: www.zorbsouth.co.uk • Tel/Fax 01929 426595
Site Address: Pine Lodge Farm, Ilsington Road, Bockhampton, Dorchester DT2 8QL
Opening Times: 10am – 5pm School Holidays, Weekends and Bank Holidays • 27/03/10 – 31/10/10

Out & about Exeter & East Devon

RYA- and British Kitesurfng Association-recognized, Edge offers a wide range of sports tuition in the estuary (kitesurfing, powerkiting, windsurfing, powerboating and paddle boarding) in sessions ranging from two-hour introductory lessons to full days on the water and three-day courses. Recommended from eight years plus, and 12 years plus for kitesurfing.

Waterfront Sports
Marina, Exmouth, EX8 1ER, T01395-276599, waterfrontsports.co.uk. Apr-Oct daily 0900-1730, Nov-Mar daily 1000-1630. £30/2 hrs, £10/ beginner board.
Windsurf specialists with a shallow Duck Pond for learners, offering two-hour starter windsurf courses (including for children aged eight to 15), and progression to certificate level.

Multi activities

Haven Banks Outdoor Education Centre
61 Haven Rd, Exeter, EX2 8DP, T01392-434668, haven-banks.co.uk. From £44-86/2 hrs.

Based at their centre on the canal basin and at Starcross Yacht Club, it offers courses and tuition for all ages and abilities in kayaking, sailing, windsurfing, rock climbing, caving and abseiling, using moor and coastal venues. Children's holiday programmes and family taster sessions with different activities morning and afternoon.

Big days out

The Amazing Maize Maze
Bickleigh, nr Tiverton, EX16 8RG, T01363-772567, getlostindevon.co.uk. Mid-Jul to Sep. £4 person, under 4s free.
An unusual option: use topical clues to find your way along twisting paths through 10 acres of maize (wellies advisable if it has been raining, and the maze may be closed when wet and slippery). There's also a riverside walk, picnic space, table tennis, football, giant chess, Jenga, pedal go-karts and other outdoor entertainment.

Devon Railway Centre & Model World
Bickleigh, nr Tiverton, EX16 8RG, T01884-855671, devonrailwaycentre.co.uk. Easter, May-Sep and Oct half term. £6.10 adult, £4.90 child (3-16), £18.80 family.
On the closed Great Western Railway branch from Exeter to Dulverton. Unlimited narrow-gauge train rides, where children can clip tickets and wave the flag to start the trains, also model railways showing some of the UK's most famous working layouts, and indoor play coaches with ball ponds, sand pits, wooden railways and toddler trucks. The under 10s can drive their own train or car, and everyone can have a go on the remote-control car circuit and try the crazy golf. There's also an Edwardian model village and museum, all set round the Victorian station, venue for the tea rooms.

Crealy: Devon's Great Adventure Park
Sidmouth Rd, Clyst St Mary, nr Exeter, T01395-233200, crealy.co.uk. Daily from 1000. £7-13.95 person, children under 92 cm free, reduced prices online for groups of 4 or more, and during winter.
This is what happens when you cross Disneyland with a farm park. Devon's Crealy will have your kids cuddling rabbits one minute, then whooping it up on a log flume the next. Older children will make straight for the Adventure Realm, where rides include the El Pastil Coaster (runaway train roller coaster), Queen Bess Pirate Ship (swing boat), Tidal Wave Terror (12-m-drop water splash), Battle of the Bears (interactive ball-dodging adventure) and Meteorite (stomach-lurching vertical-drop ride). Many of these have a minimum height restriction of 92 cm, but parents with toddlers will find tamed-down action in the Magic Realm. Meanwhile, Action Realm keeps the adrenalin pumping with its go-karts, Dino-Blaster Bumper Boats, Water Wars and Summer Soak Zone (yes, you will get wet). The three remaining realms (Animal, Farming and Natural) are the places to feed lambs, ride ponies, milk cows, tickle piglets, cuddle hamsters and ride a train

to a quiet lakeside picnic spot. On the same site are Adrenalin Games (adrenalingames.com), paintballing and a summer campsite, and a summer campsite, see page 171.

Diggerland

Cullompton, T0871-227 7007, diggerland.com. Weekends and holidays 1000-1600. £15 person, under 3s free.

Just off the M5, dig, scoop and tip to your heart's content at this earthy park, jam-packed with JCBs and including an indoor area. Parents can sigh and tap their feet or, better, join in because you're likely to be here some time. There's a bar menu at Verbeer Manor by the entrance.

Escot Gardens Maze & Park

Escot Park, Fairmile, nr Ottery St Mary, EX11 1LU, T01404-822188, escot-devon.co.uk. Daily from 1000. £6.95 adult, £5.95 child (3-15), £24 family.

The diminutive stately home doesn't offer the expected but instead the chance for kids to set up camp in the woods, and while passing through 'Jurassic Pork' (home to wild boar), leap on to the rope swing or dash aboard a hidden pirate ship. For a break, there's a birds of prey display and otter feeding, red squirrels to spot, and animal petting. Also, when it's time for more action, they can work their way out of the maze, where routes change daily. There's a good soft-play barn, workers to watch building the traditional Saxon village, and the whole family can have a go at letterboxing, with cunning clues to find the hidden stamps in the woodland; or you can frighten yourselves silly again and again on the vertical slide. There's a small farm shop and home-made food in the Coach House, plus a new children's residential summer camp, based on a Californian eco-adventure syllabus.

Seaton Tramway

Harbour Rd, Seaton, EX12 2NQ, T01297-20375, tram.co.uk. Apr-Oct daily from 1000. Return £8.50 adult, £5.85 child, free parking at Colyton.

Gleamingly restored heritage trams process along the three-mile narrow-gauge electric tramway through the Axe Valley between Colyton and Seaton, with open-topped double deckers for fine weather, enclosed saloons for the wet, and the Tramstop restaurant at Colyton station (wholesome kids' lunchboxes £3.50). Also look out for specials like guided birdwatching trips to Seaton Marshes, north of the river at Axmouth.

At Seaton you can visit the beach before strolling over the bridge to Axmouth, where there are road signs warning of the ducks. You'll pass pretty little Axe Harbour and the **Sea Discovery Centre** (EX12 4AA, T01297-24774, Apr-Oct daily),

Meet the birds at Escot Gardens Maze & Park.

Get to work at Diggerland.

Out & about Exeter & East Devon

home to creatures from giant crabs to baby sharks and conger eels in exhibitions on both the smugglers and marine life of the Jurassic Coast.

There's another nature reserve at **Colyford** (midway stop), where the common is a salt marsh regularly flooded by high tides. There's a viewing platform across the upper reaches of the estuary, where egrets fish in the creeks and lagoons, and large black-and-white shelduck can be seen grazing. In winter it's home to waders and waterfowl. Meadow pipits feed amongst the grassy tussocks, flying to overhead wires if startled. In the summer, short-winged coneheads, a rare type of bush cricket, can be heard singing in the long grass along the edges of the ditches. The ditches and pools around the reserve are full of saltwater invertebrates called isopods, which whizz about in the water.

Back in Colyton, **Waggon Wanderer** (T01297-553290, open 1000-1500, return £2.50 adult, £1.50 child, £7.30 family) is pulled by handsome Suffolk Punch horses on return trips from the tramway terminus to the town centre (summer only). Or you could stroll along a five-mile circular route, taking in part of the **East Devon Way** (devon.gov.uk/mylocalpaths), or just picnic by the river in the public gardens, feeding the ducks and perhaps spotting a kingfisher. At the tram station, on the opposite side from the platform is Colyton's **Antiques Centre**. Bike hire is available from **Soanes Cycles** in Queens Square (EX24 6JX, T01297-552308, devoncycles.net).

Don't miss Killerton

Broadclyst, EX5 3LE, T01392-881345, nationaltrust.org.uk. Gardens daily 1030-1900; house and restaurant Mar-Nov daily 1000-1700. £8 adult, £4 child, £19.75 family, lower prices for just garden or parkland.

The enormous estate (6000 acres with 20 farms) offers an outstanding network of local rights of way and footpaths with meadow flowers, 18 acres of landscaped gardens and 18th-century parklands where buzzards are regularly spotted overhead. It's a place to park the car and spend time exploring. There are lizards, grass snakes and adders in the ground, and lesser horseshoe bats roosting in the cellar, plus an Iron Age hill fort called **Dolbury Hill**, where buried treasure is rumoured to be guarded by a dragon flying over every night.

The main building, damaged in the 1920s by fire, has been refurbished to show a country house between the two World Wars. For those who like their clothes, the Paulise de Bush collection of costumes here includes more than 9000 18th- to 20th-century outfits. There's also a Victorian laundry with mangles and irons and, in the grounds, an ice house plus summerhouse called the Bear House, one-time home to a pet Canadian black bear. There are Victorian toys to play with, a quiz and trail and a good Discovery Centre with storytelling, Victorian scavenger hunts and more (at least three days a week and sometimes daily in school holidays at £5 per child).

The estate includes **Budlake**, which has a 1950s post office (£2.79 adult, £1.35 child), wash house, double-seated privy, pigsty, chicken house, cottage garden and vegetable plot; and **Broadclyst**, where you park to walk half a mile in one direction across fields to reach the thatched medieval cob house, **Markers Cottage** (T01392-461546); in the other direction is **Clyston Mill** (T01392-462425). Like the post office, they are privately rented so only open from April to November on Monday, Tuesday and Sunday from 1400 to 1700, priced at £2.70 per adult, £1.35 per child or joint £5 ticket.

If you want to spend more time here, there are five National Trust thatched holiday cottages on the estate available for self-catering, see page 19.

World of Country Life

Sandy Bay, Littleham, nr Exmouth, EX8 5BU, T01395-274533, worldofcountrylife.co.uk. Apr-Nov daily 1000-1700. £9.85 adult, £7.85 child (3-17), £32.50 family. Right at the entrance to the Devon Cliffs Holidy Park, see page 172, you could disappear here for the day. There are safari deer train rides past llama and deer (which can be hand fed), a falconry display, wooden pirate ship, complete with dock and pirate jail, flying fox, swings, trampolines, undercover outdoor slides, aviary, pet centre

Spot deer and other animals at the World of Country Life.

and animal nursery, even goat walking, plus junior play parks with net climbs, bouncy castles and ball pits. There is also a Hall of Transport with vintage vehicles and steam engines, a history of agriculture with old machinery, a Victorian street, puzzle corner and, when you've done enough, there's a restaurant, coffeeshop or pub. As well as falconry displays, **Hawkridge Birds of Prey Centre** (hawkridgebirdsofprey.com) offers a one-hour owl/bird of prey experience at £20; children's owl experiences for ages eight to 13 at £50, or junior falconer for ages 13 to 17 years at £65.

More family favourites

A La Ronde
Summer Lane, Exmouth, EX8 5BD, T01395-265514, nationaltrust.org.uk. Mar-Nov Sat-Wed 1100-1700. £6.40 adult, £3.20 child (5-17), £16 family.
Created by two cousins and inspired by their European Grand Tour, the 16-sided building is supposedly based on a basilica in Ravenna, and is decorated with a frieze of feathers and many, many shells. It's odd enough to appeal to children, and does have a grassy space outside with good views, although, being small, is for a brief visit only.

Ark Pottery
Higher Barnes, Wiggaton, nr Ottery St Mary, EX11 1PY, T1404-812628, arkpottery.co.uk. Daily 1000-1700. £10/pottery experience including postage and packaging, £4.50/cream tea.
In a former dairy building by a thatched Devon longhouse, there's a gallery plus working pottery, where you can watch traditional hand throwing of pots, along with the creation of miniature animals (good pocket money purchases). Children and adults can be provided with protective clothing and have a go on the wheel with help from the expert, getting the result posted home after firing. Ring to check potter availability.

Bicton Park Botanical Gardens
East Budleigh, Budleigh Salterton, EX9 7BJ, T01395-568465, bictongardens.co.uk. Mar-Sep daily 1000-1800, rest of year 1000-1700. £6.95 adult, £5.95 child.
Need to chill? Then this is the place, with 63 acres of fine gardens (Italian, Mediterranean, rose, fernery, hermitage, pinetum and arboretum), plus a woodland railway. Look out for the 25 champion trees, the tallest/largest of their kind in Britain. At a dizzying 41 m, the Grecian fir is the tallest ever recorded. Also, to keep the kids happy, there are play areas indoors and outdoors, mini golf and, in winter, an outdoor ice rink, along with a restaurant, plus fine 19th-century glass palm house.

Branscombe Old Bakery, Manor Mill & Forge
EX12 3DB, T01392-881691, nationaltrust.org.uk. Forge daily, free. Bakery Apr-Nov Wed-Sun 1000-1700, free. Mill Apr-Nov Sun 1400-1700, also Wed in Jul and Aug. £2.80 adult, £1.40 child.
This stone-built, thatched building was, until 1987, the last traditional working bakery in Devon. The old baking equipment, such as baking tins, storage jars and open fires, has

Out & about Exeter & East Devon

been kept and the rest of the building now operates as a tea room. Manor Mill, still in working order and recently restored, is a water-powered mill which can supply flour for the bakery. The forge is open daily and the blacksmith sells his work.

Coldharbour Mill
Uffculme, nr Cullompton, EX15 3EE, T01884-840960, coldharbourmill.org.uk. Easter-Oct daily 1100-1600, rest of year Mon-Fri. £4 adult, £2 child, £10 family.
One for mechanical enthusiasts: an 18th-century wool-spinning mill, closed only in 1981 and unchanged since 1865; much of the machinery is around 100 years old. Even the waterwheel was used until the 1970s. Both that and the horizontal steam engine are running again and a beam engine (found through the Science Museum) is steaming regularly too (check the website for dates). You can see the process from fleece to yarn, plus power-loom weaving of stair runners and tartan. On non-steam days visitors can go into the boiler and steam-engine houses, a gas retort house that produced coal gas lighting, and carpenter's workshop. Snacks and meals are available in the Gill Box restaurant open from 1000 to 1700.

Exmouth Model Railway
Queens Drive, Exmouth, EX8 2AY, T01395-278383, exmouth modelrailway.co.uk. Easter-Oct daily, winter Sat and Sun. £2.25 adult, £1.25 child (3-16), £5.50 family.
Reportedly the largest 00-gauge model railway in Britain was built over 14 years and is regularly updated. There are tankers, open wagons and coal wagons. The café is in a restored 1956 railway carriage, open daily, and there are replicas of Thomas the Tank Engine and friends that younger visitors can drive.

Knightshayes Court
Bolham, nr Tiverton, EX16 7RQ, T01884-254665, nationaltrust.org.uk. Mar-Nov Sat-Thu 1100-1700. £8.20 adult, £4.10 child, £20.50 family.
The ornate, high-Victorian interiors are one draw, but there are also outstanding grounds, with meadows to romp in and woodlands to explore, plus a newly restored kitchen garden.

Norman Lockyer Observatory
Salcombe Hill, Sidmouth, EX10 0YQ, T01395-579941, normanlockyer.org. Open from 1430 or 1930. £5 adult, £2.50 child.
Check the website for opening times and events at this historic optical observatory and science-education centre. It's run by unpaid volunteers, many retired scientists, who offer information on astronomy, meteorology, amateur radio and more. Open nights include a planetarium presentation and tour of the domes and their historic telescopes plus, perhaps, a talk in the lecture theatre and a demonstration of the Met station, showing satellite images and automatic weather recording.

Pecorama Pleasure Gardens
Beer, EX12 3NA, T01297-21542, peco-uk.com. Easter-Nov Mon-Fri 1000-1730, Sat 1000-1300. £6.60 adult, £4.50 child (4-14).
PECO are manufacturers of model railway tracks and this is an attractive showcase for their products on the hillside behind the village. Indoors is a modelling exhibition in various scales, while the gardens feature not just a wooden maze, cable slide and challenging climbing frame, but also the Beer Heights Light Railway, a narrow-gauge passenger-carrying line, powered by miniature steam and diesel locomotives. It runs for a mile through tunnels, loops and cuttings with views of the village and Lyme Bay below. When that palls, there's crazy golf, a garden-room restaurant or Pullman-car café, plus an entertainment programme of jesters, clowns and magicians.

Trains at the Exmouth Model Railway.

Off the beaten track

The Blackdown Hills

Another designated Area of Outstanding Beauty, the Blackdown Hills on the border of Devon and Somerset have no big draws. Instead they are a place to kick back and enjoy the landscape, with its windswept plateaux, green valleys and villages apparently little changed since the Second World War.

That was when the Dunkeswell airfield was a US base, with the boxer Joe Louis and even Clark Gable posted there. There's more on that at the **Dunkeswell Memorial Museum** (EX14 4PG, T01404-891943, dunkeswellmemorialmuseum.org.uk, Mar-Oct Wed-Mon 1000-1800, Nov-Feb Sat-Sun, £2 adult, £1 child), with old uniforms, kit, bits of crashed aircraft and the rest.

The nearby **air field** (T01404-891226, dunkeswellaircentre.co.uk) is still in use; a good place to watch light aircraft is from the café-bar-restaurant, which has a large window onto the runway, small children's play area and a Sunday carvery. Alternatively, eat at the Michelin-listed **Drewe Arms** (Broadhembury, EX14 3NF, T01404-841267, thedrewearms.com), which also serves sandwiches with home-made bread and parsnip crisps.

There is also the option of taking to the skies yourself. **Devon & Somerset Flight Training** (T01404-891643, dsft.co.uk) offer trips in Cessna and Piper light aircraft, flights along the Jurassic Coast, south coast or up to Minehead and back from £72 per half hour. Or for a step back in time, **Ace Flight Training** (T01404-891811, aceflight.co.uk) will take you up in an old bi-plane, generally from eight years, from £75 for 15 minutes, kitted out with flight overalls, leather jacket, goggles and helmet.

The villages and hamlets keep busy (blackdownhillsaonb.org.uk) listing events from hedgecraft days to storytelling events and stargazing evenings. Also check out the local village markets and farmers' markets, see page 175. For organized outdoor activities, contact Wildside Education, see page 162.

But this is also somewhere to just enjoy the countryside. Downloadable walking leaflets from the website (devon.gov.uk/mylocalpaths), complete with a marked-up OS map, include Walk 4 near **Hemyock**, a pretty four-mile route in Madford Valley to the ruins of the Cistercian **Dunkeswell Abbey**, in a lovely location, although little remains of the building. There's an easy, level walk of one mile, a mile north of Culmstock up **Hunters Hill** with good views. Or, for something a shade more atmospheric, try one of the Iron Age hill forts. Best known is **Hembury Fort**, close to the A373, subsequently used by the Romans; or there's **Dumpdon Hill** not far from the A303 at Monkton, the top owned by the National Trust with a couple of car parks and easy walks.

Also sample the **Herepath Trails**, alternatively called people's paths (nerochescheme.org/herepath.php), a network being created for riders and walkers, starting with a 13½-mile circuit around Staple Fitzpaine. The trails mostly follow existing public rights of way, originally ninth-century trade and communication routes between settlements.

Sleeping Exeter & East Devon

Pick of the pitches

Combe View
Branscombe, nr Seaton, EX12 3BT, T01297-680218, branscombe-camping.co.uk. Mar-Nov. From £10/pitch, £6 adult, £3 child (5-14), under 5s free.

Arrive to the moo of a cow and the honking of geese at this traditional site, ideal for families. It's spread over four fields that make one big playground and picnic area, with views over the bay and fire pits for campfires. There's a small flock of sheep, Exmoor ponies, a goat that likes to be stroked, plus free-range Berkshire pigs, and you might also spot roe deer or a fox, plus various birds. There are also two mobile homes and a touring caravan to let.

Forest Glade Holiday Park
Nr Cullompton, EX15 2DT, T01404-841381, forest-glade.co.uk. Apr-Nov. £11.50-15/pitch + 2, £3 child (10-18), £1.50 child (4-9), under 3s free.

Family-owned and run in a wide forest clearing on the edge of the Blackdown Hills, 16 acres with 80 touring pitches and holiday caravans, plus a separate, free-pitch camping field. Facilities include an indoor pool, adventure play areas, all-weather tennis, ball-games area and games room, plus a freezer-pack service. Barbecues are allowed and Abbotsford

Cycles will deliver bikes, see page 162. There's a strong environmental policy; they've won gold for the past seven years in the David Bellamy conservation award scheme.

Hook Farm
Gore Lane, Uplyme, DT7 3UU, T01297-442801, hookfarm-uplyme.co.uk. Mar-Nov. £10-24/pitch + 2, £3/additional person aged 4+.

Just outside the Devon border, 45 minutes' walk from Lyme Regis (take the hourly bus back), this terraced site looks out over green bucolic pastures and the small village, with 100 pitches in six acres. Deliberately low key and quiet at night, the play area functions as a children's meeting spot before they disappear off to make their own amusement.

Ladram Bay Holiday Park
Nr Otterton, EX9 7BX, T01395-568398, ladrambay.co.uk. Easter-Nov. £13-29/pitch + 2, £1-3.50/additional person under 16.

Another site with its own private beach (see page 159), plus 107 holiday homes and 200 pitches, run by the same family since the 1940s. The pebble beach is sandy at low tide with rock pools. There's a beach kiosk, along with an adventure playground, soft playground, indoor pool with daily kids' fun hour and daytime activities for families, plus crazy golf, amusements and evening entertainment. There's the option of staying in one of the site's mobile homes. Barbecues permitted.

Oakdown
Gatedown Lane, Weston, nr Sidmouth, EX10 0PT, T01297-680387, oakdown.co.uk. Mar-Nov. £13.50-23/pitch + 2, £3 child (5+), under 5s free.

Close to the road but very well maintained, with 150 pitches in 10 acres plus a new six-acre site. It's about a mile from the cliff tops and a steep walk down to the beach; Weston itself is 15 minutes' walk away. Landscaped into groves to give more privacy, it has a field trail to the Donkey Sanctuary or a route to Sidmouth along country lanes. There's pitch-n-putt golf, internet room, café, games room and two play areas. Slabs for barbecues are supplied.

Salcombe Regis Camping & Caravan Park
Nr Sidmouth, EX10 0JH, T01395-514303, salcombe-regis.co.uk. Mar-Nov. £11.50-17.50/pitch + 2, £2.60 child (5-15), under 5s free.

Caravans and cottages plus touring pitches on an attractive 16-acre site. Some tent pitches have sea views and it's a 20-minute walk down to the beach (no facilities but nice and wild).

Webbers Park
Castle Lane, Woodbury, nr Exmouth, EX5 1EA, T01395-232276, webberspark.co.uk. Mar-Nov. £12-18/pitch + 2, £3 child (over 3).

A family-run 20-acre five-star park near Woodbury with access to two village pubs, bistro and fish and chips, and close to the open spaces and paths of Woodbury Common. Chalets are available as well as camping.

West Middlewick Farm
Nomansland, nr Tiverton, EX16 8NP, T01884-861235, westmiddlewick.co.uk. Year round. £8-10/pitch + 2, £1 child.

A working farm, offering camping since 1933. The main site is a four-acre field with views towards Exmoor; the middle is for children to make their own entertainment; there's another no-frills field for tents only. There are often animals for cuddling, and visitors are welcome to explore the farm, which has cows, sheep, pigs and chickens. You can picnic, too, at spots like the old mill by the stream, where children make dams, or light a barbecue on the camping field. There are also two four-star log cabins.

Farm favourites

Ashridge Farm
Sandford, nr Crediton, EX17 4EN, T01363-774292, ashridgefarm.co.uk. B&B £27-35 person, £20 child (11-14), £15 child (4-10), £10/child (under 3s).
A working organic farm north of Exeter with lots of animals, arable areas, plus waymarked trails and plenty of wildlife. There's a large lawn for children to play, farm animals to feed and eggs to collect for breakfast. Accommodation is in an old piggery that has been recently converted, using natural materials where possible; with sustainable heating and hot water. There's a family room with double and bunk, twin room with disabled access and a single room.

Harton Farm
Oakford, nr Tiverton, EX16 9HH, T01398-351209, hartonfarm.co.uk. B&B £22 adult, £11 child (under 12); evening meal £12 adult, £6 child.
Welcomes families with children aged four or over in just two bedrooms, offering organic, traditional food including home-made bread and ice cream, and a chance to wander the farm with the working dogs. If children are old enough, they can join in the jobs before breakfast and supper, checking the sheep and offering the farmer a chance to explain about sheep, ewes and lambs. If a cow is in milk, they'll even teach you to milk her.

Highdown Farm
Bradninch, EX5 4LJ, T01392-881028/07739-765510, highdownfarm.co.uk. £300-530/week sleeping 4.
Holiday cottages for seven, four and two plus cot on an organic dairy farm, where you can feed the calves and watch the milking. Secure garden, cots and high chairs, play area with trampoline, football goal, swings and slide, open fields, Shetland ponies to ride; babysitting can be booked.

White Deer Camping Site
Crealy Great Adventure Park, Sidmouth Rd, EX5 1DR, T01395-233200, crealycamping.co.uk. Aug. £25/pitch + 3, £12.95 additional person, £380/tipi for 4.

Prices at this simple site (hired-in loos, showers and waste disposal) include access to the theme park (see page 164) and the option of your own pony to cosset and care for during the stay. Morning on the Farm experiences allow visitors to help milk the cows, bottle-feed the lambs and give animals their breakfast. Local farmers and producers provide farmhouse breakfasts at the **Crealy Bear Café** (open 0800-1800), served with Lavazza coffee, and barbecue packs with a 'free range fridge' to keep them in. Saturday night is Campover evening when the park stays open for play in the Adventure Zone, saying goodnight to the animals, and a stop at the bar, along with a barbecue and

Sleeping Exeter & East Devon

campfire. You can also book a pre-erected tipi with lining, ground sheet, coir matting, rugs, low table and lanterns, and for an extra £100, the luxury of sheepskins, throws, cushions and Indian mirrored hangings.

Also recommended
Axe Farm
Axemouth, EX12 4BG, T01297-24707. A basic site with flat pitches next to the river, near two pubs, plus small shop.

Best of the rest

Beer YHA
Bovey Combe, Beer, Seaton, EX12 3LL, T0845-371 9502, yha.org.uk. Year-round. £13.95 adult, £10.50 child.
Refurbished in 2009, an airy country house on the edge of Beer with large lawned garden and rooms with four, five and six beds.

Devon Cliffs Holiday Park
Sandy Bay, nr Exmouth, T0871-230 1900, haven.com, camping T0871-231 0870, caravancamping.co.uk. Camping from £35/pitch, static caravan £364-864/week.
The big draw of this all-singing, all-dancing park, reportedly the biggest in Europe, is direct access to privately owned Sandy Bay, see page 159. If that wanes the five-star facilities include spa, indoor pool with flume and play area, and outdoor multi-level pool complex. There is also an all-weather multi-sports court, adventure playground, pool tables, bike hire, bowling, climbing wall, kids' clubs, Starbucks, Burger King, entertainment day and night, and so the list goes on. As well as chalet and catered accommodation, there's a touring campsite.

Mazzard Farm
East Hill, Ottery St Mary, EX11 1QQ, T01404-815492, mazzardfarm.com. £350-975/week.
The seven cottages in this small but stylish complex in 17 acres of grounds are as green as possible without compromising luxury and convenience. Run by a family with small children of their own, it caters well to families, laying on all the kit from stair gates to sterilizers, providing ride-on toys in the courtyard, plus slide, trampoline, football pitch, and lots of open space. There's also a library of DVDs. Enjoy croissants for breakfast, burgers from the next-door farm, crumbles and juice made with apples from the orchards, vegetables from the garden, eggs from the chickens, and each cottage has its own herb pot. If you don't want to cook yourself, a local chef will do the business. You can get on-site complementary treatments as well. Bliss.

Also recommended
Alpine Park Cottages
Sidmouth Rd, Aylesbeare, EX5 2JW, T01395-233619, alpineparkcottages.co.uk. £385-600/week sleeping 2 adults and 2 children.
Centrally heated wooden lodges and chalets in five acres of lightly wooded parkland with children's games on the green, plus a field with crazy golf and football.

The Cottage Company
25a Fore St, Budleigh Salterton, EX9 6NP, T01392-201341, thecottagecompanydevon.co.uk. East Devon specialists with a small luxury range. Head office is also a shop stocking items like handmade deck chairs and windbreaks, plus beach barbecues and children's beachwear.

Milkbere Cottage Holidays
T01297-20729, milkberehols.com. An agency specializing in properties along the Jurassic Coast.

Higher Watchcombe Farm
Shute, nr Colyton, EX13 7QN, T01297-552424, higherwatchcombe.co.uk. £265-795.
Six well-sized self-catering cottages with books, DVDs, fully equipped kitchens, including washer-driers, and large, south-facing gardens and grounds including a children's play area.

Mazzard Farm courtyard.

Cool & quirky
Cuckoo Down Farm Yurts
See page 13.

Mid Devon Hire Boats & Moorings
Orchard Farm, Halbeton, nr East Manley, EX16 4NJ, T01884-252178, middevonhireboats.co.uk.
£625-955/week.
Offering a five-berth narrow boat for hire. With just 11 land-locked miles and no locks, this is very easy boating.

Tiverton Castle
Park Hill, Tiverton, EX16 6RP, T01884-253200, tivertoncastle.com.
£280-800/week.
Stay in what was once the home of the powerful medieval earls of Devon and a Plantagenet princess. There are four self-catering apartments with cot and high chair available. Originally built in 1106 by order of Henry I, public areas are open to visitors three days a week from Easter to the end of October. Holidaying here you get to enter the turret door, walk up the Jacobean staircase, enjoy the garden and its croquet, take free tours of the castle, and enjoy seasonal fruit and vegetables from the kitchen garden and even free fishing on the banks of the River Exe.

Splashing out

The Bulstone
Higher Bulstone, nr Branscombe, EX12 3BL, T01297-680446, childfriendlyhotels.com. £90-110 for 2 adults and 2 children under 11, £132-152 including dinner.
This homely and welcoming establishment boasts its own Facebook page set up by happy customers – the Bulstone Appreciation Society. Catering to those with children under eight, it's a safe haven with just 12 family units and suites, and somewhere to treat like home, with guest fridge, kettle, bottle sterilizer, microwave, full laundry service, playroom, play area, and NNEB-qualified babysitters, nappy buckets, spare cot sheets… you name it, plus home-cooked meals with high tea for the kids.

Eating Exeter & East Devon

Local goodies

Delis

B Natural
14 The Strand, Exmouth, EX8 1AD, T01395-279144.
Organic, local, environmentally friendly and ethically traded products.

Country Cheeses
Fore St, Topsham, EX3 0HD, T01392-877746, countrycheeses.co.uk.
Selling about 100 different British cheeses, most from the West Country.

Hayman's
6 Church St, Sidmouth, EX10 8LY, T01395-512877, haymansbutchers.co.uk.
Rick Stein food heroes. A family shop, known for its pies and pasties.

Honiton Dairy
60 High St, Honiton, EX14 1PQ, T01404-42075.
Dairy ice cream made on the premises (up to 40 flavours in summer), plus home-made clotted cream, biscuits, honey and Ivor Dewdney pasties.

Treloars Delicatessen
38 High St, Crediton, EX17 3JP.
A local food hero, selling bread and baked goods, cheese and dairy produce, meats, preserves and home-cooked dishes.

Trumps of Sidmouth
8 Fore St, EX10 8AQ, T01395-512446.
An old-fashioned grocer's that also runs a café. It's a fun place to visit, although there's a premium to be paid.

Vinnicombe's Bakery
60 High St, Sidmouth, EX10 8EH, T01395-513379.
Traditional bakers and confectioners.

Woozies Deli
Diamond House, Fore St, Beer, EX12 3NA, T01297-20707.
Offering alternatives to the chippie next door.

Farm shops

Berry Farm
Four Elms Hill, Harpford, nr Sidmouth, EX10 0FE, T07969-024749. May-Sep and Dec.
Farm shop and pick-your-own with sea views, offering light lunches, home-made cakes and more, using farm produce, plus East Hill Pride butchers.

Culm Valley Farm Shop
Willand Rd, Cullompton, Devon, EX15 1AP, T01884-38513.
Fruit and vegetables.

Darts Farm Shopping Village
Clyst St George, nr Topsham, EX3 0QH, T01392-878200, dartsfarm.co.uk.
An operation to rival the supermarkets with not just food from the farm (still in operation) and surroundings. There are good meat and cheese counters, plus vegetables, fruit, biscuits, bread and imports such as Italian food, a toy department and other retailers, including a big Cotswold Camping outlet. An RSPB observation centre looks out over the marshes and down the estuary. There are also animals, including donkeys, rabbits, alpacas and pot-bellied pigs.

Exe Valley Farm Shop
Thorverton, nr Crediton, EX5 5LZ, T01392-861239.
Fruit and vegetables, organic produce, local meat, preserves, West Country cheeses, Darts Farm vegetables, local eggs and breads, gluten-free products, milk, household groceries, plus odds and ends like local jewellery and original surfboards.

Folly End Farm Shop
Rewe, EX5 4DY, T01392-861406.
A small simple outlet on the A396 just north of Rewe, selling cakes, bread, some meat and other basics.

Joshua's Country Harvest Store
Gosford Rd, Ottery St Mary, EX11 1NU, T01404-815473, joshuasharveststore.co.uk.
North of Ottery, slightly old-fashioned but large and with a food hall specializing in own-baked cakes, tasty ready meals, deli items, local and organic produce, beer, wine and cider, and more.

Little Turberfield Farm Shop
Sampford Peverell, nr Tiverton, EX16 7EH, T01884-820908. Tue-Thu 0800-1700, Fri 0800-1730, Sat 0800-1530. Local fruit and vegetables, plus meat, own sausages, burgers and faggots, local cheese and preserves.

Millers Farm Shop
Kilmington, nr Axminster, EX13 7RA, T01297-35290, millersfarmshop.com. On the A35 west of Axminster, a barely converted barn, has rows of food, including home-grown vegetables, meat from local producers, a local fish stall, local cakes, bread, cheeses and preserves, drink and imports; including wine.

Oaklands Farm Shop, Café, Vineyard & Winery
Monkton, nr Honiton, EX14 9QH, T01404-47442, blackdownhills-vineyard.co.uk.
Just off the A303, a small outlet for home-reared meat and poultry, ready meals such as chicken, bacon and tarragon pie, and cakes, plus café serving Lavazza coffee, and outdoor space with home-made food and English wine.

Pynes Farmshop
South Farm, nr Budleigh Salterton, EX9 7AZ, T01395-443329. Mon-Sat 0900-1730, Sun 1000-1500.
An attractive new shop on a courtyard with other businesses, selling dried goods, vegetables, eggs, meat, etc.

Quickes Farm Shop
Home Farm, Newton St Cyres, nr Crediton, EX5 5AY, T01392-851000, quickes.co.uk. Mon-Sat 0900-1700. The retail outlet for multiple award-winning cheese, plus own butter and ice cream and other West Country produce, such as frozen meats, including game, handmade chocolates, honey and eggs.

Royal Oak Farm
Nr Stockland, EX14 9LF, T01404-831223, royaloakfarm.co.uk.
Based around a small 17th-century farmhouse, a shop with grass-fed beef, free-range pork, chicken, pick-your-own soft fruit and vegetables, and more, plus morning coffees, light lunches served between 1200 and 1400 (£6.50) and award-winning cream teas served on bone china, all home-made. A good place to park, take a circular walk and return for refuelling.

Quick & simple

Boston Tea Party
Monkton House, 53 High St, Honiton, EX14 1PW, T01404-548739, bostonteaparty.co.uk.
One of a group of well-liked family-friendly West Country cafés, serving local and Fairtrade produce; a place to read the newspaper at wooden tables or on leather sofas. Mini West Country Breakfast for kids £3.25.

Market days

Farmers' markets
Cullompton, second Saturday.
Crediton, first Saturday.
Exeter, Fore St, Thursday; South St third Saturday; quayside last Wednesday.
Exmouth, second Wednesday.
Honiton, third Thursday.
Killerton, March-October third Saturday.
Ottery St Mary, first Friday.
Seaton, usually third Friday.
Topsham, usually third Sunday.

General markets
All Saints, second Saturday.
Axminister, Thursday.
Charmouth, Monday.
Churchinford, first Saturday.
Exeter, Sidwell St, Monday-Saturday.
Exmouth, second Wednesday.
Hemyock, third Saturday.
Honiton, Tuesday and Saturday, cattle market Monday.
Luppitt, Friday.
Ottery St Mary, last Saturday.
Stockland, last Saturday.
Tiverton, pannier market, third Wednesday.
Yarcombe, second Saturday.

Capel's of Exmouth
11 Imperial Rd, EX8 1BY, T01395-263645.
Offering popular fish and chips, smart but small and unpretentious, not far from the train station. £4.25 medium cod and chips, £3.40 for a child's portion.

Eating Exeter & East Devon

The Lamb Inn
The Square, Sandford, nr Crediton, EX17 4LW, T01363-773676, lambinnsandford.co.uk. Open from 0900. There's good food such as bangers and mash £7.50, a garden on three levels, even a small weekend cinema (ring for the programme) and smart accommodation, too.

The Longboat Café
Marine Parade, Budleigh Salterton, EX9 6NS, T01395-445619. The old boathouse offers tea, coffee and sandwiches, plus home-made cakes. There are proposals to turn it into something smarter and larger.

Mason's Arms
Branscombe, EX12 3DJ, T01297-680300, masonsarms.co.uk. A fine old pub with outside seating as well as a fire. You could just have a drink and snack, or restaurant-style, food such as mussels £5.95, garlic roasted lamb £12.25. It gets very busy so booking is advisable.

The Otter Inn
Colaton Raleigh, T01395-568434, otterinn.co.uk. One of the most child-friendly pubs in the area with a play table inside and play area out, sometimes with a bouncy castle.

Fish & chips

The Beer Fish & Chip Shop
Fore St, EX12 3JQ, T01297-625774. A very plain takeaway joint that uses produce straight off the boat.

Particularly recognized for fish. Scampi, chips and salad £9.95, sausage and mash with red onion jam £8.95.

Pottery Shop & Milkshake Bar
30 High St, Honiton, EX14 1PU, T01404-42106, honitonpottery.co.uk/Milkshakebar.html. A 1950s diner theme, complete with jukebox, and a chance for

children and adults to paint their own pottery. Offering an all-day breakfast, burgers and fries from £4.60 and 40-plus milkshakes and pancakes from £1.70, home-made cakes and ice cream desserts. Eat in, on the patio, or take away.

River Cottage Canteen
Trinity Sq, Axminster, EX13 5AN, T01297-631862, rivercottage.net. Canteen Mon 1000-1600, Tue-Sat 0900-2130, Sun 1030-1500, book for Sun and evenings. Deli Mon-Sat 0830-1700, Sun 1000-1630.
Serves from breakfast through lunch, tea to dinner, showcasing local and organic food and drink producers. BLT in a bap with chips £6.95, soup £5, delicious chips and sea salt £3, cream tea £4.50. The deli stocks basics through to award-winning pies, charcuterie and local cheeses. There are weekly tastings and regular events. Children are also welcome at River Cottage HQ for Sunday events and special courses.

Taste of Sidmouth
Old Fore St, Sidmouth, EX10 8AR, T01395-512634, tasteofsidmouth.co.uk.
A tea room (cream tea £3.75) also serving snacks like a chunk of pork pie £2.50, but, above all, recommended for outstanding ice cream at £1.40 for a large scoop, in Italian-with-a-Devon-twist style.

Thirsty Farmer
Whimple, EX5 2QQ, T01404-822287, thirstyfarmer.co.uk.
Just off the A30, a village pub where kids can roam and which starts serving at 1800. Prices from £6.25 for baguettes and wraps.

Posh nosh

The Globe
Fore St, Topsham, EX3 0HR, T01392-873471, globehotel.com.
As well as the restaurant, there's a café serving not just baguettes and snacks but smoked haddock with a cheesy potato sauce, lemon goujons, and fish of the day and chips. Smaller portions are available for children. The local folk club meets here on Sunday evenings. There's attractive accommodation too, including family rooms from £90 and from £7.50 per child.

The Holt
Honiton, T01404-47077, theholt-honiton.com.
Owned by the Otter Brewery family and nicely refurbished with downstairs bar and papers, and upstairs restaurant (best to book). There are fancier mains like warm ham hock salad with crispy polenta, beetroot and herbs £7.50, as well as daily panini and fries £5.50, and puddings from the intriguing, such as chocolate and beet cake with raspberry sauce and vanilla sour cream £5.50, to the traditional, like treacle tart and clotted cream £5.

Michael Caines Café Bar
Abode Exeter, Royal Clarence Hotel, Cathedral Yard, EX1 1HD, T01392-223626, michaelcaines.com. Daily 1000-2200.
Food from the Michelin-starred chef at non-Michelin prices, such as £14.95 for a two-course lunch, complete with petits fours. Not for ADHD kids but, if they can sit still, a chance to show fine dining and enjoy really fancy desserts. There are outside tables in the yard and live jazz some evenings.

Salty Monk
Sidford, EX10 9QP, T01395-513174, saltymonk.co.uk. Lunches Thu-Sun.
Prize-winning and Michelin-listed with a strong emphasis on locally sourced food, cooked on request for children. As well as the formal restaurant, there are cream teas daily £6.25, or full teas £10.50 in the old-fashioned sitting room, plus accommodation from £55 per person.

Grown-ups' stuff Devon

Inroads

Getting there
By car For North Devon turn off the M5 on to the A361 at Tiverton towards Barnstaple. For other areas, continue to the end of the motorway. Turn immediately to the coast on the A379 for Dawlish, Teignmouth and neighbouring resorts. Turn inland on the A30 for the north part of Dartmoor. For destinations further west, continue on the A38, turning off quickly on to the A380 to reach Torbay.

East Devon may be best reached from London and the east by the A303 (becoming the A30), which connects with the M3 south of London. However, the A303 continues through Exeter, which can become congested so is best avoided if you're travelling further.

Travelling time to Exeter by car is estimated as 3½ hours from London, 1½ hours from Bristol and three hours from Birmingham. **AA Roadwatch** (T84322 from a mobile or T0906-888 4322 from a landline) provides 24-hour traffic information, including any problem weather, which may cause further delays.

As with Exeter, you often find tailbacks on the outskirts of Plymouth, particularly at rush hour, including on the A386 towards Tavistock, but also on the dual carriageway A38 east towards the South Hams.

Another problem area is Totnes, where, in summer, you can face tailbacks as far as Paignton. In North Devon the bottleneck is Barnstaple.

By coach **Megabus** (T09001-600900, megabus.com) Operated by Stagecoach to Exeter and Plymouth, low-cost long-distance bus fares.
National Express (T08717-818181, nationalexpress.com) Serving Exeter and Plymouth.

By train **British Rail** (T0845-748 4950/08457-484950, nationalrail.co.uk) Travelling time from London to Exeter is two hours 10 minutes, from Bristol one hour 10 minutes and from Birmingham 2½ hours. Routes to Exeter from London are via Taunton or on much slower trains via Basingstoke, Salisbury and Yeovil. From Exeter there are services on to Torquay and Paignton (the last section particularly scenic), or via Totnes to Plymouth.
Cross Country Trains (T0844-811 0124, crosscountrytrains.co.uk) Based at Birmingham with routes to Exeter and further via the south coast to Plymouth.
First Great Western (T08457-000125, firstgreatwestern.co.uk) Operating from Paddington.
Megatrain (T0900-160 0900, megatrain.com) Low-cost intercity rail travel operated by Stagecoach on Southwest Trains with services to Exeter, Honiton, Axminster and Plymouth.
Southwest Trains (T0845-600 0650, southwesttrains.co.uk/SWTrains) Run by Stagecoach, with Waterloo as its hub; the single-track service from London to Exeter is approximately hourly.

Boredom busters

Invest in stories from talkingbooks.co.uk or audiohome.co.uk. There are also rental services, travellerstales.co.uk, rental.audiobooksonline.co.uk, as well as your local library. Harry Potter, *Swallows and Amazons*, and Just William titles are good choices for family listening.

Break the journey

There are two main routes to Devon. One is via the M5 motorway, certainly best for North Devon and if travelling from the Midlands, the northwest, and also from London on the M4. The other, for East Devon, is via the A303 (becoming the A30) which connects with the M3 south of London.

If you need a better break than a motorway service station, here are some alternatives.

A303

Cadbury Castle Despite the chocolate name, an Iron Age hill fort, surrounded by four terraced earthworks and ditches, considered by some the site of King Arthur's Camelot. It's visible from the road, on the south side close to South Cadbury.

Farmer Giles Farmstead (farmergiles.co.uk) South of the A303, a working farm with play areas inside and outdoors.

Fleet Air Arm Museum (fleetairarm.com) Covering 100 years of flying in the Royal Navy, and including the first British-built Concorde; you can climb into the cockpit. There's also a children's playground.

Hawk Conservancy (hawk-conservancy.org) Four miles west of Andover, with 150 birds of prey in 22 acres including woodland and meadows.

Montacute (nationaltrust.org.uk) Fabulous Elizabethan stone house near Yeovil, including period portraits from the National Portrait Gallery (great if covering the Tudors at school).

Popham Little Chef (littlechef.co.uk/heston.php) Made famous by the TV programmes covering Heston Blumenthal's efforts at improvement.

Stonehenge (english-heritage.org.uk) Right by the road, you could just wave as you go by, but there is also an activity sheet for children aged five to nine to get a bit more out of it.

Stourhead (nationaltrust.org.uk) Perfect English landscape garden around a circular lakeside walk with fabulous trees, also pub and grand house, good café and small farm shop.

White Sheet Fort A couple of acres near the small town of Mere, the site of a Neolithic causeway and Iron Age camp, and chalkland site of Special Scientific Interest.

M4

Avebury Stone Circle (nationaltrust.org.uk) A World Heritage Site offering a family fun trail and regular events. Unlike Stonehenge, you can picnic among the stones and there's a museum too, if you fancy.

Barbury Castle About five miles south of Swindon, a 12-acre park with Iron Age hill fort, plus round barrows, Celtic field systems and 18th- to 19th-century flint workings.

Bowood House (bowood-house.co.uk) A stately home at Calne south of the M4, with parkland and impressive adventure playground.

Uffington Castle White Horse and Dragon Hill (english-heritage.org.uk) North of the M4, west of Wantage, along the ridgeway, a large Iron Age hill fort and natural mound, plus the oldest chalk-cut hill figure in Britain, at least 3000 years old.

Stonehenge.

M5

Crook Peak and **Shute Shelve Hill** (nationaltrust.org.uk) Open space just west of the M5, not far from Cheddar.

Haresfield Beacon (nationaltrust.org.uk) Three miles northwest of Stroud on the Cotswold escarpment.

Robinswood Hill Country Park (T01452-38333) Two miles south of Gloucester, of the A4173, 250 acres of countryside with rarebreed farm and waymarked nature and geology trails, Wildlife Trust visitor centre.

Spetchley Park (spetchleygardens.co.uk) Three miles east of Worcester. No dedicated play area but ducks, geese, squirrels, peacocks and acres of space.

Worcester Woods (worcestershire.gov.uk) Approximately 100 acres of woodland, plus meadows, play space, café and picnic area, reached from junction 7.

Grown-ups' stuff Devon

Getting around

By bus A growing number of routes are being created to cater for visitors. The **Transmoor Link** runs between Exeter and Plymouth and the Cross Moor Link between Bovey Tracey and Okehampton, via Moretonhampstead, with five trips a day at weekends. Special tickets include the **Dartmoor Sunday Rover** that runs from October to mid-May (£6 adult, £4 child, £16 family including 3 children). It covers travel across the Devon tourist train and bus network, making Sunday a good day to try public transport. The **Haytor Hoppa** (dartmoor-npa.gov.uk, Jun-Nov; £2 person, £5 family) is a circular bus route that operates several times a day so you don't have to double back but can take linear walks across the moor.

First Group (T0845-600 1420, firstgroup.com/devon) provides bus services across North Devon with a travel shop at Barnstaple Bus Station, and around Plymouth as well as the **CoastLinX53** (devon.gov.uk/x53_coastlinx) that serves the Jurassic Coast from Exeter.

Stagecoach Southwest (Exeter T01392-427711, Torquay T01803-664500, Barnstaple T01271-329089, stagecoachbus.com/southwest) operates travel shops at Exeter Bus Station, Paignton Bus Station and 15 Victoria Parade, Torquay. There are also local ticket agents.

By car A key requirement to driving in Devon is the ability to reverse in narrow spaces. As many of the roads are single track, this is a particular issue in peak season.

Another problem is parking on the coast. It's best to time visits for early morning or late afternoon to increase chances of finding a space, and consider avoiding smaller villages like Branscombe at peak times. Also make sure you have plenty of change for daily parking charges of up to £5.

Bear in mind that away from larger centres you may have to travel some distance to find a petrol station, and do not count on being able to use your mobile phone, particularly in the valleys and dips.

By train Travelling around Devon on public transport can make a lot of sense. It can also be fun, with the **Riviera Line**, south from Exeter, dashing not just past but sometimes through the waves from Dawlish to Teignmouth on a route past Starcross, Dawlish, Dawlish Warren, Teignmouth, Newton Abbot, Totnes, Ivybridge and on to Plymouth. First Great Western and South West Trains operate services (see page 178).

The **Tarka Line** (special deals on family tickets) travels through the valleys of the rivers Yeo and Taw past Crediton and Mid Devon to connect with Barnstaple, where there are bus links to main resorts. It's one of the prettiest lines in the country and some tickets allow you to break your journey and explore on foot or by bike. Summer Sundays only there is an additional branch service from Crediton to Okehampton.

First Great Western, which runs the Tarka Line, also operates the **Tamar Valley Line**, see page 68. Ranger tickets, giving

Ballooning

With seven balloons flying twice a day from flight areas from Salisbury to Cornwall, Aerosaurus Balloons near Exeter (T01404-823102, ballooning.co.uk) are one of the biggest UK operators. To catch the right currents, check-in either half an hour after sunrise or two to three hours before sunset. It's hands on – everyone getting the balloon rigged and inflated – and flights last one hour covering a 20-mile radius from Tiverton, Exeter, Plymouth, and Launceston just across the Cornish border. The recommended minimum age (to see over the side of the basket) is seven years. It's weather dependent, so booking two or three alternative dates is advised, then calling a few hours before to check the flight is on. The main flying season is late March to early November, but flights do run in the winter also. Prices range from £99-120 for adults and £99 for children aged seven to 12 years.

Maps

Standard road maps are of limited use and, if planning to walk, you will definitely benefit from Ordnance Survey maps or Explorer (1:25,000). Landranger maps come with a tough waterproof coating. If you only need a small area you may be able to access this online at ordnancesurvey.co.uk.

freedom of a branch line for the day, are available for both lines at £7.50 per adult for the Tarka Line and £4.50 per adult for the Tamar Valley Line. Children aged five to 15 pay half price. GroupSave allows up to four to travel for the price of two adults plus additional children at £1.

Also look for other tourist services including the **Dartmoor Railway**, see page 36, **South Devon Railway**, see page 67, and the **Paignton and Dartmouth Steam Railway**, see pages 66 and 96. And for more information check out **Great Scenic Railways of Devon and Cornwall** at carfreedaysout.com, which includes Trails from the Tracks with suggested walks from the different railways.

Local travel information
Traveline Southwest (travelinesw.com, T0871-200 2233) offers details of bus and rail services at 10 pence per minute.

Hiking & biking routes

Hike it
There has been a big effort to make it easy to walk in Devon with plenty of resources to help.
Devon County Council (devon.gov.uk/walking) Walks plus maps. Interactive maps (gis.devon.gov.uk) Include maps of footpaths across the region.
Mid Devon (middevon.gov.uk/index.cfm?articleid=130) Leaflets on walks in Mid Devon.
Ordnance Survey Explore (explore.ordnancesurvey.co.uk) Walk suggestions, shown on OS maps, searchable by location.
Richard Knight (richkni.co.uk/dartmoor/index.html) Walking on Dartmoor plus photos of things to look for.
South West Coast Path (T01392-383560, southwestcoastpath.com) Walks search facility, gradient and suitability indicated.
West Country Walks (westcountrywalks.com) By a journalist from the Western Morning News, searchable by area and style.

Bike it
The network of cycle routes is growing, sometimes overlapping with walking paths. For more on routes see devon.gov.uk/cycling, with downloadable routes.
Buzzard Cycle Route Regional Route 52, a circular route in East Devon taking in Sidmouth, Seaton, Axminster, Honiton, Woodbury and Exmouth, plus northern branch.
Coastal Route Between Totnes and Salcombe.
Devon Coast to Coast Between Ilfracombe and Plymouth.

Drake's Trail (drakesdartmoor.co.uk) Launched March 2009, walking and cycling routes for all ages with off-road cycling on the old railway between Tavistock and Plymouth, a smart steel bridge across the River Tavy leading to a route across open moor at Roborough Down before reaching the wooded valleys of the River Meavy and eventually the River Plym.
Moorlands Route Between Totnes and the edge of Plympton via Ivybridge.
National Route 2 A long-distance route planned between St Austell and Dover, crossing Devon between Plymouth and Seaton.
Stop Line Way National Route 33 in East Devon, past old pill boxes, tank traps and gun emplacements.
Sustrans (sustrans.org.uk) Information on national routes current and planned, and any closures; the website also sells maps and guides.
West Country Way From Bristol to Lands End.

181

Grown-ups' stuff Devon

Tots to teens

Babies (zero to 18 months)
More and more accommodation is laying on all the facilities you need and, at this stage, you can tuck them into a backpack and go for a stroll along the coast path or across the moors. There's also the option of hiring a baby seat or trailer for a bike ride. When it comes to amusing them, there are plenty of safe animals to pet and places where they can discover the joy of sand.

Toddlers/pre-school (18 months to four years)
Younger ones will still fit into backpacks for walks and child seats and trailers on biking trips, or even start to do a little peddling themselves with a tag-a-long. They will now take more interest in animals, maybe enjoying a whole day at one of the many zoos or petting centres, and of course you can also start rock pooling and crabbing.

Kids (four to 12 years)
Young enough to be enthusiastic, old enough to take a real interest, this is when you can start really exploring. You could go letterboxing on Dartmoor (page 31), or get pedalling, catch seafaris to look for seals and dolphins (pages 60 and 92) and look out for wildlife both in the wild and in zoos and aquaria, the best being in Plymouth (page 72). You can also take them to castles and forts, from Francis Drake's Buckland Abbey (page 70) to prehistoric Blackbury Camp (page 152). There are countless trains and boats to ride, and all the thrills of the theme parks like Woodlands (page 68), Milky Way (page 130), the slightly less manic Big Sheep (page 128), or better still Escot, with its challenging maze and scary drop slide (see page 165).

Teenagers (13 years+)
Devon has plenty of places where teens can feel independent but remain in a safe environment, including countryside campsites, small villages, quiet beaches, and off-the-beaten-track attractions like Dingles (page 36), where they can ride the dodgems to their hearts' content. If they need a physical outlet take them surfing (page 125), cycling, quad biking (pages 94, 123 and 163), or really put them through their paces with one of the tree-surfing sites (pages 33 and 93), or rock climbing, caving and more at an outdoor activity centre. They might take to letterboxing, but you could also get them navigating with map and compass (page 34), or give them a day in the company of a bird of prey, learning how to work with a real wild beast (pages 32 and 121). Quieter options include basket or willow weaving (page 35) or, when they want the classic holiday attractions, you can ferry them off to places like Crealy (page 164).

Special needs
Devon caters to everyone, offering new, extra accessible walking paths (see the leaflet *Accessible Devon and Easy-Going Dartmoor Routes* and devon.gov.uk/accessibletrailsindevon.pdf). The reservoirs are particularly easy to get around. Increasingly, accommodation, including campsites, caters to all, as do tourist attractions (see visitdevon.co.uk/site/accommodation/accessibledevon). **Accessible South West**, accessiblesouthwest.co.uk, is a directory of places to stay and visit for those with disabilities.

Single parents
Camping is ideal for single-parent families as it offers plenty of opportunity for your kids to meet and hang out with others. There are a number of organizations catering for single parents with small children in Devon. **Mango** (mangokids.co.uk) has reasonably priced group holidays for single-parent families at the Royal Hotel in Woolacombe. **Evolve** (e.volve.org.uk) offers help with reducing holiday costs for single parents, while the **Single Parent Travel Club** (sptc.org.uk) is also a good support network.

Cliff jumping with H2Outdoor.

Grown-ups' stuff Devon

Festivals

Over the summer months almost every village has a summer fair or fête, small scale, with activities like ferret racing and flower shows. Larger events on offer are:

February
Animated Exeter, exeter.go.uk. Half-term animation festival.
Dartmouth Comedy Festival, visitdevon.co.uk.

April
Budleigh Salterton, budleigh-festival.org.uk. Jazz weekend.
Exeter Festival of South West England Food and Drink, vistsouthwest.co.uk/foodfestival.

May
Appledore Visual Arts Festival, appledorearts.org.
Braunton Carnival.
Budleigh Salterton Gala Week, visitbudleigh.com.
Dartmouth Music Festival, T01803-833943, dartmusicfestival.co.uk.
Devon Country Show, Exeter, devoncountryshow.co.uk.
Geopark Festival
Honiton Festival, thehonitonfestival.co.uk. Bi-annual with classical music and visual arts.
Hunting of the Earl of Rone Festival, Combe Martin. Re-enactment of an ancient legend.
North Devon and Exmoor Walking Festival, walkingnorthdevon.co.uk. Guided walks.
Salcombe Regis Country Fair

June
Axe Vale Festival, axevalefestival.org.uk.
Croyde Viking Festival.
Crediton Festival.
Exmouth Kite Festival, exmouthrotaryclub.co.uk/kite-festival. With dedicated campsite.
Gold Coast Oceanfest, goldcoastoceanfest.co.uk. Surf and music festival. See page 15.
Ilfracombe Victorian Week, ilfracombevictoriancelebration.org.uk.
Kingsbridge Music Festival, kingsbridge.info.
Lynton and Lynmouth Music Festival, llama.org.uk. Free three-day event. See page 15.
North Devon Festival, northdevonfestival.org, northdevontheatres.org.uk/north_devon_festival.asp. Dance, fairs, theatre, music, comedy and nature events, many free.
Ottery St Mary Pixie Day, pixieday.org. On the Saturday closest to midsummer children dress as pixies to re-enact an old legend, followed by entertainment and fireworks.
Robey Steam Fair, Tavistock, therobeytrust.co.uk.
Shaldon International Music, shaldon-village.co.uk.
Teignmouth Folk Festival, see page 15.

July
Brixham Buccaneers, brixhambuccaneers.co.uk. Activities like soak the pirate, treasure hunts, pirate cruises, and more – including an award for the best-dressed pirates.
Brixham Regatta.
Budleigh Salterton Festival, budleigh-festival.org.uk. Two-week music festival.
Chagford Arts Festival, chagfordartsfestival.com.
Chagstock, see page 15.
Combe Martin Music Festival, combemartinmusicfestival.vpweb.co.uk.
Crabbing Cup, Dartmouth Quay.
East Devon Heath Week, Aylesbeare, eastdevonaonb.org.uk. Including family activities.
Exeter Summer Festival, exeter.gov.uk/summerfestival.
Hot Pennies, Honiton, honitontic.org.uk. Warmed pennies are scattered from pub windows.
Gold Coast Ocean Fest (details from T01271-344248 or northdevonhspice.org.uk under fund-raising events). Annual sandcastle competition at Woolacombe.
Kingsbridge Fair Week and Carnival, kingsbridgefairweek.co.uk.
Lifeboat Week. All along the coast in July.
Mid Devon Show, Tiverton, middevonshow.co.uk. One-day show with attractions like the Rockin' Horse Stunt Team.

Sandcastle Competition, Woolacombe.
Tavistock Carnival, tavistockdevon.com.
Teignmouth Carnival, teignmouthcarnival.co.uk.
Woolsery Agricultural Show, woolseryshow.org.uk.

August
Agricultural Show, Honiton, honitonshow.co.uk. One-day show with livestock competitions.
Appledore and Instow Regatta.
Beer Regatta, beer-devon.co.uk. With distinctive beer luggers.
Bideford Folk Festival, bidefordfolkfestival.co.uk. Week-long.
Bideford Regatta.
Blackstock Hills Music, blackdownbeerfestival.com. Welcoming families.
Branscombe Air and Classic Car Day, axevalleyholidays.co.uk.
British Firework Championship Final, Plymouth waterfront, britishfireworks.co.uk.
Chagford Agricultural Show, T01647-24306, chagfordshow.com.
Children's Festival, Paignton, T01803-208861.
Combe Martin Carnival Week, visitcombemartin.com.
Dartmoor Folk Fesitval, see page 15.
Dawlish Carnival, dawlish.net.
English Sheep Dog Trails and Country Fayre, Filleigh, englishnational-sheepdogtrials.co.uk, isds.org.uk.

Escot Beautiful Days Festival, beautifuldays.org.
Ilfracombe Carnival, visitilfracombe.co.uk.
Hartland Carnival, hartlandcarnival.com.
Holsworthy Agricultural Show, visitholsworthy.co.uk.
Honiton Hill Rally, Stockland, honitontic.org.uk. Vintage cars and motorcycles.
Mortehoe Scarecrow Festival.
North Devon Show, northdevonshow.com.
Okehampton and District Agricultural Show, T01837-861322, okehamptonshow.co.uk.
Paignton Regatta, paigntonregatta.org.uk.
Plymouth Flavour Fest, plymouth.gov.uk/favourfest.html.
Royal Regatta, Dartmouth, dartmouthregatta.co.uk.
Sidmouth Folk Week, sidmouthfolkweek.co.uk. International event including children's tent.
Sidmouth Regatta.
Seaton Carnival, seatontic.com.
Teignmouth Regatta. Nine days including Shaldon water carnival.
Torbay Regatta, torbayweek.co.uk. Yachts, dinghy racing and more.

September
Abbfest, Newton Abbot, abbfest.org. Food, drink and music.
Appledore Book Festival, appledorebookfestival.co.uk. Includes family events.
Axminster Carnival, axminsterholidays.co.uk.
Barnstaple Fair and Carnival.
Bideford Carnival.
Kingsbridge Agricultural Show, kingsbridgeshow.co.uk.
Sidmouth, Sidbury Fair Week, sidmouth.gov.uk.
Sidmouth Carnival.
Tavistock Food Festival. Morwellham Quay, tavistockfoodfestival.co.uk.
Widecombe Fair, widecombe-in-the-moor.com.

October
Exmoor Food Festival, exmoorfoodfestival.co.uk.
Exmouth Carnival, exmouth-guide.org.uk.
Honiton and District Carnival, honitontic.org.uk.
Ottery St Mary Carnival, ottertourism.org.uk.
Tavistock Goosey Fair. No geese but around 200 stalls and traders.

Chagstock Festival.

Grown ups' stuff Devon

Essentials

Health
For minor accidents go to the nearest casualty department, or there are accident and emergency units at:
Derriford Hospital, Plymouth, T01752-202082.
North Devon District Hospital, Barnstaple, T01271-322577.
Royal Devon and Exeter Hospital, Exeter, T01392-411611 (also NHS walk-in clinic).
Torbay District General Hospital, Torquay, T01803-614567.
Taunton and Somerset Hospital, Taunton, T01823-333444.
For other enquiries phone **NHS Direct 24-hours** (T0845-4647) or there are **NHS walk-in centres** at 31 Sidwell Street, Exeter, EX4 6NN, T01392-276892; and Plymouth GP Health Centre, Mount Gould Hospital, Mount Gould Road, PL4 7QD, T0845-155 8100.

Shopping
Exeter is the main big shopping centre in the region. Support the local area by spending your money with local businesses rather than the big chains. That way you get a taste of local life, and your money helps keep it going. If you want old-fashioned shops where those serving you understand what they are selling, Devon is the place for you, with centres like Tavistock shining examples of what a bustling market town can still feel like. Even smaller centres can meet most requirements. Chagford, for example, boasts a couple of retro, everything-you-want-is-in-here-somewhere establishments. Also try the shops of Ottery St Mary, or Fields of Sidmouth, an Are You Being Served-style store.

Beach gear Beach gear is sold everywhere along the coast, including newsagents and even some cafés such as the **Venus Café** and **Mill Café** on Wembury beach. If it's surfer stuff you want, Woolacombe alone boasts Billabong, RipCurl and Saltrock. In Croyde, **Chapel Farm** (Cott Lane, off Hobbs Hill, T01271-890429, chapelfarmcroyde.co.uk) makes a point of selling long and short wetsuits from the smallest child upwards, along with beach shoes, buckets and spades, kites and balls.

Camping gear Many of the camp shops listed sell relevant supplies or, for camping equipment, there's **Ashby's Leisure Superstore** at East Charleton between Kingsbridge and Dartmouth (T01548-531625, ashbysonline.co.uk) selling camping gear plus wetsuits, body boards, etc. **Mounts Farm Touring Park** (East Allington, nr Totnes, TQ9 7QJ, T01548-521591,

Fantastic Family Holidays!
Choose from over 60 locations in Devon
For a brochure, please call
0844 847 1103
and QUOTE GA120
www.hoseasons.co.uk/dwk

BEST PRICE GUARANTEE

Hoseasons

mountsfarm.co.uk, Mar-Oct) is right next to the A381 and the shop sells a wide range of camping accessories. **Kountry Kit** (22-23 West St, Tavistock, T01822-613089, kountrykit.com) is another specialist; others are **Devon Outdoor** (37 Bear St, Barnstaple, EX32 7BZ, T01271 268277), **Moor & Tor** (Fore St, Bovey Tracey, TQ13 9AB, T01626 835522), **OK Leisure** (Fore St, Okehampton) and **Southface** (Fore St, Kingsbridge).

Chainstores Bigger name chains like **Mothercare** are found in Plymouth, Barnstaple, Torquay and Exeter.

Groceries Check out the local stores, including **Gilletts**, a group that owns 12 Spar supermarkets across North and South Devon (gillettsspar.com), or **John's** supermarket at Appledore and Instow, **Cawthornes** in Braunton, and **Berrynarbor Community Stores**. Also try shopping at petrol stations like those in the **Holliss** group in South Devon (look for BP stations with Spar stores), which stock local produce. There are also Co-op stores (now including Somerfield) in centres as small as Moretonhampstead. You can also order deliveries in advance from **Riverford Organics** (T0845-6002311, riverford.co.uk). Other suppliers are listed by chapter.

Toys There are some good toyshops in the smaller centres including **The Tree House** in Salcombe (61B Fore St), selling toys including seaside items, **Honiton Toyshop** (85-87 High St), **Kaleidoscope** in Tavistock (Brook St), **Toyday** in Totnes (71 High St, toyday.co.uk) and **Hullabaloo** (77 High St), also in Totnes, offering traditional toys, plus a limited selection at Bovey Tracey's marble museum, see page 37. However, best of all is the excellent toyshop at **Dartington Cider Press Centre** (dartington.org/cider-press-centre).

Weather & tides
With sea on both sides and two moors, you can see very changeable weather in Devon. For forecasts try bbc.co.uk/weather. **Weathercall Devon** and Cornwall, T09068-500404, is a 24-hour regional summary followed by a five-day weather forecast.

North Devon tides are particularly strong with rises of up to 15 m in the Bristol Channel. Check timings at bbc.co.uk/weather/coast/tides.

Local food

It's not difficult to find seriously good, local food in Devon. Ingredients celebrated by Slow Food Devon include clotted cream (apparently first gifted by the monks of Tavistock Abbey as thanks for help with repairs), Dittisham Ploughman plums, farmhouse cheeses, Dartmouth crab, Red Ruby and South Devon cattle, Exmoor Horn sheep, venison, cider, apples, wine, swede, early cauliflowers, Landkey Mazzards (cherries) and Clovelly herrings, although any seafood is generally excellent; the Teign and Avon estuaries are particularly known for mussels and oysters.

Also look out for local brands like Luscombe Organic drinks, Heron Valley juices, Quickes cheese (quickes.co.uk), plus Burts Potato Chips (burtschips.com).

For parents who love beer, CAMRA lists almost 30 independent brewers in the county, so plenty to sample when visiting the pubs, and the whole family can do comparative tastings of local ice creams, see page 22.

October is food-celebration month, particularly on Dartmoor and in Dartmouth. For more information see lovethefavour.co.uk and food-mag.co.uk.

Index

A

accommodation 186
  camper vans 17
  camping 40, 42, 74, 100, 136, 170
  Dartmoor 40
  East Devon 170
  historical 19
  holiday parks 139, 172
  North Devon 136
  Okehampton YHA 43
  South Devon 74
  Torbay Coast 100
  YHA 42, 77, 140
  yurts 13
A La Ronde 167
Amazing Maize Maze 164
Anstey's Cove 88
Appledore 113
archery 120
Ark Pottery 167
Arlington Court 130
arts and crafts 35, 41, 77, 155
Avon Estuary 63

B

Babbacombe 88
Babbacombe Cliff Railway 88
Babbacombe Model Village 97
Baggy Point 111
ballooning 180
Bantham 58
Barricane 111
basket making 35
beaches 5, 58, 88, 114, 158
beach gear 186
Becky Falls Woodland Park 36
Beer 155, 158
Beesands 56, 58
Berry Head 95
Berry Pomeroy Castle 97
Bicton Park Botanical Gardens 167
Bideford 113
Bigbury-on-Sea 58
Big Sheep 128
birds 87, 95, 121, 134, 135, 160, 167
Blackbury Camp 152
Blackdown Hills 169
Blackmore, RD 119
Blackpool Sands 58
Boat Cove 89
boat trips 60, 63, 92, 120, 160, 161
  See also ferries
books 23
Borough Farm 130
Bovisand 58
bowling 90
Bradley 97
Branscombe 155, 158
Branscombe Old Bakery, Manor Mill and Forge 167
Braunton Burrows 112
Brixham 89
Breakwater Beach 89
Broadsands 114
Buckland Abbey 70
Bucks Mills 114
Budleigh Salterton 158
bushcraft 60, 162
Bygones 97

C

camper vans 17
camping 5, 42
  Dartmoor 40
  East Devon 170
  North Devon 136
  South Devon 74
  Torbay Coast 100
  wild 42
camping gear 186
canoeing 60, 162
Canonteign Falls 36
Castle Drogo 35
Challaborough 58
Children's Poetry Trail 87
Churston Cove 89
cinemas 41, 71, 90, 133, 155
climbing 32, 33, 34, 43, 64, 76, 93, 120, 123, 164, 172
Clovelly 130
Coldharbour Mill 168
Coleton Fishacre 97
Combe Martin Bay 114
Combe Martin Museum 130
Compton Castle 97
Coryton Cove 89
crabbing 20
Crealy Adventure Park 164
Croyde Bay 114
cycling 32, 93, 121, 126, 153, 160, 161, 162, 181
  Granite Way 31
  Haldon Forest Park 99
  South Devon 57
  Tarka Trail 126

D

Dartington Crystal 130
Dartington Hall 77
Dartmeet 31
Dartmoor 25-81
  eating 46
  letterboxing 31
  map 26
  reservoirs 30
  safety 39
  sleeping 40
  visitor centres 38
  walking 38
Dartmoor Railway 36
Dartmoor Zoo 66
Dartmouth Castle 57
Dawlish 89
Dawlish Warren 87, 90
delis 46, 78, 102, 142, 174
Devon Railway Centre and Model World 164
Diggerland 165
Dingles Fairground Heritage Centre 36
Dittisham 56
Donkey Sanctuary 153
Dunkeswell Abbey 169
Dunkeswell airfield 169
Dunkeswell Memorial Museum 169

E

East Devon 147-177
  beaches 158
  eating 174
  map 148
  sleeping 170
East Portlemouth 58
Eggesford Forest 113
Erme Plym Trail 57
Escot Gardens Maze and Park 165

Exe Estuary 160
Exe River 160
Exeter 156
　city tours 156
　eating 157
　Guildhall 156
　Phoenix 157
　Quay House Visitor
　　Centre 157
　Royal Albert Memorial
　　Museum 157
　St Nicholas Priory 157
　St Peter's
　　Cathedral 156
　Underground
　　Passages 156
Exeter Ship Canal 153
Exmoor 118
Exmoor Pony
　Society 118
Exmoor Zoo 131
Exmouth 158
Exmouth Model
　Railway 168

F

falconry 32, 121
farmers' markets 46,
　79, 102, 144, 175
farm shops 46, 78, 102,
　142, 174
farm stays 44, 75, 141, 171
ferries 60, 63, 92, 93, 161
festivals 15, 184
Finch Foundry 36
Fire Beacon Hill 154
fish and chips 103,
　143, 176
Fishcombe Cove 89
fishing 121
food 46, 78, 102, 143, 174
　local 187

G

games 22
geopark 86
Glen Lyn Gorge 111
Global Geopark 86
Gnome Reserve 131
Gold Coast
　Ocean Fest 110
Goodrington Sands 87
Grand Western
　Canal 153
Granite Way 31
Greenway 56
Greenway Estate 97
groceries 187

H

Haldon Forest Park 99
Hallsands 56
Hartland Quay 110, 114
Haytor 38
health 186
HiFlyer 97
High Moorland
　Visitor Centre 38
high wires 33, 93, 123
Holocombe 91
Hope Cove 58
Hope's Nose 86
horse riding 32, 62, 93,
　121, 162
hospitals 186
Hound Tor 30
House of Marbles 37
Hughes, Ted 87

I

ice cream 22
Ilfracombe 111
　Aquarium 131
　Capstone 114

indoor activities 71,
　133, 155
Instow 115

J

Jacob's Ladder 159
Jurassic Coast 152

K

karting 94
kayaking 122
Kents Cavern 98
Killerton 166
Knightshayes
　Court 168

L

Ladram Bay 159
Landmark Trust 19
Lannacombe 58
Lee Bay 115
letterboxing 31
Living Coasts 96
llama walks 34, 124, 163
Lorna Doone 119
Lundy Island 134
Lydford Gorge 37
Lynmouth 111, 115
Lynton 111
Lynton and Barnstaple
　Railway 131

M

Maidencombe 88
markets 144, 175
　See also farmers'
　　markets
Milky Way 130
Mill Bay 58
Miniature Pony
　Centre 37

Modbury 70
Morwellham Quay 66
multi-activity centres
　34, 64, 94, 123
museums 41, 71,
　90, 133, 155
　Combe Martin 130
　Dunkeswell
　　Memorial 169
　Hartland Quay 110
　Morwellham Quay 66
　Royal Albert
　　Memorial 157

N

National Marine
　Aquarium Plymouth 72
National Trust 5, 19
　A La Ronde 167
　Arlington Court 130
　Bradley 97
　Branscombe Old
　　Bakery, Manor Mill
　　and Forge 167
　Buckland Abbey 70
　Castle Drogo 35
　Coleton Fishacre 97
　Compton Castle 97
　Finch Foundry 36
　Greenway Estate 97
　Killerton 166
　Knightshayes
　　Court 168
　Lydford Gorge 37
　Overbeck's 70
　Powderham
　　Castle 96
　Saltram House 73
　Watersmeet 111, 118
navigation 34
Ness Cove 91
Ness Point 86

189

Newton
 Poppleford 154
Norman Lockyer
 Observatory 168
Northam Burrows
 Country Park 110
North Devon 105-145
 beaches 114
 eating 142
 map 106
 sleeping 136
North Sands 59

O

Oddicombe Beach 88
Okehampton YHA 43
Old Corn Mill 131
Ottery St Mary 154
Overbeck's 70

P

Paignton and Dartmouth
 Steam Railway 66, 96
Paignton Zoo 96
paintballing 140,
 163, 165
Pecorama Pleasure
 Gardens 168
Pennywell Farm 66
Peppercombe 115
Plymouth 58, 72
 Barbican 72
 eating 73
 National Marine
  Aquarium 72
 Saltram House 73
 Smeaton's Tower 73
 Waterfront 57
Plymouth Sound 57
Plym Valley
 Cycle Track 57
 poetry trail 87

Postbridge 31, 38
Powderham Castle 96
powerboating 62, 94
Preston Sands 91
Prickly Ball Farm 98
Putsborough Sands 116

Q

quad biking 94, 163
Quince Honey Farm 131

R

railways 66, 67, 68, 96,
 131, 168
reservoirs 30
restaurants and cafés
 46, 79, 102, 143, 175
Revelstoke
 Carriage Drive 57
RHS Garden
 Rosemoor 131
River Beach 91
River Dart
 Country Park 43
River Exe 160
Rockham Bay 116
rock pooling 20, 59, 110
Roundham Head 86
RSPB 5, 160
Isley Marsh 113

S

safety 39
sailing 62, 64, 94
Salcombe 59, 63
 North Sands 59
 South Sands 59
Salcombe Estuary 56
Salcombe Regis 159
Saltern Cove 86
Saltern Cove Trail 87

Sandy Bay 159
Sandymere 116
Saunton 116

Seaton 159
Seaton Tramway 165
Shaldon 86, 91
Shaldon
 Wildlife Trust 98
Sharpham Vineyard 71
Shelly Beach 159
Ship Canal, Exeter 153
Shoalstone Beach 89
shopping 186
Sidmouth 159
single parents 182
Slapton Ley 67
Slapton Sands 59
Soar Mill Cove 59
South Devon 51-81
 beaches 58
 eating 78
 map 52
 sleeping 74
South Devon
 Railway 67
South Milton 59
South Sands 59
special needs 182
Speke's Mill Mouth 110
Spirit of Adventure 43
Splashdown
 Quaywest 96
Start Point
 Lighthouse 57
St Mary's Bay 89
Stover Country Park 87
surfing 64, 125
swimming
 indoors 41, 71,
  90, 133, 155
 outdoors 34, 62,
  94, 163

T

Tamar Valley Line 68
Tapeley Park 132
Tarka the Otter 111
Tarka Trail 121, 126
Taverner's Farm 98
Ted Hughes
 Poetry Trail 87
teenagers 182
Teignmouth 91
Templer Way 86
Thurlestone 59
tides 187
toddlers 182
Topsham 160
Torbay Coast 83
 beaches 88
 eating 102
 map 84
 sleeping 100
Torrington 1646 132
toyshops 187
traditional skills 35
TRAIL 86
trains 161
transport 161
 getting around 180
 getting there 178
treasure hunting 21
Treasure Trails 21
Tunnels Beaches 116

V

Valley of the Rocks 111

W

Walkers Chocolate
 Emporium 132
walking 181
 Avon Estuary Walk 63
 Dartmoor 38

Dart Valley Trail 56
Exe Estuary 160
North Devon 113
Plymouth
  Waterfront 57
Tarka Trail 126
Templer Way 86
Watcombe Beach 88
Watermouth Castle 132
Watersmeet 111
Exmoor 118
water sports 64, 94,
  124, 164
weather 187
Wembury 59
Weston Mouth 159
Wildersmouth 114
wildlife 21, 124
Wildlife and
  Dinosaur Park 132
Williamson, Henry 111
willow working 35
Wonwell 59
Woodlands
  Leisure Park 68
Woody Bay 115
Woolacombe
  Sands 117
World of Country
  Life 166
Wringcliff 117

Y

YHA
  Beer 172
  Dartmoor 42
  Hartland 140
  Okehampton 43
  Salcombe 77
yurts 13

Image credits

Kate Calvert 28, 29, 36, 37, 38, 45, 48, 56, 63, 75, 85, 102, 128, 131, 150, 160, 165.

Will Grey 13, 22, 42, 43, 44, 55, 91, 92, 95, 114, 125, 126, 133, 135, 153, 167, 168.

Neville Stanikk 1, 104, 110, 111, 112, 113, 118, 122, 129, 145.

Julius Honnor 50, 54.

Alan Murphy 16.

Crown Copyright 2, 99.

O Connors Campers 10, 17.

luxurydevonyurts.co.uk 12, 13.

Matt & Sarah Smith Pg 14, 185.

Lynton & Lynmouth
  Music Festival 15.

Classic Campervan Hire 17.

The Landmark Trust 18, 19.

Usborne Publishing Ltd 21.

Penguin Group 23.

Frances Lincoln
  Children's Book 23.

dartmoor.co.uk 30, 32, 39, 49.

Harford Bridge Holiday Park 41.

Dave Willis 47.

Julius Honnor 50, 54.

Helpful Holidays 58.

wildwise.co.uk 61.

Discovery Surf School 64.

woodlandspark.com 68.

Neil Hope 72, 73.

Kents Cavern 98.

Crown Copyright 99.

The Cary Arms 100.

Langstone cliff Hotel 101.

North Devon+ 108, 109, 114, 116, 181.

Woolacombe Bay Hotel 117.

Ilfracombe Princess 120

H2Outdoor 123, 183.

Mazzard Farm 151, 173.

Escot 152, 165.

Wildside education 162.

istock
Sierraskye: 4; Kodachrome25: 67, 88; Snowshill: 70; Moorefam: 82; Creativeye99: 144; pelvidge: 155.

Shutterstock
Hicki: 19; David Hughes: 19, 140, 169; KariDesigns: 20; Daniel Gale: 24; swinner: 33; Sacha Khamnei-Brooks: 76; Monkey Business Images: 79, 177; OlegD: 81; Hal-P: 94; Bodil1955: 141; Martin Garnham: 146; Erthan Day: 156; Becky Stares: 158; Joe Gough: 176; David Young: 178; Andresr: 179; Graeme Dawes: 187.

HEMIS
Ingolf Pompe: 134.

Front cover
Stephen Shepherd/Alamy.

Back cover
Will Gray, Escot.

Credits

Footprint credits

Project editor: Felicity Laughton
Text editor: Alison Smith
Picture editors: Angus Dawson, Kassia Gawronski
Proofreader: Sophie Jones
Layout & production: Angus Dawson
Maps: Kevin Feeney

Managing Director: Andy Riddle
Commercial Director: Patrick Dawson
Publisher: Alan Murphy
Publishing Managers: Felicity Laughton, Jo Williams
Digital Editor: Alice Jell
Design: Mytton Williams
Marketing: Liz Harper, Hannah Bonnell
Sales: Jeremy Parr
Advertising: Renu Sibal
Finance & administration: Elizabeth Taylor

Print

Manufactured in India by Nutech

Every effort has been made to ensure that the facts in this guidebook are accurate. However, travellers should still obtain advice from consulates, airlines, etc about travel and visa requirements before travelling. The authors and publishers cannot accept responsibility for any loss, injury or inconvenience however caused.

Footprint Feedback

We try as hard as we can to make each Footprint guide as up to date as possible but, of course, things always change. If you want to let us know about your experiences – good, bad or ugly – then don't delay, go to www.footprintbooks.com and send in your comments.

Publishing information

Footprint Devon with Kids, 1st edition
© Footprint Handbooks Ltd, April 2010

ISBN 978-1-906098-97-1
CIP DATA: A catalogue record for this book is available from the British Library

® Footprint Handbooks and the Footprint mark are a registered trademark of Footprint Handbooks Ltd

Published by Footprint

6 Riverside Court
Lower Bristol Road
Bath BA2 3DZ, UK
T +44 (0)1225 469141
F +44 (0)1225 469461
discover@footprinttravelguides.com
footprinttravelguides.com

Distributed in North America by

Globe Pequot Press, Guilford, Connecticut

Ordnance Survey® This product includes mapping data licensed from Ordnance Survey® with the permission of the Controller of Her Majesty's Stationery Office. © Crown Copyright. All rights reserved. Licence No. 100027877.

All rights reserved. No part of this publication may be reproduced, stored in a retrieval system, or transmitted, in any form or by any means, electronic, mechanical, photocopying, recording, or otherwise without the prior permission of Footprint Handbooks Ltd.

Acknowledgements

The families of those who write about travel with kids contribute more than most to the writer's efforts, so thanks to mine for all their input. Thanks also to all the professionals, not least the team at Footprint but also Richard Drysdale, Jessica Whistance, Pat Edgar, Andrew Savery, Anne Tattersall, Ruud Jansen Venneboer, Claire Toze, Richard Ball and Kevin Monaghan, as well as the many kind and helpful people we met in Devon, who all contributed invaluable ideas, information and advice in writing this book.